MONTGOMERY COUNTY COMMUNITY COLLEGE

3 0473 00052557 9

W9-BCG-335

QC
6
M5913

Moszkowski, A.
Conversations with
Einstein.

DATE DUE

MAR 1 1977			
12/5/72			
NOV 2 7 1978			
APR 1 1979			
MAY 2 6 1993			
JUN 2 1994			
Jul 19, 1994			
MAY 2 1996			
MAY 6 1996			

j

THE LIBRARY
MONTGOMERY COUNTY COMMUNITY COLLEGE

DEMCO

CONVERSATIONS WITH EINSTEIN

CONVERSATIONS WITH EINSTEIN

by

ALEXANDER MOSZKOWSKI

Translated by

HENRY L. BROSE

Introduction by

HENRY LE ROY FINCH

HORIZON PRESS   NEW YORK

Copyright © 1970, by Horizon Press
Library of Congress Catalog Card Number: 74-132324
ISBN 0-8180-0215-8
Printed in the United States of America

QC
6
M5913

29268

EXTRACT FROM THE AUTHOR'S PREFACE

THE book which is herewith presented to the public has few contemporaries of a like nature ; it deserves special attention inasmuch as it is illuminated by the name *Albert Einstein*, and deals with a personality whose achievements mark a turning-point in the development of science.

Every investigator, who enlarges our vision by some permanent discovery, becomes a milestone on the road to knowledge, and great would be the array of those who have defined the stages of the long avenue of research. One might endeavour, then, to decide to whom mankind owes the greater debt, to Euclid or to Archimedes, to Plato or to Aristotle, to Descartes or to Pascal, to Lagrange or to Gauss, to Kepler or to Copernicus. One would have to investigate—as far as this is possible—in how far each outstanding personality was in advance of his time, whether some contemporary might not have had the equal good fortune to stumble on the same discovery, and whether, indeed, the time had not come when it must inevitably have been revealed. If we then further selected only those who saw far beyond their own age into the illimitable future of knowledge, this great number of celebrities would be considerably diminished. We should glance away from the milestones, and fix our gaze on the larger signs that denote the lines of demarcation of the sciences, and among them we should find the name of Albert Einstein. We may find it necessary to proceed to a still more rigorous classification ; Science, herself, may rearrange her chronological table later, and reckon the time at which Einstein's doctrine first appeared as the beginning of an important era.

This would in itself justify—nay, render imperative—the writing of a book *about* Einstein. But this need has already been satisfied on several occasions, and there is even now a considerable amount of literature about him. At the end of this generation we shall possess a voluminous library composed entirely of books about Einstein. The present book will differ from most of these, in that Einstein here occurs not only objectively but also subjectively. We shall, of course, speak of him here too, but we shall also hear him speak himself, and there can be no doubt that all who are devoted to the world thought can but gain by listening to him.

The title agrees with the circumstance to which this book owes its birth. And in undertaking to address itself to the circle of readers as to an audience, it promises much eloquence that came from Einstein's own lips, during hours of social intercourse, far removed from academic purposes and not based on any definite scheme intended for instruction. It will, therefore, be neither a course of lectures nor anything similar aiming at a systematic order and development. Nor is it a mere phonographic record, for this is made impossible if for no other reason than that whoever has the good fortune to converse with this man, finds every minute far too precious to waste it in snatching moments to take shorthand notes. What he has heard and discussed crystallizes itself in subsequent notes, and to some extent he relies on his memory, which would have to be extraordinarily lax if it managed to forget the essentials of such conversations.

But these essentials could not be attained by clinging closely to the exact terms of utterance. This would be a gain neither for the scheme of the book nor for the reader who wishes to follow a great thinker in all the ramifications of his ideas. It must be reiterated that this book is intended neither as a textbook nor as a guide leading to a complete system of thought ; nor, above all, is it in any way due to Einstein, nor desired by him. Any value and attraction of the book is rather to be sought in its kaleidoscopic nature, its loose connexion, which expresses a general meaning without being narrowed to pedantic limits by a restriction to literal repetition. It is just this absence of the method that is rightly demanded of a textbook, which may enable these conversations to pass on to the world a little of the pleasure which they originally gave me. Perhaps they will even be sufficient to furnish the reader with a picture of the eminent scientist, sufficient to give him a glimpse of his personality, without demanding a detailed study to secure this end. Even here I should like to state that the range of Einstein's genius extends much further than is generally surmised by those who have busied themselves only with the actual physical theory. It sends out rays in all directions, and brings into view wonderful cosmic features under his stimulus—features which are, of course, embedded in the very refractory mathematical shell of his physics which embraces the whole world. But only minds of the distant future, perhaps, will be in a position to realize that *all* our mental knowledge is illuminated by the light of his doctrine.

Einstein's mission is that of a king who is pursuing building operations on a large scale ; carters and workmen, each in their own line, receive employment for decades ahead. But apart from the technical work, there may still be room for non-technical account, which, without following a definite programme, yet pursues a definite object, to offer Einsteiniana in an easily intelligible and ever-changing form, to represent him, as it were, wandering over fields and meadows, and every now and then stooping to pluck some problem in the guise of a flower. Seeing that he granted me the pleasure of accompanying him on these excursions, it was not within my sphere to expect in addition that he would direct his steps according to a preconceived plan. Often enough the goal vanished, and there remained nothing but the pleasure of the rambles themselves with the consciousness of their purpose. As Schopenhauer remarks, one who walks for leisure can never be said to be making detours; and this holds true independently of the nature of the country that happens to be traversed at the moment. If I just now mentioned walks on meadowy slopes, this is not to be understood literally. In Einstein's company one encounters from moment to moment quite suddenly some adventure which destroys our comparison with idyllic rambles. Abysmal depths appear, and one has to pass along dangerous pathways. It is at these moments that unexpected views present themselves, and many strips of landscape that, according to our previous estimate, appeared to be situated on higher slopes, are now discovered reposing far below. We are familiar with the "Wanderer Fantasie" of Schubert; its tonal disposition is realistic, conforming to Nature, yet its general expression is transcendental: so is a ramble with Einstein; he remains firmly implanted in reality, but the distant views that he points out stretch into transcendental regions. He seems to me to be essentially as much an artist as a discoverer, and if some sense of this heaven-sent combination of gifts should be inspired by this book, it alone would justify the publication of these talks.

TRANSLATOR'S NOTE

IT is scarcely necessary to enlarge on the scope and design of the present book, which manifest themselves at a glance.

The author merits our thanks for making accessible to us material about Einstein which, in the ordinary course of events, would ever remain unknown. An account of Einstein's work would be incomplete without a sketch of his personality. Mr. Moszkowski invites us to ramble with Einstein into realms not confined to pure physics. Many subjects that have a peculiar interest at the present critical stage of the world's history receive illuminating attention. It is hoped that the appearance of the book in English will stimulate further interest in the thought-world of a great scientist.

Warm thanks are due to Mr. Raymond Kershaw, B.A., and to my sister, Miss Hilda Brose, for help in reading the manuscript and the proofs.

HENRY L. BROSE

OXFORD, 1921

CONTENTS

INTRODUCTION

EINSTEIN'S place as one of the three or four greatest minds in the history of science is already well-established. But future historians may also see him as something else—a phenomenon of the twentieth century. They may find themselves wondering how it happened that an abstract scientist, whose work could be understood only by a relative handful of people, should nevertheless have become an idol of millions so that his name and face were known all over the globe.

That this puzzled Einstein himself is evident from several comments in his writings, including this:

> It strikes me as unfair, and even in bad taste, to select a few individuals for boundless admiration, attributing superhuman powers of mind and character to them. This has been my fate, and the contrast between the popular estimate of my powers and achievements and the reality is simply grotesque. The awareness of this strange state of affairs would be unbearable but for one pleasing consolation: it is a welcome symptom in an age which is commonly denounced as materialistic, that it makes heroes of men whose goals lie wholly in the intellectual and moral sphere. This proves that knowledge and justice are ranked above wealth and power by a large section of the human race.[1]

These words do not really tell us what caught the popular imagination. With characteristic modesty Einstein may have overlooked the main point. For was the main point not perhaps that Einstein himself appeared as something of a living demonstration that science and goodness could, after all, go together, a demonstration the more needed the more threaten-

[1]Einstein, *Ideas and Opinions* (New York, 1954) , p. 5.

ing and inhuman science had seemed to become? We must not forget that the picture of the mad scientist had already firmly lodged itself in popular mythology. What could be more reassuring than this benign and kindly figure whose very appearance showed that he was that essential thing—a *good man*?

It may be, in other words, that it was not so much knowledge as goodness which the millions craved, and that in this respect Einstein's popularity may have been little different from that of many a saint in the religious tradition, although indeed here was also something new—a saint of science. Men everywhere had only to look at that extraordinary face with its purity and unworldliness to know that here was a man who did not belong to the ordinary realm of human affairs. It was the face of a visionary preoccupied with some other reality.

When we look at the pictures of Einstein as a young man, before age had begun to cast its shadows of sorrow over that face, we see also, however, something else of the greatest importance, a quality which can perhaps best be called "expectancy." We see a face which is, as it were, "leaning forward," not imposing itself, but alert with great *confidence* and *expectation*. Toward the end of his life, at the age of 67, Einstein concluded his *Autobiographical Notes* with this sentence:

> This exposition has fulfilled its purpose if it shows the reader how the efforts of a life hang together and why they have led to expectations of a definite form.[2]

The expectations—were they not perhaps always there, even if the form was not always known? And was it not perhaps the aim of the efforts and the struggle, not so much to *give* them form, but to permit them to take form, to permit their form to emerge, so that the world might, if it could, answer to them?

In contemplating such creative achievements we may be reminded of the statement of the mathematician Gauss, applicable far beyond the realm of mathematics: *I have the result, only I do not yet know how to get to it*. This points to the "positional" character of thinking, the ability of the creative mind to occupy a position without knowing where it is or where the road to it lies, yet never doubting that that is where

[2]In Paul Arthur Schilpp (ed.), *Albert Einstein: Philosopher Scientist* (Evanston, Ill., 1949), p. 95.

it has to go. Thinking indeed has this power to anticipate it-self, to divine its end from its expectations, leaping at once to its furthest outpost as to something already long remembered.

The quality of inner necessity in Einstein's work, the con-ditions which made it possible and the almost inconceivable cost in struggle and commitment—these we can learn, not only from Einstein's own writings, but from the writings of those who knew him. For this latter we have to turn to a small num-ber of memoirs and biographies, of which the present book by Alexander Moszkowski is one of the most important.[3] Mosz-kowski's book has a unique position because it is the first full-scale picture of Einstein, the first introduction to the man when he was just turning forty, had already accomplished his greatest work, and was just about to start on the way to world-wide fame.

What were the components of Einstein's genius? Perhaps the two most important were noted by the physicist Leopold Infeld, who worked with Einstein at Princeton and who wrote about him in his own autobiography *Quest*:

> The greatness of Einstein lies in his tremendous imagination, in the unbelievable obstinacy with which he pursues his problems.[4]

Infeld was inclined to attribute more even to the "unbeliev-able obstinacy" than to the "tremendous imagination."

> Einstein devoted ten years of his life to this problem [that of gravita-tion] when no one else was interested in it....To ponder on a prob-lem for ten years without any encouragement from the outside requires strength of character. This strength of character, perhaps more than his great intuition and imagination, led to Einstein's sci-entific achievements.[5]

No one, however, will minimize that imagination, the imagination which re-formed our conception of the universe. The original formulation of the Special Theory of Relativity

[3]See especially the following: Philipp Frank, *Einstein, His Life and Times,* translated from the German by George Rosen (New York, 1947) ; Dimitri Mari-anoff and Pamela Wayne, *Einstein, An Intimate Study of a Great Man* (New York, 1944) ; David Reichinstein, *Albert Einstein, A Picture of His Life and His Conception of the World* (Prague, 1934) ; Anton Reiser, *Albert Einstein, a Bio-graphical Portrait* (New York, 1930) ; Antonina Vallentin, *Einstein: A Biog-raphy,* translated from the French by M. Budberg (London, 1954) . And see also W. Cahn, *Einstein, a Pictorial Biography* (New York, 1955) ; Einstein *Lettres à Maurice Solovine* (Paris, 1956); and B. Kuznetsov, *Einstein* (Moscow, 1965) .

[4]Leopold Infeld, *Quest: The Evolution of a Scientist* (London, 1942) , p. 208.

[5]*Ibid.,* p. 219.

involved an imaginative feat unparalleled in human thought. It involved accepting an all but inconceivable paradox (the constancy of the velocity of light) and then revising all the rest of physics (including especially the conceptions of space and time) to fit it. When asked many years later how he had come to formulate this theory, Einstein is said to have replied: "By refusing to accept an axiom."[6] The axiom was *absolute simultaneity*—that events appearing to occur at the same time may be said without further specification actually to occur *at the same time*. But bound up with it was something even more deeply axiomatic, absolute space and absolute time, Newton's apparently unalterable cosmic framework.

The imaginative leap made by Einstein may be said to have been to "physicalize" space and time, to bring them, as it were, fully into the physical world, so that they no longer functioned as merely the *setting* for the world, but became actual *parts* of the physical world interacting with matter and motion. Space and time were "dethroned" and endowed with physical and changeable properties.[7] They lost their immemorial "untouchability" and began to enter the domain of the comprehensible (for, of course, the transformation has not yet been completed).

If Einstein's second great step—the General Theory of Relativity—did not have the same seeming logical inevitability as the Special Theory, it was none the less an equally unparalleled feat. Through it gravitation appeared as a structural or geometrical phenomenon, which varied and changed in definite ways, instead of the occult force of Newton's theory. This step, after it had been taken, appeared as a natural extension of the field concept of Faraday and Maxwell, but only a mind of the caliber of Einstein's would have been able to imagine such an extension.

We cannot, of course, separate these achievements of scientific imagination from the "unbelievable obstinacy" and the intensity of expectation. Einstein's total energies were always

[6] Marianoff, *op. cit.*, p. 148.

[7] See especially Einstein, *Sidelights on Relativity*, translated by G. B. Jeffery and W. Perrett (London, 1922). When asked by his nine-year-old son why he was famous, Einstein is said to have replied: "You see, son, when a blind bug crawls along the surface of a sphere, it doesn't notice that its path is curved. I was fortunate enough to notice this." (Kuznetsov, *op. cit.*, p. 200)

turned in the direction of unremitting questioning, and the answers were actually won inch by inch over periods of many years as the questions themselves underwent change after change. Infeld observed:

> The most amazing thing about Einstein was his tremendous vital force directed toward one and only one channel: that of original thinking, of doing research. Slowly I came to realize that in exactly this lies his greatness.[8]

The precondition for this obstinacy, this struggle, its life-long cost, was an inner isolation and solitude which few men could have endured, but which had become the very air Einstein breathed and which had to be that if his single-minded devotion to scientific thought was to be possible.[9]

Einstein himself commented on this inner isolation, saying:

> Arrows of hate have been shot at me too, but they never hit me, because somehow they belonged to another world with which I have no connection whatsoever. I live in that solitude which is painful in youth, but delicious in the years of maturity.[10]

His son-in-law described it this way:

> Regardless of how many surround him, he is always alone—not lonely, but alone. Einstein does not need people. He receives them with warmth and kindliness, but they are in no way necessary to him. You see this in his eyes when he leaves them; the expression is already one of extreme contemplation, and he is barely aware he has been with them; the line of his thinking is unbroken.[11]

Einstein's own words confirm this:

> My passionate sense of social justice and social responsibility has always contrasted oddly with my pronounced lack of need for direct contact with other human beings and human communities. I am truly a "lone traveler" and have never belonged to my country, my friends, or even my immediate family with my whole heart; in the face of all these ties, I have never lost a sense of distance and a need for solitude—feelings which increase with the years.[12]

---

[8]Infeld, *op. cit.*, p. 212.

[9]I recall a comment made by the mathematician L. E. J. Brouwer, one of the great figures of twentieth-century mathematics, after he had returned from a visit with Einstein at Princeton and was giving his impressions. "Nothing can distract Einstein from his own line of thought," Brouwer said. "He seems to be listening to what other people say, but his mind is always on his own thoughts."

[10]*Out of My Later Years* (New York, 1955) , p. 5.

[11]Marianoff, *op. cit.*, p. 134. This book contains many inaccuracies and must be used with a great deal of caution.

[12]*Ideas and Opinions* (New York, 1954) , p. 9.

We turn now to Einstein's philosophy, which was for him both a conception of the world and a way of life. His inner isolation and complete dedication to thought were an expression of a life-long striving to rise above the "merely personal," to achieve liberation from the self in order to contemplate the vast impersonal truths of nature. In the *Autobiographical Notes* he expresses this in terms strongly reminiscent of Spinoza:

> Out yonder there was this huge world, which exists independently of us human beings and which stands before us like a great, eternal riddle, at least partially accessible to our inspection and thinking. The contemplation of this world beckoned like a liberation, and I soon noticed that many a man whom I had learned to esteem and admire had found inner freedom and security in devoted occupation with it.[13]

Einstein found, as Spinoza did, that the human qualities of modesty, equanimity, universality, equality and kindness were actually promoted by a sense of the vast impersonality of truth and of a natural law and harmony far beyond human hopes, fears and wishes.

Einstein formulated this philosophical position with great clarity and in clear-cut distinction to other philosophies. It may be summarized as follows: (1) there is a reality independent of human knowledge; (2) this reality is intrinsically harmonious and lawful, though it appears to us as a vast riddle; (3) it involves at its basis universal causality; (4) it is knowable by means of "free constructions" of the human mind which express these relations; (5) these "free constructions" begin and end in experience, but they are not derived from experience, and they are not "forms of thought"; (6) there is no free will and no personal or moral God.

The crux of this, it will be seen, is Einstein's *causalism,* his belief in causality as the objective *ratio* of the world and the *sine qua non* of science. In this respect Einstein is indeed the heir of Spinoza and belongs squarely to the great tradition of seventeenth-century rationalism. The philosopher Hume, who, we may say, upset that particular apple cart for Kant, failed to upset it for Einstein after he had broken away from the early

[13]Schilpp, *op. cit.,* p. 5.

influence of Mach. The following words of Einstein, for example, are pure Spinoza:

> ...the scientist is possessed by the sense of universal causation. The future, to him, is every whit as necessary and determined as the past. There is nothing divine about morality, it is a purely human affair. His religious feeling takes the form of rapturous amazement at the harmony of natural law, which reveals an intelligence of such superiority that, compared with it, all the systematic thinking and acting of human beings is an utterly insignificant reflection.[14]

What is important in the history of twentieth-century science is that Einstein continued to defend universal causality even when virtually the entire scientific community had abandoned it in its strict form by accepting the "principle of indeterminacy" in quantum physics. He continued to assert that indeterminacy was only a temporary expedient and that there could be no *complete* description in science without full causality.[15]

Causality (or natural laws expressing causal relations), was for Einstein the "objectivity" of the world, its invariant independent reality. The "longing for pure knowledge," which he said lies at the root of science, is the longing to discover these hidden relations, which we are never able to discover completely, but which are the answer to the riddle that the world presents to us. To abandon the belief in universal causality was for him tantamount to giving up the belief in the ultimate rationality and harmony, the search for which was the very nerve of science.

Equally strong was a second philosophical position—Einstein's refusal to try to base science upon sense experience and his repudiation of philosophies which attempted to do this, philosophies of phenomenalism and logical positivism. In the Schilpp volume in which he was attacked by the quantum physicists Einstein was assailed on this point too, and at the end in his "Reply to Criticisms" he wrote:

> "Being" is always something which is mentally constructed by us, that is, something which we freely posit (in the logical sense). The justification of such constructs does not lie in their derivation from what is given by the senses. Such a type of derivation (in the sense

---

[14]*The World As I See It* (New York, 1949), p. 29.
[15]This matter is discussed at length in the Schilpp volume where Einstein takes up the cudgels against Born, Pauli, Heitler, Bohr and Margenau.

of logical deducibility) is nowhere to be had, not even in the domain of pre-scientific thinking. The justification of the constructs, which represent "reality" for us, lies alone in their quality of making intelligible what is sensorily given...[16]

Later in the same Reply he points out that there is *no* way of formulating satisfactorily the relation between the world as experienced and the conceptual systems of science.[17]

We are faced, therefore, with the impossibility of "explaining" concepts in terms of sense experience or of "reducing" conceptual knowledge to what is "immediately given" to our senses. There simply does not exist any logical relation between these two—the world-experienced and the world-thought-about.

> I do not consider it legitimate to mask the logical independence of the concept of perceptible experience. The connection is not analogus to that of beef tea and beef, but rather to that of the cloakroom ticket number and the overcoat.... The fact is that we are dealing with freely formed concepts which, with a sufficient certitude for practical use, are intuitively bound up with complexes of perceptible experiences, in such a way that in no matter what given case of experience, there is no uncertainty as to the application or non-application of the statement.[18]

Here is the mystery of how theory can apply to the world, or how we are able to comprehend the world; how it is that our abstract concepts, seemingly ever further removed from the world as experienced, nevertheless "apply" to it, "represent" it, "comprehend" it. Einstein found this the greatest mystery of all, and he did not think that we will ever understand it:

> The very fact that the sum total of our perceptible experiences is such that by means of thought it can perhaps be regulated (operation with concepts, creation and use of definite functional relations between them, coordination of perceptible experiences with these concepts) ; this fact I admit bewilders us completely and we shall never understand it. It can be said that "the eternal mystery of the world" is its "comprehensibility."[19]

Finally, besides his disagreement with the quantum physicists, the phenomenalists and the logical positivists, Einstein found himself in opposition to various forms of idealism and

[16]Schilpp, *op. cit.*, p. 669.

[17]*Ibid.*, p. 680.

[18]Quoted in Hilaire Cuny, *Albert Einstein, The Man and His Theories* (London, 1963) , p. 129.

[19]*Ibid.*, p. 126.

also to the traditional religions. There is an unforgettable picture of Einstein and the Indian poet Rabindranath Tagore, who visited him in Berlin and at the Einstein summer home in Caputh.[20] As Marianoff reported their conversation:

> "This world," went on Tagore, "is a human world. The scientific view of it is only that of the scientific man. Therefore, the world apart from us humans does not exist; it is a relative world, depending for its reality upon our consciousness. There is a standard of reason which gives it truth—the standard of the eternal man, whose experiences are made possible through our experiences."...
>
> "I agree with the conception of beauty as being inseparate from man, but I do not agree with this conception as pertaining to truth," went on Einstein.
>
> "Why not?" inquired Tagore. "Truth is realized through man."
>
> There was a long pause. Then Einstein said very quietly and softly: "I cannot prove my conception is right, but that is my religion."[21]

Truth, *independent of man,* independent of consciousness, independent of sense experience, independent of morality—this was Einstein's "religion." It brought him into conflict with Tagore because ultimately it rested upon and preserved the separation between man and the world which has characterized Western thought in its fundamental divergence from the monisms of the East. While some have objected to Einstein (as they objected to Spinoza) using the word "God" to mean, not the *creator* of the universe, but the *intelligibility* of the universe,[22] in the context of the discussion with the East, represented by the poet Tagore, it is the *independent reality* of this "intelligibility" which is the critical factor, and this is signalized (in however heterodox a fashion) by the use of the term "God." To this extent, and *only to this extent,* Einstein, like Spinoza, belonged to the Biblical tradition.

When, however, we counterpose Einstein to the orthodox Jewish-Christian tradition, an altogether different picture emerges. For a God who is the impersonal "rationality" of the universe may be the God of philosophy (or of some philosophy), but he is not the God of Abraham, Isaac and the prophets. He is not the source of faith, and he does not "speak to

20Frank, *op. cit.,* p. 115.
21Marianoff, *op. cit.,* p. 75.
22e.g., Kuznetsov, *op. cit.,* pp. 53-66.

the prophets." He may be in some way the God of Nature, but he is not the God of History; and he may be the God of Truth, but he is not the God of Life.

Even though Einstein brought to science essentially religious attitudes and emotions, including the attitudes of cosmic awe and wonder and a devout humility before the harmony of the world, it cannot be said that he overcame the fundamental disparity between religion and science. The picture of the universe implied by theoretical physics remained as much at variance with what seemed to be the presuppositions of religion as it had since the beginnings of modern science. In the Einstein universe living organisms, as well as human life and personality, remained as strange and inexplicable as in any of the great seventeenth-century systems. We might indeed be more awestruck than ever by the marvelous mathematical harmony of the world, but we would also be more puzzled than ever about what this has to do with the living soul.

There is one additional aspect of Einstein's conception of science which must, however, not be overlooked. This is the emphasis upon the scientific aim of theoretical simplicity and the dictum which prescribes that, all other factors being equal, the *simpler* hypothesis is always to be preferred. Einstein wrote of this in one place thus:

> The aim of science is, on the one hand, as complete a comprehension as possible of the connection between perceptible experiences in their totality, and, on the other hand, the achievement of this aim *by employing a minimum of primary concepts and relations.*[23] (Italics in original.)

The demand for increasing simplicity of explanation appears to be met by the development of science itself, and the Special and General Theories of Relativity may both be said to represent decisive steps in this direction. Einstein compared the work of the theoretical physicist to a man solving "a well-constructed crossword puzzle" where many words might be suggested, but in the end "a single word really resolves the riddle in all its forms."[24] It might be added that the puzzle of nature would attain its finally simplest form if indeed it consisted of

[23]Cuny, *op. cit.*, p. 128.
[24]*Ibid.*, p. 129.

no more than one word for all its empty places (with synonyms, as it were, in the "different" places) .

Is there any connection between simplicity as the aim of science and simplicity in the personal and moral sphere? It has been said that common sense is the prerogative of the good, and the bad are destroyed by their lack of it. We may wonder if something similar does not apply to truth—that truth is the the prerogative of the simple, and only those who are in a certain sense without guile are able to recognize it. In the case of someone like Einstein we cannot but feel that there is indeed an inner and necessary connection between the extraordinary theoretical simplicity of his work and the personal simplicity of the man himself. We feel that only someone himself so simple could have conceived such ideas.

And if we think about it, it is this (involving, as it does, also the notion of purity) , which probably has the most to do with the question of the relations between science and morality and science and religion. Here what Einstein was spoke more unanswerably than anything he said.

HENRY LEROY FINCH

Sarah Lawrence College
June, 1970

CHAPTER I

PHENOMENA IN THE HEAVENS

Proclamation of the New Mechanics.—Verification of Theoretical Results.
—Parallels with Leverrier.—Neptune and Mercury.—Testing the Theory of
Relativity.—The Solar Eclipse of 1919.—The Programme of an Expedition.
—The Curved Ray of Light.—Refinement of Calculation and Measurement.—
Stellar Photography.—The Principle of Equivalence.—The Sun Myth.

O N the 13th October 1910 a memorable event took
place in the Berlin Scientific Association: Henri
Poincaré, the eminent physicist and mathematician,
had been announced to give a lecture in the rooms of the
institute " Urania " ; an audience of rather meagre dimensions
assembled. I still see him before me in my mind's eye, a
scholar who was snatched away in the prime of his creative
period, a man whose external appearance did not suggest the
light of genius, and whose carefully trimmed beard reminded
one rather of the type of a practising barrister. He walked
up and down the platform, accompanying his speech with
gestures marked by an easy elegance. There was no sign of
an attempt to force a doctrine. He developed his thesis, in
spite of the foreign language, in fluent and readily intelligible
terms.

It was at this lecture that we heard the name Albert
Einstein pronounced for the first time.

Poincaré's address was on the New Mechanics, and was
intended to make us acquainted with the beginning of a
tendency which, he himself confessed, had violently disturbed the equilibrium of his former fundamental views. He
repeatedly broke the usually even flow of his voice to indicate,
with an emphatic gesture, that we had perhaps arrived at a

critical, nay epochal, point marking the commencement of a new era of thought.

" Perhaps " was a word he never failed to emphasize. He persistently laid stress on his doubts, differentiated between hardened facts and hypotheses, still clinging to the hope that the new doctrine he was expounding would yet admit of an avenue leading back to the older views. This revolution, so he said, seemed to threaten things in science which a short while ago were looked upon as absolutely certain, namely, fundamental theorems of classical mechanics, for which we are indebted to the genius of Newton. For the present this revolution is of course only a threatening spectre, for it is quite possible that, sooner or later, the old established dynamical principles of Newton will emerge victoriously. Later in the course of his lecture he declared repeatedly that he felt a diffidence akin to fear at the sight of the accumulating number of hypotheses, and that it seemed to border on the impossible to attempt to arrange them into a system.

It is a matter of complete indifference how the revelations of Poincaré affected us individually ; if I may infer from my own case, there is only one word to express it—staggering ! Oblivious of the doubts of the lecturer, I was swept along under the impetus of this new and mighty current of thought. This awakened two wishes in me : to become acquainted with Einstein's researches as far as lay within my power, and, if possible, to see him once in person. In me the abstract had become inseparable from the concrete personal element. The presentiment of the happy moment in the future hovered before my vision, whispering that I should hear his doctrine from his own lips.

Several years later Einstein was appointed professor of the Academy of Sciences with the right of lecturing at the University of Berlin. This brought my personal wish within reach. Trusting to good fortune, I set about materializing it. In conjunction with a colleague I wrote him a letter asking him to honour with his presence one of the informal evenings instituted by our Literary Society at the Hôtel Bristol. Here he was my neighbour at table, and chatted with me for some hours. Nowadays his appearance is known to every one through the innumerable photos which have appeared in the papers. At that time I had never seen his countenance before, and I became absorbed in studying his features, which struck me as being those of a kindly, artistically inclined, being, in nowise suggesting a professor. He seemed vivacious and unrestrained in conversation, and, in response to our request, willingly touched upon his own subject as far as the place and occasion allowed, exemplifying Horace's saying, " Omne tulit punctum, qui miscuit utile dulci, tironem delectando pariterque monendo." It was certainly most delightful. Yet at moments I was reminded of a male sphinx, suggested by his highly expressive enigmatic forehead. Even now, after a warm acquaintanceship stretching over years, I cannot shake off this impression. It often overcomes me in the midst of a pleasant conversation interspersed with jests whilst enjoying a cigar after tea ; I suddenly feel the mysterious sway of a subtle intellect which captivates and yet baffles the mind.

At that time, early in 1916, only a few members of the Literary Society divined who it was that was enjoying their hospitality. In the eyes of Berlin, Einstein's star was beginning its upward course, but was still too near the horizon to be visible generally. My own vision, sharpened by the French lecture and by a friend who was a physicist, anticipated events, and already saw Einstein's star at its zenith, although I was not even aware at that time that Poincaré had in the meantime overcome his doubts and had fully recognized the lasting importance of Einstein's researches. I had the instinctive feeling that I was sitting next to a Galilei. The fanfares sounded in the following years as a sign of appreciation by his contemporaries were only a fuller instrumentation of the music of destiny which had vibrated in my ears ever since that time.

I recollect one little incident : one of these lovers of literature, who was, however, totally ignorant of natural science, had accidentally seen several learned articles dealing with Einstein's Reports for the Academy, and had preserved the cuttings in his pocket-book. He considered this a fitting opportunity for enlightenment. Surely a brief question would suffice to guide one through these intricate channels. " Professor, will you kindly tell me the meaning of potential, invariant, contravariant, energy-tensor, scalar, relativity-postulate, hyper-Euclidean, and inertial system ? Can you explain them to me in a few words ? "—" Certainly," said Einstein, " those are merely technical expressions ! " That was the end of the little lesson.

Far into the night three of us sat in a café while Einstein gently lifted the veil from his newest discovery for the benefit of my journalist friend and myself. We gathered from his remarks that a Special Theory of Relativity formed a prelude to a general theory which embraced the problem of gravitation in its widest sense, and hence also the physical constitution of the world. What interested me apart from this theme, which was, of course, only touched upon lightly, was the personal question in its psychological aspect.

" Professor," said I, " such investigations must involve enormous mental excitement. I imagine that there lurks behind every solved problem ever and again some new problem with a threatening or a fascinating aspect, as the case may be, each one calling up a tumult of emotion in its author. How do you succeed in mastering this difficulty ? Are you not continually tormented by restless thoughts that noisily invade your dreams ? Do you ever succeed at all in enjoying undisturbed slumber ? "

The very tone in which the answer was given showed clearly how free he felt himself of such nervous troubles which usually oppress even the mediocre thinker. It is fortunate that such affections do not penetrate to his high level. " I break off whenever I wish," he said, " and banish all difficulties when the hour for sleep arrives. Thinking during dreams, as in the case of artists, such as poets and composers, by which they weave the thread of day on into the night, is quite foreign to me. Nevertheless, I must confess that at the very beginning, when the special theory of relativity began to germinate in me, I was visited by all sorts of nervous conflicts. When young I used to go away for weeks in a state of confusion, as one who at that time had yet to overcome the stage of stupefaction in his first encounter with such questions. Things have changed since then, and I can assure you that there is no need to worry about my rest."

" Notwithstanding," I answered, " cases may arise in which a certain result is to be verified by observation and experiment. This might easily give rise to nerve-racking experiences. If, for instance, a theory leads to a calculation which does not agree with reality, the propounder must surely feel considerably oppressed by this mere possibility. Let us take a particular event. I have heard that you have made a new calculation of the path of the planet Mercury on the basis of your doctrine. This must certainly have been a laborious and involved piece of work. You were firmly convinced of the theory, perhaps you alone. It had not yet been verified by an actual fact. In such cases conditions of great psychological tension must surely assert themselves. What in Heaven's name will happen if the expected result does not appear ? What if it contradicts the theory ? The effect on the founder of the theory cannot even be imagined ! "

" Such questions," said Einstein, " did not lie in my path. That result could not be otherwise than right. I was only concerned in putting the result into a lucid form. I did not for one second doubt that it would agree with observation. There was no sense in getting excited about what was self-evident."

Let us now consider several facts of natural science, apart from this chat, but suggested by it, which caused Einstein little excitement, but the whole world generally, so much the more. By way of illustration we shall link them up with the result of a forerunner who, like Einstein, fixed on paper what should happen in the heavens.

Formerly, whenever one wished to play a particularly effective trump card in favour of research work it was customary to quote the achievement of the French astronomer Leverrier who, pen in hand, established the material existence of a planet at that time quite unknown and unnoticed. Certain disturbances in the orbit of the planet Uranus, which was regarded as being the most distant of the wandering stars, at that time had caused him to believe in the certainty of the existence of a still more distant planet, and by using merely the theoretical methods of celestial mechanics in connexion with the problem of three bodies he succeeded in revealing what was hidden behind the visible constellations. He reported the result of his calculations to the Berlin Observatory about seventy-five years ago, as it was at that time in possession of the best instruments. It was then that the amazing event happened : on the very same evening an observer in Berlin, Gottfried Galle, discovered the predicted new star almost exactly at the point of the heavens for which it was prophesied, only half the moon's diameter from it. The new planet Neptune, the farthest outpost of our solar system, reposed as a prisoner in his telescope ; the seemingly undiscoverable star had capitulated in the face of mental efforts of a mathematical scholar, who, in reasoning meditation, had sketched his curves in the quiet atmosphere of his study.

This was certainly bewildering enough, but nevertheless this incredible result which stirred the imagination so strongly was directly rooted in reality, lay on the path of research, followed of necessity from the laws of motion known at that time, and disclosed itself as a new proof of the doctrines of astronomy which had long been recognized as supreme and incontestable. Leverrier had not created these, but had found them ready ; he applied them with the mind of genius. Anyone who nowadays is sufficiently trained to work through the highly complicated calculation of Leverrier has every reason to marvel at a work which is entirely mathematical throughout.

Our own times have been marked by an event of still greater significance.

Irregularities had shown themselves in observation of the heavens that could not be explained or grasped by the accepted methods of classical mechanics. To interpret them, ideas of a revolutionary nature were necessary. Man's view of the plan according to which the universe is mapped out had to be radically reformed to bring within comprehension the problems that presented themselves in macroscopic as well as in microscopic regions, in the courses of the stars as well as in the motions of the ultimate constituents of the atom of material bodies, incapable of being directly observed. The goal consisted in bringing those doctrines in which truth had been proclaimed in its essential features, but not exhaustively, by the genius of Copernicus, Galilei, Kepler, and Newton, to their conclusion by penetrating as far as possible into the mysteries of the structure of the universe. This is where Einstein comes forward.

Whereas the outermost planet Neptune had bowed to the

accepted laws, by merely disclosing his presence, Mercury, the innermost planet, preserved an obstinate attitude even in the face of the most refined calculations. These always led to an unaccountable remainder, a disagreement, which seemed very small when expressed in numbers and words, and yet enclosed a deep secret. Wherein did this disagreement consist ? In a difference of arc which had likewise been discovered by Leverrier and which defied explanation. It was only a matter of about forty-five insignificant quantities, seconds of arc, which seemed vanishingly small since this deviation did not occur within a month or a year, but was spread over a whole century. By just so much, or rather so little, the rotation of Mercury's orbit differed from what might be termed the allowable astronomical value. Observation was exact, calculation was exact ; why, then, the discrepancy ?

It was thus inferred that there was still some hidden unexplored factor which had to be taken into account in the fundamental principles of celestial mechanics. The formerly invisible Neptune confirmed the old rule by appearing. Mercury, which was visible, opposed the rule.

In 1910 Poincaré had touched upon this embarrassing question, mentioning that here was a possibility of testing the new mechanics.

He declined the suggestion of some astronomers that this was again a Leverrier problem and that there must exist another undiscovered planet still nearer the sun and disturbing Mercury's orbit. He also refused to accept the assumption that the disturbance might be caused by a ring of cosmic matter distributed round the sun. Poincaré divined that the new mechanics could supply the key to the enigma, but, obviously to be quite conscientious, he expressed his presentiment in very cautious terms. On that occasion he said that some special cause had yet to be found to explain the anomaly of Mercury's behaviour ; till that was discovered one could only say that the new doctrine could not be regarded as in contradiction to astronomical facts. But the true explanation was gradually drawing near. Five years later, on 18th November 1915, Albert Einstein presented to the Prussian Academy of Sciences a paper which solved this riddle which, expressed in seconds, seemed so insignificant and yet was of such enormous importance in its bearing on fundamental questions. He proved the problem was solved quite accurately if the general Theory of Relativity he had founded was accepted as the only valid basis for the phenomena of cosmic motions.

Many would at this point express a wish to have the essence of the doctrine of relativity explained in an easily intelligible manner. Indeed, some would go even further in their desire, and would ask for a simple description in a few succinct sentences. This, measured in terms of difficulty and possibility, would be about equivalent to wishing to learn the history of the world by reading several quarto pages of manuscript or a novelette. But even if we start at long range and use elaborate materials for our description, we should have to give up the idea that this knowledge may be gained with playful ease. For this doctrine, inasmuch as it discloses the relationship between mathematical and physical events, emerges out of mathematics, which thus limits the mode of its representation. Whoever undertakes to present it in a form in which it is easily intelligible, that is quite unmathematical and yet complete, is engaged in an impossible venture; he is like one who would whistle Kepler's Laws on the flute or would elucidate Kant's Critique of Pure Reason by means of coloured illustrations. In all frankness we must confess once and for all that whenever popular accounts are attempted they can be only in the nature of vague suggestions removed from the domain of mathematics. But even such indications have a fruitful result if they succeed in focusing the attention of the reader or the hearer so that the connexions, the Leitmotivs, so to speak, of the doctrine, are at least suggested.

It must therefore suffice if we place the conception of approximation in the foreground here as in other parts of this book. Till quite recently Newton's Equations of Motion were used as a foundation for verifying astronomical occurrences. These are symbolical representations expressed as formulæ that contain in an exceedingly simple form the law of mass attraction. They express the comprehensive principle that the attraction is directly proportional to the mass and inversely proportional to the square of the distance ; so that the moving force is doubled when the mass is doubled, whereas if the distance is double, the force is only a quarter as great, if the distance is trebled, the force becomes one-ninth as great.

According to the Theory of Relativity this fundamental law is not wrong or invalid, but no longer holds fully if pursued to its last inferences. In applying corrections to it, new factors occur, such as the ratio of given velocities to the velocity of light, and the new geometry which operates with " world-lines " in space which, amalgamated with the dimension of time, is regarded as a quadruply extended continuum. Einstein has actually supplemented these fundamental equations for the motion of masses so that the original form states the true condition of affairs only approximately, whereas Einstein's equations give the motion with very great accuracy.

The above-mentioned essay of Einstein is carried out as if the structure bequeathed to us by Newton required the addition of a final, very delicate pinnacle. For the mathematician this pinnacle is given as a combination of signs, representing a so-called " Elliptic Interval." Such an interval is a very weird construction, and the man who will make it apprehended by the general reader is yet to be born. When Lord Byron said :

> " And Coleridge, too, has lately taken wing,
> But like a hawk encumbered with his hood,—
> Explaining Metaphysics to the nation—
> *I wish he would explain his Explanation.*"
> *(Dedication to " Don Juan.")*

he had still a sure footing in intelligibility, compared with the non-mathematician, who demands an explanation for such a construction. And what a complex of mathematical dangers must be overcome even before the question of the meaning of this integral is crystallized out !

But now the explanation had arrived and could be evaluated, if only approximately. Before we give the result, let us just describe at least one technical term, namely, " Perihelion." It is that point of a planetory orbit which lies nearest the sun. This orbit is an ellipse, that is, an elongated curved line in the interior of which one distinguishes a major axis in the direction of elongation, and a minor axis perpendicular to the former at its middle point. The perihelion of a planetory orbit is at one of the end points of the major axis.

In time the perihelion alters its position in space, advancing in the same sense as the orbit is traversed. It would naturally be assumed that the amount of this advance as measured astronomically would agree with the calculation resulting from Newton's theory. But this was not the case. An unaccountable remainder was left over, which astronomers ascertained to be 45 seconds (of arc) per 100 years, with a possible fluctuation of plus or minus 5 seconds. Thus, if the new result were found to lie between 40 and 50 seconds, the new theory would henceforth have to be regarded as the only valid one.

It happened just as Einstein predicted : calculation according to his theory shows that for the planet Mercury the perihelion should advance 43 seconds per 100 years. This signifies full agreement with observation and fully removes the former apparent difficulty. Whereas Leverrier in his time had pointed out a new planet, Einstein brought to view something far more important : a new truth.

It was a test of accuracy so dazzling that it alone would have sufficed to prove the correctness of Einstein's Principles. Yet, a second test, fraught with graver and more far-reaching consequences, presented itself—a test which could be applied only several years later, and which developed into a scientific event of the highest importance.

For at the same time that Einstein solved the problem of Mercury, he had investigated the path of light-rays according to his revolutionary method, and had arrived at the conclusion that every ray under the influence of a gravitational field, as, for example, in the neighbourhood of the sun, must become curved. This daring announcement gave a new possibility of putting the theory to a practical test during the total eclipse of the sun on 29th May 1919. For, when the disc of the sun is obscured, the stars that are closest to it become visible (even to the naked eye). They may be photographed, and the distances of the points of light on the negative allow us to detect whether the rays from the stars in passing the massive body of the sun have actually been deflected by the amount prophesied by Einstein.

Once again current thought encountered a sharp corner, and "common sense," which furnishes its own certificate of merit, threatened to become rebellious. How now ? A ray from a star could be curved ? Does not this contradict the elementary conception of the straight lines, that is, the shortest lines, for which we have no better picture than just these rays ? Did not Leonardo da Vinci define the straight line by means of the term *linea radiosa*.

But such supposedly self-evident facts have no longer a place in the space-time world. The point was to test whether a physical anomaly which had been predicted actually existed. If the deflection of the rays really happened, it should manifest itself in the distances between the stars on the photographic plate being greater than one would expect from their actual position.

For the curvature has its concave side towards the sun, as is easy to see, once the phenomenon is regarded as possible. It is as if the ray were directly subject to gravitation. Let us take two stars, one on each side of the sun. On account of the concavities the eye receives rays from them under a greater visual angle than if the rays were straight, and interprets this angle as denoting a greater distance between the sources of light, that is, it sees the two stars farther apart than in the case of rectilinear propagation.

By how much farther apart ? The preceding calculation and the subsequent direct observation demanded incredible delicacy of measurement. If we suppose the whole arc of the heavens divided into easily picturable units such as degrees, then the apparent width of the moon is about half a degree. We may still easily imagine the thirtieth part of this, namely, a minute of arc. But the sixtieth part of the latter, the second of arc, vanishes almost out of the range of sense-perception. And it was just this minute measure that came into question, for the theory which had been developed from pure thought predicted a deflection of $1\frac{7}{10}$ seconds of arc. This corresponds to about a hairbreadth when seen at a distance of 17 yards, or to the thickness of a match at a distance of over half a mile.

One of the greatest problems of the most comprehensive science depended on this unthinkably small measure.

In no sense did Einstein himself entertain a possibility of doubt.

On repeated occasions before May 1919 I had opportunities of questioning him on this point. There was no shadow of a scruple, no ominous fears clouded his anticipations. Yet great things were at stake.

Observation was to show " the correctness of Einstein's world system " by a fact clearly intelligible to the whole world, one depending on a very sensitive test of less than two seconds of arc.

" But, Professor," said I, on various occasions, " what if it turns out to be more or less ? These things are dependent on apparatus that may be faulty, or on unforeseen imperfections of observation." A smile was Einstein's only answer, and this smile expressed his unshakeable faith in the instruments and the observers to whom this duty was to be entrusted.

Moreover, it is to be remarked that no great lengths of time were available for comfortable experimentation in taking this photographic record. For the greatest possible duration of a total eclipse of the sun viewed at a definite place amounts to less than eight minutes, so that there was no room for mishaps in this short space of time, nor must any intervening cloud appear. The kindly co-operation of the heavens was indispensable—and was not refused. The sun, in this case the darkened sun, brought this fact to light.

Two English expeditions had been equipped for the special occasion of the eclipse—one to proceed to Sobral and the other to the Island of Principe, off Portuguese Africa ; they were sent officially with equipment provided in the main by the time-honoured Royal Society. Considering the times, it was regarded as the first symptom of the revival of international science, a praiseworthy undertaking. A huge apparatus was set into motion for a purely scientific object with not the slightest relation to any purpose useful in practical life. It was a highly technical investigation whose real significance could be grasped by only very few minds. Yet interest was excited in circles reaching far beyond that of the professional scientist. As the solar eclipse approached, the consciousness of amateurs became stirred with indefinite ideas of cosmic phenomena. And just as the navigator gazes at the Polar

Star, so men directed their attention to the constellation of Einstein, which was not yet depicted in stellar maps, but, from which something uncomprehended, but undoubtedly very important, was to blaze forth.

In June it was announced that the star photographs had been successful in most cases, yet for weeks, nay for months, we had to exercise patience. For the photographs, although they required little time to be taken, took much longer to develop and, above all, to be measured ; in view of the order of smallness of the distances to be compared, this was a difficult and troublesome task, for the points of light on the plate did not answer immediately with Yes or No, but only after mechanical devices of extreme delicacy had been carefully applied.

At the end of September they proclaimed their message. It was in the affirmative, and this Yes out of far-distant transcendental regions called forth a resounding echo in the world of everyday life. Genuinely and truly the $1\frac{7}{10}$ seconds of arc had come out, correct to the decimal point. These points representing ciphers, as it were, had chanted of the harmony of the spheres in their Pythagorean tongue. The transmission of this message seemed to be accompanied by the echoing words of Goethe's " Ariel " :

> " With a crash the Light draws near !
> Pealing rays and trumpet-blazes,—
> Eye is blinded, ear amazes."

Never before had anything like this happened. A wave of amazement swept over the continents. Thousands of people who had never in their lives troubled about vibrations of light and gravitation were seized by this wave and carried on high, immersed in the wish for knowledge although incapable of grasping it. This much all understood, that from the quiet study of a scholar an illuminating gospel for exploring the universe had been irradiated.

During that time no name was quoted so often as that of this man. Everything sank away in face of this universal theme which had taken possession of humanity. The converse of educated people circled about this pole, could not escape from it, continually reverted to the same theme when

pressed aside by necessity or accident. Newspapers entered
on a chase for contributors who could furnish them with short
or long, technical or non-technical, notices about Einstein's
theory.   In all nooks and corners social evenings of instruction
sprang up, and wandering universities appeared with errant
professors that led people out the three-dimensional misery
of daily life into the more hospitable Elysian fields of four-
dimensionality.   Women lost sight of domestic worries and
discussed co-ordinate systems, the principle of simultaneity,
and negatively-charged electrons.   All contemporary questions
had gained a fixed centre from which threads could be spun to
each.   Relativity had become the sovereign password.   In
spite of some grotesque results that followed on this state of
affairs it could not fail to be recognized that we were watching
symptoms of mental hunger not less imperative in its demands
than bodily hunger, and it was no longer to be appeased by
the former books by writers on popular science and by mis-
guided idealists.

And whilst leaders of the people, statesmen, and ministers
made vain efforts to steer in the fog, to arrive at results serviceable to the nation, the multitude found what was expedient for
it, what was uplifting, what sounded like the distant hammer-
ing of reconstruction.   Here was a man who had stretched his
hands towards the stars ; to forget earthly pains one had but
to immerse oneself in his doctrine.   It was the first time for
ages that a chord vibrated through the world invoking all eyes
towards something which, like music or religion, lay outside
political or material interests.

The mere thought that a living Copernicus was moving in
our midst elevated our feelings.   Whoever paid him homage
had a sensation of soaring above Space and Time, and this
homage was a happy augury in an epoch so bare of brightness
as the present.

. . . .

As already remarked, there was no lack of rare fruits among
the newspaper articles, and a chronicler would doubtless have
been able to make an attractive album of them.   I brought
Einstein several foreign papers with large illustrations which
must certainly have cost the authors and publishers much
effort and money.   Among others there were full-page beauti-

fully coloured pictures intended to give the reader an idea of the paths pursued by the rays from the stars during the total eclipse of the sun. These afforded Einstein much amusement, namely, *e contrario*, for from the physical point of view these pages contained utter nonsense. They showed the exact opposite of the actual course of the rays inasmuch as the author of the diagrams had turned the convex side of the deflected ray towards the sun. He had not even a vague idea of the character of the deflection, for his rays proceeded in a straight line through the universe until they reached the sun, where they underwent a sudden change of direction reminiscent of a stork's legs. The din of journalistic homage was not unmixed with scattered voices of dissent, even of hostility. Einstein combated these not only without anger but with a certain satisfaction. For indeed the series of unbroken ovations became discomfiting, and his feelings took up arms against what seemed to be developing into a star-artist cult. It was like a breath of fresh air when some column of a chance newspaper was devoted to a polemic against his theory, no matter how unfounded or unreasoned it may have been, merely because a dissonant tone broke the unceasing chorus of praise. On one occasion he even said of a shrill disputant, " The man is quite right ! " And these words were uttered in the most natural manner possible. One must know him personally if one is to understand these excesses of toleration. So did Socrates defend his opponents.

In our conversation we returned to the original question, and I asked whether there was no means of making the deflection of the ray intelligible to an average person.

Einstein replied : " In a very superficial manner this is certainly possible." And with a few strokes on the paper, which I shall here try to describe in words, he gave his explanation in terms something like the following :

This square is to denote the cross-section of a closed box which we imagine to be situated somewhere in the universe. Inside it there lives a physicist who makes observations and draws inferences from them. In the course of time he perceives, what is familiar to all of us, that every body not supported and left to itself, for example, a stone that is released, drops to the floor with uniform acceleration, that is, with a steady increase of velocity in going downwards. There are *two* ways open to him to explain this phenomenon.

Firstly, he might suspect—and this suspicion would be most likely to occur to him—that his box was resting on some body in the heavens. For if indeed the box were a cave in some part of the world, the falling of the stone would suggest nothing unusual; it would be quite self-evident to every occupant, and quite explicable to the physicist according to Galilei's (or Newton's) Laws for Falling Bodies. He need not necessarily restrict himself to the Earth, for if the box happened to be on some other star, this phenomenon of falling would likewise occur, with greater or less speed, and the body would certainly fall with uniform acceleration. Thus the physicist could say : this is an effect of gravitation, exhibiting the property of weight which I explain to myself as usual, as due to the attraction of a heavenly body.

Secondly, another idea might strike him. For we stipulated nothing about the position of the box, and assumed only that it was to exist "somewhere in the universe." The physicist in the box might reason as follows :

Supposing I am separted by incalculable distances from every attracting heavenly body, and supposing gravitation existed neither for me nor for the stone which I release from my hand, then it would still be possible for me to give a complete explanation of the phenomena I observe. I should only have to assume that the body is moving with uniform acceleration "upwards." The motion previously interpreted by me as a falling "downwards" need not take place at all. The stone, as an *inert* body, could persist in its position (relative to the box or the observer), and would, in spite of this, show exactly the same behaviour when the box moves with acceleration upwards as if it were falling with increasing velocity downwards.

Now since our physicist has no system which might serve for reference and orientation, and since in his box which is shut off from the universe he has no means at his disposal of determining whether he is in the sphere of influence of an attracting heavenly body or not, both the above explanations are feasible for him and both are equally valid, and it is impossible for him to come to a decision in his choice. He can interpret the acceleration in either way, as being upwards or downwards, connected to one another by relativity ; a fundamental reason for preferring one interpretation to the other cannot be furnished, since the phenomenon of falling is represented unchanged whether he assumes the stone to be falling and the box to be at rest, or vice versa. This may be generalized in these words :

At every point of the world the observed acceleration of a body left to itself may be interpreted either as a gravitational *or* as an inertial effect—that is, from the point of view of physics we may assert with equal right that the system (the box, the complex defining the orientation) from which I observe the event is accelerated, or that the event takes place in a gravitational field. The equal right to these two views is called the " Principle of Equivalence " by Einstein. It asserts the equivalence or the identity of inertial and gravitational mass. If we familiarize ourselves with this identity, an exceedingly important road to knowledge is opened up to our consciousness. We arrive at the inevitable conclusion that every inertial effect that we perceive in bodies, the most essential quality of it, itself so to speak in its persistent nature, is to be traced back to the influence to which it is subjected by other bodies. When this has become clear to us, we feel impelled to inquire how a ray of light would behave under the influence of gravitation. Hence we return to our physicist in the box, and we now know that as a consequence of the Principle of Equivalence we are free to assume either that an attracting heavenly body, such as the sun, is situated somewhere below the box, or to refer the phenomena to the box regarded as being accelerated upwards. In the box we distinguish the floor, the ceiling, four walls, and among these again, according to the position we take up, the wall on the left and its opposite one on the right.

We now imagine a marksman to be outside the box and having no connexion with us, being poised freely in space, and suppose him to fire out of a horizontal gun at the box so that the bullet pierces both the wall on the left and the wall on the right. Now, if everything else were to remain at rest, the holes in both walls would be equally distant from the floor, and the bullet would move in a straight line parallel to the floor and to the ceiling. But, as we have seen, all events happen as if the box itself moved with constant acceleration. The bullet that requires time to pass from one wall to the other thus finds that when it reaches the wall on the right the latter has advanced a little, so that the resulting hole is a little lower than that on the left wall. This means that the flight of the bullet, according to our observation in the interior of the box, is no longer rectilinear. In fact, if we trace the bullet from point to point, we should find that for us, situated in the box, it would describe a line bent downwards, with its concave side to the floor.

Exactly the same thing happens with a ray of light which is emitted by a source outside in a horizontal direction and which traverses the space between the walls (supposed transparent). Only the velocity would be different. In the course of its flight the ray would move like a projectile that is whizzing along at the rate of 180,000 miles per second. But provided sufficiently delicate means of measurement are applied, it should still be possible to prove the existence of an infinitesimal deflection from the rectilinear horizontal path, an insignificant concavity towards the floor.

Consequently this curvature of the light-ray (say, from a star) must also be perceptible in places where it is subject to the influence of a gravitational field. If we drop our imaginary picture of the box, the argument is in nowise altered. A ray from a star which passes close by the sun seems to our perception to be bent in towards the sun, and the order of this deflection can be determined if sufficiently delicate instruments be used. As above remarked, it is a question of detecting a difference of 1·7 seconds of arc, which is to be manifested as a distance on the photographic plate, and is actually found to be present.

The fact that scientists are able to detect this appears in itself a marvel of technical precision far in advance of " splitting hairs," for in comparison a single hair is, in this case, to be removed to a considerable distance if we are to use it to give an idea of the size of angle under consideration. Fortunately stellar photography has been developed so wonderfully that in every single case extraordinarily accurate results are got even from preliminary measurements.

In ordinary astronomical practice it is usually found that

a millimetre in linear measure on the plate corresponds to a minute of arc. This means that the sun's disc itself has a diameter of 3 centimetres on the photograph. The stars appear as tiny dots, which may be sharply differentiated in an enlargement. Stars of the fourteenth order of magnitude and beyond it become visible, whereas the naked eye cannot see those of order higher than the sixth. A grating whose lines are $\frac{1}{100}$ millimetre wide is copied on to the plate to make the measurement more accurate, so that the positions of objects can be ascertained with certainty to within a few tenths of a second of arc. Thus the problem which was to be solved by the solar eclipse of 1919 lay within the realm of possibility as regards our means of measurement.

A copy of this photograph had been sent to Einstein from England, and he told me of it with evident pleasure. He continually reverted to the delightful little picture of the heavens, quite fascinated by the thing itself, without the slightest manifestation of a personal interest in his own success. Indeed, I may go further and am certainly not mistaken in saying his new mechanics did not even enter his head, nor the verification of it by the plate ; on the contrary, he displayed that disposition of the mind which in the case of genius as well as in that of children shows itself as *naïveté*. The prettiness of the photograph charmed him, and the thought that the heavens had been drawn up as for parade to be a model for it.

All things are repeated in the history of life. In these happenings, which mark the 29th May 1919 as a red-letter day in the history of science, we recognize a revival of the Sun Myth, unperceived by the individual, but as an expression of the universal consciousness, just as when Copernicus converted the geocentric picture of the universe into a heliocentric one, the Sun Myth again sprang into life ; the symbolization of faith in the light-giving and heat-giving star. This time it has arisen, purified of all dross, scarcely perceptible to our senses, like an aureole spun about the sun by far-distant sources of light, in honour of a principle, and even if most of us do not yet know what a " system of reference " means, yet for many such a system has unconsciously evolved, a thought-system serving as a reference for the development of their knowledge when they thought or spoke of Einstein.

CHAPTER II

BEYOND OUR POWER

Useful and Latent Forces.—Connexion between Mass, Energy, and Velocity of Light.—Deriving Power by Combustion.—One Gramme of Coal.—Unobtainable Calories.—Economics of Coal.—Hopes and Fears.—Dissociated Atoms.

29th March 1920

WE spoke of the forces that are available for man and which he derives from Nature as being necessary for his existence and for the development of life. What forces are at our disposal ? What hopes have we of elaborating our supply of these forces ?

Einstein first explained the conception of energy, which is intimately connected with the conception of mass itself. Every amount of substance (I am paraphrasing his words), the greatest as well as the smallest, may be regarded as a store of power, indeed, it is essentially identical with energy. All that appears to our senses and our ordinary understanding as the visible, tangible mass, as the objective body corresponding to which we, in virtue of our individual bodies, abstract the conceptual outlines, and become aware of the existence of a definite copy is, from the physical point of view, a complex of energies. These in part act directly, in part exist in a latent form as strains which, for us, begin to act only when we release them from their state of strain by some mechanical or chemical process, that is, when we succeed in converting the potential energy into kinetic energy. It may be said, indeed, that we have here a physical picture of what Kant called the "thing in itself." Things as they appear in ordinary experience are composed of the sum of our direct sensations ; each thing acts on us through its outline, colour, tone, pressure, impact, temperature, motion, chemical behaviour, whereas the thing in itself is the sum-total of its energy, in which there is an enormous predominance of those energies which remain latent and are quite inaccessible in practice.

But this " thing in itself," to which we shall have occasion to refer often with a certain regard to its metaphysical significance, may be calculated. The fact that it is possible to calculate it takes its origin, like many other things which had in no wise been suspected, in Einstein's Theory of Relativity.

Quite objectively and without betraying in the slightest degree that an astonishing world-problem was being discussed, Einstein expressed himself thus :

" According to the Theory of Relativity there is a calculable relation between mass, energy, and the velocity of light. The velocity of light (denoted by c, as usual) is equal to $3 \cdot 10^{10}$ cm. per second. Accordingly the square of c is equal to 9 times 10^{20} cm. per second, or, in round numbers, 10^{21} cm. per second. This c^2 plays an essential part if we introduce into the calculation the mechanical equivalent of heat, that is, the ratio of a certain amount of energy to the heat theoretically derivable from it ; we get for each gramme $20 \cdot 10^{12}$ that is, 20 billion calories."

We shall have to explain the meaning of this brief physical statement in its bearing on our practical lives. It operates with only a small array of symbols, and yet encloses a whole universe, widening our perspective to a world-wide range !

To simplify the reasoning and make it more evident we shall not think of the conception of substance as an illimitable whole, but shall fix our ideas on a definite substance, say coal.

There seems little that may strike us when we set down the words :

" One Gramme of Coal."

We shall soon see what this one gramme of coal conveys when we translate the above-mentioned numbers into a language to which a meaning may be attached in ordinary life. I endeavoured to do this during the above conversation, and was grateful to Einstein for agreeing to simplify his argument by confining his attention to the most valuable fuel in our economic life.

Once whilst I was attending a students' meeting, paying homage to Wilhelm Dove, the celebrated discoverer took us aback with the following remark : When a man succeeds in climbing the highest mountain of Europe he performs a task which, judged from his personal point of view, represents something stupendous. The physicist smiles and says quite simply, " Two pounds of coal." He means to say that by burning 2 lb. of coal we gain sufficient energy to lift a man from the sea-level to the summit of Mont Blanc.

It is assumed, of course, that an ideal machine is used, which converts the heat of combustion without loss into work. Such a machine does not exist, but may easily be imagined by supposing the imperfections of machines made by human hands to be eliminated.

Such effective heat is usually expressed in calories. A calorie is the amount of heat that is necessary to raise the temperature of a gramme of water by one degree centigrade. Now the theorem of the Mechanical Equivalent, which is founded on the investigations of Carnot, Robert Mayer, and Clausius, states that from one calorie we may obtain sufficient energy to lift a pound weight about 3 feet. Since 2 lb. of coal may be made to yield 8 million calories, they will enable us to lift a pound weight through 24 million feet, theoretically, or, what comes to the same approximately, to lift a 17-stone man through 100,000 feet, that is, nearly 19 miles : this is nearly seven times the height of Mont Blanc.

At the time when Dove was lecturing, Einstein had not yet been born, and when Einstein was working out his Theory of Relativity, Dove had long passed away, and with him there vanished the idea of the small value of the energy stored in substance to give way to a very much greater value of which we can scarce form an estimate. We should feel dumbfounded if the new calculation were to be a matter of millions, but actually we are to imagine a magnification to the extent of billions. This sounds almost like a fable when expressed in words. But a million is related to a billion in about the same way as a fairly wide city street to the width of the Atlantic Ocean. Our Mont Blanc sinks to insignificance. In the above calculation it would have to be replaced by a mountain 50 million miles high. Since this would lead far out into space, we may say that the energy contained in a kilogramme of coal is sufficient to project a man so far that he will never return, converting him into a human comet. But for the present this is only a theoretical store of energy which cannot yet be utilized in practice.

Nevertheless, we cannot avoid it in our calculations just as we cannot avoid that remarkable quantity c, the velocity of light that plays its part in the tiny portion of substance as it does in everything, asserting itself as a regulative factor in all world phenomena. It is a natural constant that preserves itself unchanged as 180,000 miles per second under all conditions, and which truly represents what appeared to Goethe as " the immovable rock in the surging sea of phenomena," as a phantasm beyond the reach of investigators.

It is difficult for one who has not been soaked in all the elements of physical thought to get an idea of what a natural constant means ; so much the more when he feels himself impelled to picture the constant, so to speak, as the rigid axis of a world constructed on relativity. Everything, without exception, is to be subjected not only to continual change (and this was what Heraclitus assumed as a fundamental truth in his assertion *panta rhei*, everything flows), but every length-measurement and time-measurement, every motion, every form and figure are dependent on and change with the position of the observer, so that the last vestige of the absolute vanishes from whatever comes into the realm of observation. Nevertheless, there is an absolute despot, who preserves his identity inflexibly among all phenomena—the velocity of light, c, of incalculable influence in practice and yet capable of measurement. Its nature has been characterized in one of the main propositions of Einstein stated in 1905 : " Every ray of light is propagated in a system at rest with a definite, constant velocity independent of whether the ray is emitted by a body at rest or in motion." But this constancy of the omnipotent c is not only in accordance with world relativity : it is actually the main pillar which supports the whole doctrine ; the further one penetrates into the theory, the more clearly does one feel that it is just this c which is responsible for the unity, connectivity, and invincibility of Einstein's world system.

In our example of the coal, from which we started, c occurs as a square, and it is as a result of multiplying 300,000 by itself (that is, forming c^2) that we arrive at the thousands of milliards of energy units which we associated above with such a comparatively insignificant mass. Let us picture this astounding circumstance in another way, although we shall soon see that Einstein clips the wings of our soaring imagination. The huge ocean liner *Imperator*, which can develop a greater horse-power than could the whole of the Prussian cavalry before the war, used to require for one day's travel the contents of two very long series of coal-trucks (each series being as long as it takes the strongest locomotive to pull). We now know that there is enough energy in two pounds of coal to enable this boat to do the whole trip from Hamburg to New York at its maximum speed.

I quoted this fact, which, although it sounds so incredibly fantastic, is quite true, to Einstein with the intention of justi-fying the opinion that it contained the key to a development which would initiate a new epoch in history and would be the panacea of all human woe. I drew an enthusiastic picture of a dazzling Utopia, an orgy of hopeful dreams, but immediately noticed that I received no support from Einstein for these visionary aspirations. To my disappointment, indeed, I perceived that Einstein did not even show a special interest in this circumstance which sprang from his own theory, and which promised such bountiful gifts. And to state the conclusion of the story straight away I must confess that his objections were strong enough not only to weaken my rising hopes, but to annihilate them completely.

Einstein commenced by saying : " At present there is not the slightest indication of when this energy will be ob-tainable, or whether it will be obtainable at all. For it would presuppose a disintegration of the atom effected at will —a shattering of the atom. And up to the present there is scarcely a sign that this will be possible. We observe atomic disintegration only where Nature herself presents it, as in the case of radium, the activity of which depends upon the con-tinual explosive decomposition of its atom. Nevertheless, we can only establish the presence of this process, but cannot pro-duce it ; Science in its present state makes it appear almost impossible that we shall ever succeed in so doing."

The fact that we are able to abstract a certain number of calories from coal and put them to practical use comes about owing to the circumstance that combustion is only a molecular process, a change of configuration, which leaves fully intact the atoms of which the molecules are composed. When carbon and oxygen combine, the elementary constituent, the atom, remains quite unimpaired. The above calculation, "mass multiplied by the square of the velocity of light," would have a technical significance only if we were able to attack the interior of the atom ; and of this there seems, as remarked, not the remotest hope.

Out of the history of technical science it might seem possible to draw on examples contradictory to this first argument which is soon to be followed by others equally important. As a matter of fact, rigorous science has often declared to be impossible what was later discovered to be within the reach of technical attainment—things that seem to us nowadays to be ordinary and self-evident. Werner Siemens considered it impossible to fly by means of machines heavier than air, and Helmholtz proved mathematically that it was impossible. Antecedent to the discovery of the locomotive the "impossible" of the academicians played an important part ; Stephenson as well as Riggenbach (the inventors of the locomotive) had no easy task to establish their inventions in the face of the general reproach of craziness hurled at them. The eminent physicist Babinet applied his mathematical artillery to demolish the ideas of the advocates of a telegraphic cable between Europe and America. Philipp Reis, the forerunner of the telephone, failed only as a result of the "impossible" of the learned physicist Poggendorff ; and even when the practical telephone of Graham Bell (1876) had been found to work in Boston, on this side of the Atlantic there was still a hubbub of "impossible" owing to scientific reasons. To these illustrations is to be added Robert Mayer's mechanical equivalent of heat, a determining factor in our above calculations of billions ; it likewise had to overcome very strong opposition on the part of leading scientists.

Let us imagine the state of mankind before the advent of machines and before coal had been made available as a source of power. Even at that time a far-seeing investigator would have been able to discover from theoretical grounds the 8000 calories mentioned earlier and also their transformation into useful forces. He would have expressed it in another way and would have got different figures, but he would have arrived at the conclusion : Here is a virtual possibility which must unfortunately remain virtual, as we have no machine in which it can be used. And however far-sighted he may have been, the idea of, say, a modern dynamo or a turbine-steamer would have been utterly inconceivable to him. He would not have dreamed such a thing. Nay, we may even imagine a human being of the misty dawn of prehistoric ages, of the diluvial period, who had suddenly had a presentiment of the connexion between a log of wood and the sun's heat, but who was yet unaware of the uses of fire ; he would argue from his primordial logic that it was not possible and never would be possible to derive from the piece of wood something which sends out warmth like the sun.

I believe now, indeed, that we have grounds for considering ourselves able to mark off the limits of possibility more clearly than the present position of science would seem to warrant. There is the same relation between such possibilities and absolute impossibilities as there is between Leibniz's *vérités de fait* and the *vérités éternelles*. The fact that we shall never succeed in constructing a plane isosceles triangle with unequal base angles is a *vérité éternelle*. On the other hand, it is only a *vérité de fait* that science is precluded from giving mortal man eternal life. This is only improbable in the highest degree, for the fact that, up to the present, all our ancestors have died is only a finite proof. The well-known Cajus of our logic books need not die ; the chances of his dying are only $\frac{n}{n+1}$, where we denote the total of all persons that have passed away up to this moment by n. If I ask a present-day authority in biology or medicine what evidence there is that it will be possible to preserve an individual person permanently from death, he would confess : not the slightest. Nevertheless, Helmholtz declared : " To a person who tells me that by using certain means the life of a person may be prolonged indefinitely I can oppose my extreme disbelief, *but I cannot contradict him absolutely*."

Einstein himself once pointed out to me such very remote possibilities ; it was in connexion with the following circumstance. It is quite impossible for a moving body ever to attain a velocity greater than that of light, because it is scientifically inconceivable. On the other hand, it is conceivable, and therefore within the range of possibility, that man may yet fly to the most distant constellations.

There is, therefore, no absolute contradiction to the notion of making available for technical purposes the billions of calories that occurred in our problem. As soon as we admit it as possible for discussion, we find ourselves inquiring what the solution of the problem could signify. In our intercourse we actually arrived at this question, and discovered the most radical answer in a dissertation which Friedrich Siemens has written about coal in general without touching in the slightest on these possibilities of the future. I imagine that this dissertation was a big trump in my hand, but had soon to learn from the reasoned contradiction of Einstein that the point at issue was not to be decided in this way.

Nevertheless, it will repay us to consider these arguments for a moment.

Friedrich Siemens starts from two premises which he seemingly bases on scientific reasoning, thus claiming their validity generally. They are : Coal is the measure of all things. The price of every product represents, directly or indirectly, the value of the coal contained in it.

As all economic values in over-populated countries are the result of work, and as work presupposes coal, capital is synonymous with coal. The economic value of each object is the sum-total of the coal that had to be used to manufacture the object in question. In over-populated states each wage is the value of the coal that is necessary to make this extra life possible. If there is a scarcity of coal, the wages go down in value ; if there is no coal, the wages are of no value at all, no matter how much paper money be issued.

As soon as agriculture requires coal (this occurs when it is practised intensively and necessitates the use of railways, machines, artificial manures), coal becomes involved with food-stuffs. Thanks to industrialism, coal is involved in clothing and housing, too.

Since money is equivalent to coal, proper administration of finance is equivalent to a proper administration of coal resources, and our standard of currency is in the last instance a coal-currency. Gold as money is now concentrated coal.

The most advanced people is that which derives from one kilogramme of coal the greatest possibilities conducive to life. Wise statesmanship must resolve itself into wise administration of coal. Or, as it has been expressed in other words elsewhere : " We must think in terms of coal."

These fundamental ideas were discussed, and the result was that Einstein admitted the premises in the main, but failed to see the conclusiveness of the inferences. He proved to me, step by step, that Siemens' line of thought followed a vicious circle, and, by begging the question, arrived at a false conclusion. The essential factor, he said, is man-power, and so it will remain ; it is this that we have to regard as the primary factor. Just so much can be saved to advantage as there is man-power available for purposes other than for the production of coal from which they are now released. If we succeed in getting greater use out of a kilogramme of coal by better management, then this is measurable in man-power, with which one may dispense for the mining of coal, and which may be applied to other purposes.

If the assertion : " Coal is the measure of all things," were generally valid, it should stand every test. We need only try it in a few instances to see that the thesis does not apply. For example, said Einstein : However much coal we may use, and however cleverly we may dispose of it, it will not produce cotton. Certainly the freightage of cotton-wool could be reduced in price, but the value-factor represented by man-power can never disappear from the price of the cotton.

The most that can be admitted is that an increase of the amount of power obtained from coal would make it possible for more people to exist than is possible at present, that is, that the margin of over-population would become extended. But we must not conclude that this would be a boon to mankind. " A maximum is not an optimum."

He who proclaims the maximum without qualification as the greatest measure of good is like one who studies the various gases in the atmosphere to ascertain their good or bad effect on our breathing, and arrives at the conclusion : the nitrogen in the air is harmful, so we must double the proportion of oxygen to counteract it ; this will confer a great benefit on humanity !

* Armed with this striking analogy, we can now subject the foundation of Siemens' theory to a new scrutiny, and we shall then discover that even the premises contain a trace of the *petitio principii* that finally receives expression in the radical and one-sided expression : " Coal is everything."

As if built on solid foundations this first statement looms before us : Coal is solar energy. This is so far indisputable. For all the coal deposits that are still slumbering in the earth were once stately plants, dense woods of fern, which, bearing the burden of millions of years, have saved up for us what they had once extracted as nutrition from the sun's rays. We may let the parallel idea pass without contention : In the beginning was not the Word, nor the Deed, but, in the beginning was the Sun. The energy sent out by the sun to the earth for mankind is the only necessary and inevitable condition for deeds. Deeds mean work, and work necessitates life. But we immediately become involved in an unjustifiable subdivision of the idea, for the propounder of the theory says next : ". . . Coal is solar energy, therefore coal is necessary if we are to work . . ." and this has already thrust us from the paths of logic ; the prematurely victorious ergo breaks down. For, apart from the solar energy converted into coal, the warmth of our mother planet radiates on us, and furnishes us with the possibility of work. Siemens' conclusion, from the point of view of logic, is tantamount to : Graphite is solar energy ; hence graphite is necessary, if we are to be able to work. The true expression of the state of affairs is : Coal is,

* The parts included between * . . . * are to be regarded as supplementary portions intended to elucidate the arguments involved in the dialogue. In many points they are founded on utterances of Einstein, but also contain reflections drawn from other sources, as well as opinions and inferences which fall to the account of the author, as already remarked in the preface. One will not get far by judging these statements as right or wrong, for even the debatable view may prove itself to be expeditious and suggestive in the perspective of these conversations. Wherever it was possible, without the connexion being broken, I have called attention to the parts which Einstein corrected or disapproved of. In other places I refrained from this, particularly when the subject under discussion demanded an even flow of argument. It would have disturbed the exposition if I had made mention of every counter-argument of the opposing side in all such cases while the explanation was proceeding along broad lines.

for our present conditions of life, the most important, if not the exclusive, preliminary for human work.

And when we learn from political economy that "in a social state only the necessary human labour and the demand for power-installations which require coal, and hence again labour for their production, come into question," this in no way implies the assertion, as Siemens appears to assume, that coal can be made out of labour. But it does signify that work founded on the sun's energy need not necessarily be reducible to coal. And this probably coincides with Einstein's opinion, which is so much the more significant, as his own doctrine points to the highest measure of effect in forces, even if only theoretically.*

Nevertheless, it is a fact that every increase in the quantity of power derived, when expressed per kilo, denotes a mitigation of life's burdens ; it is only a question of the limits involved.

Firstly, is technical science with its possibilities, as far as they can be judged at present, still able to guarantee the future for us ? Can it spread out the effective work so far that we may rely peacefully on the treasures of coal slumbering in the interior of the earth ?

Evidently not. For in this case we are dealing with quantities that may be approximately estimated. And even if we get three times, nay ten times, as many useful calories as before, there is a parallel calculation of evil omen that informs us : there will be an end to this feast of energy.

In spite of all the embarrassments due to the present shortage of coal we have still always been able to console ourselves with the thought that there is really a sufficiency, and that it is only a question of overcoming stoppages. It is a matter of fact that from the time of the foundation of the German Empire to the beginning of the World War coal production had been rising steadily, and it was possible to calculate that in spite of the stupendous quantities that were being removed from the black caves of Germany, there remained at least 2000 milliards of marks in value (taken at the nominal rate, that is, £100,000,000,000). Nevertheless, geologists and mining experts tell us that our whole supply will not last longer than 2000 years, in the case of

England 500 years, and in that of France 200 years. Even if we allow amply for the opening up of new coal-fields in other continents, we cannot get over the fact that in the prehistoric fern forests the sun has stored up only a finite, exhaustible amount of energy, and that within a few hundred years humanity will be faced with a coal famine.

Now, if coal were really the measure of all things, and if the possibility of life depended only on the coal supply, then our distant descendants would not only relapse into barbarity, but they would have to expect the absolute zero of existence. We should not need to worry at all about the entropy death of the universe, as our own extinction on this earthly planet beckons to us from an incomparably nearer point of time.

At this stage of the discussion Einstein revealed prospects which were entirely in accordance with his conviction that the whole argument based on the coal assumption was untenable. He stated that it was by no means a Utopian idea that technical science will yet discover totally new ways of setting free forces, such as using the sun's radiation, or water power, or the movement of the tides, or power reservoirs of Nature, among which the present coal supply denotes only one branch. Since the beginning of coal extraction we have lived only on the remains of a prehistoric capital that has lain in the treasure-chests of the earth. It is to be conjectured that the interest on the actual capital of force will be very much in excess of what we can fetch out of the depositories of former ages.

To form an estimate of this actual capital, entirely independent of coal, we may present some figures. Let us consider a tiny water canal, a mere nothing in the watery network of the earth, the Rhine-falls at Schaffhausen, that may appear mighty to the beholder, but only because he applies his tourist's measure instead of a planetary one. But even this bagatelle in the household of Nature represents very considerable effectual values for us : 200 cubic metres spread over a terrace 20 metres high yield 67,000 horse-power, equivalent to 50,000 kilowatts. This cascade alone would suffice to keep illuminated to their full intensity 1,000,000 glow-lamps, each of 50 candle-power, and according to our present tariff we should have to pay at least 70,000 marks (£3500 nominally) per hour. The coal-worshipper will be more impressed by a different calculation. The Rhine-falls at Schaffhausen is equivalent in value to a mine that yields every day 145 tons of the finest brown coal. If we took the Niagara Falls as an illustration, these figures would have to be multiplied by about 80.

And by what factor would we have to multiply them, if we wished to get only an approximate estimate of the energy that the breathing earth rolls about in the form of the tides ? The astronomer Bessel and the philosopher-physicist Fechner once endeavoured to get at some comparative picture of these events. It required 360,000 men twenty years to build the greatest Egyptian pyramid, and yet its cubical contents are only about the millionth of a cubic mile, and perhaps if we sum up everything that men and machinery have moved since the time of the Flood till now, a cubic mile would not yet have been completed. In contrast with this, the earth in its tidal motion moves 200 cubic miles of water from one quadrant of the earth's circumference to another *in every quarter of a day*. From this we see at once that all the coal-mines in the world would mean nothing to us if we could once succeed in making even a fraction of the pulse-beat of the earth available for purposes of industry.

If, however, we should be compelled to depend on coal, our imaginations cling so much more closely to that enormous quantity given by the expression mc^2, which was derived from the theory of relativity.

The 20 billion calories that are contained in each gramme of coal exercise a fascination on our minds. And although Einstein states that there is not the slightest indication that we shall get at this supply, we get carried along by an irresistible impulse to picture what it would mean if we should actually succeed in tapping it. The transition from the golden to the iron age, as pictured in Hesiod, Aratus, and Ovid, takes shape before our eyes, and following our bent of continuing this cyclically, we take pleasure in fancying ourselves being rescued from the serfdom of the iron and of the coal age to a new golden age. A supply, such as is piled up in an average city storing-place, would be sufficient to supply the whole world with energy for an immeasurable time. All the troubles and miseries arising from the running of machines, the mechanical production of wares, house-fires would vanish, and all the human labour at present occupied in mining coal would become free to cultivate the land, all railways and boats would run almost without expense, an inconceivable wave of happiness would sweep over mankind. It would mean an end of coal-, freight-, and food-shortage ! We should at last be able to escape out of the hardships of the day, which is broken up by strenuous work, and soar upwards to brighter spheres where we would be welcomed by the true values of life. How alluring is the song of Sirens chanted by our physics with its high " C," the velocity of light to the second power, which we have got to know as a factor in this secret store of energy.

But these dreams are futile. For Einstein, to whom we owe this formula so promising of wonders, not only denies that it can be applied practically, but also brings forward another argument that casts us down to earth again. Supposing, he explained, it were possible to set free this enormous store of energy, then we should only arrive at an age, compared with which the present coal age· would have to be called golden.

And, unfortunately, we find ourselves obliged to fall in with this view, which is based in the wise old saw $\mu\eta\delta\grave{\epsilon}\nu$ $\check{\alpha}\gamma\alpha\nu$, *ne quid nimis*, nothing in excess. Applied to our case, this means that when such a measure of power is set free, it does not serve a useful purpose, but leads to destruction. The process of burning, which we used as an illustration, calls up the picture of an oven in which we can imagine this wholesale production of energy, and experience tells us that we should not heat an oven with dynamite.

If technical developments of this kind were to come about, the energy supply would probably not be capable of regulation at all. It makes no difference if we say that we only want a part of those 20 billion calories, and that we should be glad to be able to multiply the 8000 calories required to-day by 100. That is not possible, for if we should succeed in disintegrating the atom, it seems that we should have the billions of calories rushing unchecked on us, and we should find ourselves unable to cope with them, nay, perhaps even the solid ground, on which we move, could not withstand them.

No discovery remains a monopoly of only a few people. If a very careful scientist should really succeed in producing a practical heating or driving effect from the atom, then any untrained person would be able to blow up a whole town by means of only a minute quantity of substance. And any suicidal maniac who hated his fellows and wished to pulverize all habitations within a wide range would only have to conceive the plan to carry it out at a moment's notice. All the bombardments that have taken place ever since fire-arms were invented would be mere child's play compared with the destruction that could be caused by two buckets of coal.

At intervals we see stars light up in the heavens, and then become extinguished again ; from these we infer that world catastrophes have occurred. We do not know whether it is due to the explosion of hydrogen with other gases, or to collisions between two stellar bodies. There is still room for the assumption that, immeasurably far away in yonder regions of celestial space, something is happening which a malevolent inhabitant of our earth, who has discovered the secret of smashing the atom, might here repeat. And even if our imaginations can be stretched to paint the blessings of this release of energy, they certainly fail to conjure up visions of the disastrous effects which would result.

Einstein turned to a page in a learned work of the mathematical physicist Weyl of Zürich, and pointed out a part that dealt with such an appalling liberation of energy. It seemed to me to be of the nature of a fervent prayer that Heaven preserve us from such explosive forces ever being let loose on mankind !

Subject to present impossibility, it is possible to weave many parallel instances. It is conceivable that by some yet undiscovered process alcohol may be prepared as plentifully and as cheaply as ordinary water. This would end the shortage of alcohol, and would assure delirium tremens for hundreds of thousands. The evil would far outweigh the good, although it might be avoidable, for one can, even if with great difficulty, imagine precautionary measures.

War technique might lead to the use of weapons of great range, which would enable a small number of adventurers to conquer a Great Power. It will be objected : this will hold vice versa, too. Nevertheless, this would not alter the fact that such long-range weapons would probably lead to the destruction of civilization. Our last hope of an escape would be in a superior moral outlook of future generations, which the optimist may imagine to himself as the *force majeure*.

There are apparently only two inventions, in themselves triumphs of intellect, against which one would have no defence. The first would be thought-reading made applicable to all, and with which Kant has dealt under the term " thinking aloud." What is nowadays a rare and very imperfect telepathic " turn " may yet be generalized and perfected in a manner which Kant supposed not impossible on some distant planet. The association and converse of man with his fellows would not stand the test of this invention, and we should have to be angels to survive it even for a day.

The second invention would be the solution of this mc^2-problem, which I call a problem only because I fail to discover a proper term, whereas so far was it from being a problem for Einstein that it was only in my presence he began to reckon it out in figures from the symbolic formula. To us average beings a Utopia may disclose itself, a short frenzy of joy followed by a cold douche : Einstein stands above it as the pure searcher, who is interested only in the scientific fact, and who, even at the first knowledge of it, preserves its essentially theoretical importance from attempts to apply it practically. If, then, another wishes to hammer out into a fantastic gold-leaf what he has produced as a little particle of gold in his physical investigations, he offers no opposition to such thought-experiments, for one of the deepest traits of his nature is tolerance.

A. Pflüger, one of the best qualified heralds of the new doctrine, has touched on the above matter in his essay, *The Principle of Relativity*. Einstein praised this pamphlet ; I mentioned that the author took a view different from that of Einstein, of the possibility of making accessible the mc^2. In discussing the practical significance of this eventuality, Pflüger says : " It will be time to talk of this point again a hundred years hence." This seems a short time-limit, even if none of us will live to be present at the discussion. Einstein smiled at this pause of a hundred years, and merely repeated, " A very good essay ! " It is not for me to offer contradictions ; and, as far as the implied prognostication is concerned, it will be best for mankind if it should prove to be false. If the optimum is unattainable, at least we shall be spared the worst, which is what the realization of this prophecy would inflict on us.

Some months after the above discussion had first been put to paper, the world was confronted by a new scientific event. The English physicist Rutherford had, with deliberate intention, actually succeeded in splitting up the atom. When I questioned Einstein on the possible consequences of this experimental achievement, he declared with his usual frankness, one of the treasures of his character, that he had now occasion to modify somewhat the opinion he had shortly before expressed. This is not to mean that he now considered the practical goal of getting unlimited supply of energy as having been brought within the realm of possibility. He gave it as his view that we are now entering on a new stage of development, which may perhaps disclose fresh openings for technical science. The scientific importance of these new experiments with the atom was certainly to be considered very great.

In Rutherford's operations the atom is treated as if he were dealing with a fortress : he subjects it to a bombardment and then seeks to fire into the breach. The fortress is still certainly far from capitulating, but signs of disruption have become observable. A hail of bullets caused holes, tears, and splinterings.

The projectiles hurled by Rutherford are alpha-particles shot out by radium, and their velocity approaches two-thirds that of light. Owing to the extreme violence of the impact, they succeeded in doing damage to certain atoms enclosed in evacuated glass tubes. It was shown that atoms of nitrogen had been disrupted. It is still unknown what quantities of energy are released in this process. This splitting up of the atom carried out with intention can, indeed, be detected only by the most careful investigations.

As far as practical applications are concerned, then, we have got no further, although we have renewed grounds for hope. The unit of measure, as it were, is still out of proportion to the material to be cut. For the forces which Rutherford had to use to attain this result are relatively very considerable. He derived them from a gramme of radium, which is able to liberate several milliard calories, whereas the net practical result in Rutherford's experiment is still immeasurably small. Nevertheless, it is scientifically established that it is possible to split up atoms of one's own free will, and thus the fundamental objection raised above falls to the ground.

There is also another reason for increased hope. It seems feasible that, under certain conditions, Nature would automatically continue the disruption of the atom, after a human being had intentionally started it, as in the analogous case of a conflagration which extends, although it may have started from a mere spark.

A by-product of future research might lead to the transmutation of lead into gold. The possibility of this transformation of elements is subject to the same arguments as those above about the splitting up of the atom and the release of great quantities of energy. The path of decay from radium to lead lies clearly exposed even now, but it is very questionable whether mankind will finally have cause to offer up hymns of thanksgiving if this line from lead on to the precious metals should be continued, for it would cause our conception of the latter to be shattered. Gold made from lead would not give rise to an increase in the value of the meaner metal, but to the utter depreciation of gold, and hence the loss of the standard of value that has been valid since the beginning of our civilization. No economist would be possessed of a sufficiently far-sighted vision to be able to measure the consequences on the world's market of such a revolution in values.

The chief product would, of course, be the gain in energy, and we must bear this in mind when we give ourselves up to our speculations, however optimistic or catastrophic they may be. The impenetrable barrier " impossible " no longer exists. Einstein's wonderful " Open Sesame," mass times the square of the velocity of light, is thundering at the portals.

And mankind finds a new meaning in the old saw : One should never say *never* !

CHAPTER III

VALHALLA

I HAD made up my mind to question Einstein about a number of famous men, not concerning mere facts of their lives and works, for these details were also procurable elsewhere, and, moreover, I was not ignorant of them, but what attracted me particularly was to try to discover how the greatness of one might be compared with that of another. This sometimes helps us to see a personality in a different light and from a new perspective, which leads us to assign to him a new position in the series of orders of merit.

I had really sketched out a list for this purpose, including a great number of glorious names from the annals of physics and regions just beyond : a table, as it were, from which one might set up a directory for Valhalla ! It seemed to me a pleasing thought to roam through this hall of celebrities in company with Einstein, and to pause at the pedestal of the busts of the great, who, in spite of their number, are still too few, far too few, in comparison with the far too many who populate the earth like so many factory-produced articles. If we set to work to draw up a list of this sort, we soon find that there is no end to these heroes of Valhalla, and we are reminded of the hall of fame of the Northern Saga, of the mythological Valhalla, whose ceiling was so high that the gable was invisible, and whose extent was so great that anyone wishing to enter could choose from five hundred and forty entrances.

In reality our little excursion was far from taking these dimensions, the chief reason being probably that we had begun at Newton. However attractive it may be to hear Einstein talk of Newton, a disadvantage arises in that we find it hard to take leave of his bust situated at the main portal, and that we continually revert to it even when we call to mind the remaining paths free for our choice and stretching out of sight.

Reality, even figuratively, offered a picture which differed considerably from the measures of greatness apportioned by legendary accounts. In Einstein's workroom, certainly, a visitor encounters portraits, not busts, and it would be rash to speak of this little collection of portraits as of a miniature museum. No, it is certainly not that, for its catalogue numbers only to three. But here they act as a trinity with a special significance under the gaze of Einstein, who looks up to them with reverence. To him their contribution of thought is immeasurable ; Faraday, Maxwell with his rich coils of hair, and between them, Newton with his flowing wig, represented in an excellent English engraving, whose border consists of symbolic insignias encircling his distinguished-looking countenance.

.   .   .   .

According to Schopenhauer, the measure of reverence that one can feel is a measure of one's own intrinsic value. Tell me how much respect you can feel, and I shall tell you what is your worth. It is certainly not necessary to emphasize this quality specially in the case of Einstein, for there are other points of vantage from which we may form an estimate of his excellence. Nevertheless, I make special mention of the circumstance to give an indication of the difference between a revolutionary discoverer and revolutionary pioneers in other fields. It is particularly noticeable that inborn respect is seldom found in modernists of Art. The only means of propaganda known to them consists in a passionate denunciation of what has been developed historically by gradual and patient effort ; their retrospect consists of unmitigated contempt ; they profess to be disciples only of what is most recent, remaining confined within the narrow circle surrounding their own ego. The horizon of the discoverer has a different radius. He takes over responsibility for the future by never ceasing his offerings at the altar of the Past. There is probably no discoverer who is devoid of this characteristic, but I should like to emphasize that, among all the scientists with whom I am acquainted, no one recognizes the merit of others so warmly as Einstein. He becomes carried away with enthusiasm when he talks of great men, or of such as appear great to him. His Valhalla is not, of course, the same as that favoured by Encyclopædias, and many a one whom we rank as a Sirius among men is to be found lower than the sixth order of magnitude in Einstein's list. Nevertheless, the number of selection of constellations is no mean one, and the reverence that was originally inspired by reasoned thought has become infused in his temperament and become a part of his emotional self.

One need only mention the name of Newton—and even this is scarcely necessary, for Newton seems always near at hand ; if I happen to start with Descartes or Pascal, it does not take long before we arrive at Newton. ἄνδρα μοῖ ἔννεπη !

Once we began with Laplace ; and it seemed almost as if the " Traité de la méchanique céleste " was to become the subject of discussion. But Einstein left his seat, and, taking up a position in front of his series of portraits on the wall, he meditatively passed his hand through his hair, and declared :

" In my opinion the greatest creative geniuses are Galilei and Newton, whom I regard in a certain sense as forming a unity. And in this unity Newton is he who has achieved the most imposing feat in the realm of science. These two were the first to create a system of mechanics founded on a few laws and giving a general theory of motions, the totality of which represents the events of our world."

Interrupting his remarks, I asked : " Can Galilei's fundamental law of inertia (Newton's First Law of Motion) be said to be a law deduced from experience ? My reason for asking is that the whole of natural science is a science of experience, and not merely something based on speculation. It might easily suggest itself to one that an elementary law like that of Galilei or Newton could be derived from our everyday experience. But, if this is the case, how is it that science had to wait so long before this simple fact was discovered ? Experience is as old as the hills ; why did the law of inertia not make its appearance at the very beginning, when Nature was first subjected to inquiry ? "

"By no means!" replied Einstein. "The discovery of the law of rectilinear motion of a body under no external influences is not at all a result of experience. On the contrary! A circle, too, is a simple line of motion, and has often been proclaimed as such by predecessors of Newton, for example, by Aristoteles. It required the enormous power of abstraction possessed only by a giant of reason to stabilize rectilinear motion as the fundamental form."

To this may be added that before and even after the time of Galilei, not only the circle but also other non-rectilinear lines have been regarded even by serious thinkers as the primary lines given by Nature ; these thinkers even dared to apply their curvilinear views to explaining world phenomena that could be made clear only after Galilei's abstraction had been accepted.

I asked whether the theory of gravitation was already implicitly contained in Galilei's Laws of Falling Bodies. Einstein's answer was in the negative : the gravitational theory falls entirely to the credit of Newton, and the greatness of this intellectual achievement remains unimpaired even if the efforts of certain forerunners are recognized. He mentioned Robert Hooke, whom, among others, Schopenhauer sets up against Newton, with absolute injustice and from petty feelings of antipathy, which takes its origin from Schopenhauer's unmathematical type of mind. The vast difference between Hooke's preliminary attempts at explaining gravitation, and Newton's monumental structure, was beyond his power of discernment.

*Schopenhauer (vol. ii. of the *Parerga*) uses two arguments to discredit Newton. Firstly, he refers to two original works, both of which he misinterprets ; secondly, he undertakes a psychological analysis of Newton. He uses psychological means, which would be about equally reasonable as applying the Integral Calculus to proving facts of Ethical Psychology, and he arrives at the conclusion that priority in discovering the law of gravitation is due to some one else ; Hooke is pictured as having been treated like Columbus : we now hear of "America," and likewise "Newton's Gravitational System"!

Schopenhauer has, however, quite forgotten that he himself, some pages earlier, trumpeted forth Newton's imperishable fame with the words : " To form an estimate of the great value of the gravitational system which was at least completed and firmly established by Newton, we must remind ourselves how entirely nonplussed about the origin of the motion of celestial bodies thinkers had previously been for thousands of years." That bears the ring of truth. Newton's greatness can be grasped only if thousands of years are used as a measure.

Whereas Schopenhauer argued from grounds drawn from psychology and the principle of universal knowledge, his antagonist Hegel, who was still more vague in these fields, sought to dispense with both Newton and Kepler by calling to his aid the so-called pure intuition of the curved line. In an exposition of truly comical prolixity, such as would have delighted the hearts of scholiasts, he proves that the ellipse must represent the fundamental type of planetary motion, this being quite independent of Newton's laws, Kepler's observations, and resulting mathematical relationships. And Hegel actually succeeds, with a nebulous verbosity almost stultifying in its unmeaningness, in paraphrasing Kepler's second law in his own fashion. It reads like an extract from some carnival publication issued by scientists in a bibulous mood to make fun of themselves.

But these extravagances, too, serve to add lustre to Newton, for his genius shines out most brilliantly when it is a question of expressing clearly, and without assumptions, a phenomenon of cosmic motion. Here there are no forerunners, not even with regard to his own law of gravitation. Newton showed with truly triumphant logic that Kepler's second law belongs to those things that are really self-evident.

This law, taken alone, offers considerable difficulties to anyone who learns of it for the first time. Every planet describes an ellipse ; that is accepted without demur. But the uninitiated will possibly or even probably deduce from this that the planet will pass over equal lengths of arc in equal times. By no means, says Kepler ; the arcs traversed in equal times are unequal. But if we connect every point of the elliptic path with a definite point within the curve (the focus of the ellipse) by means of straight lines, each of which is called a radius vector, we get that the areas swept out by the radius vector in equal times (and not the arcs) are equally great.

Why is this so ? This cannot be understood *a priori*. But

one might argue that since the attraction of the sun is the governing force, this will probably have something to do with Newton's law of gravitation, in particular with the inverse square of the distance. And one might further infer that, if a different principle of gravitation existed, Kepler's law would assume a new form.

A fact amazing in its simplicity here comes to light. Newton states the proposition : " According to whatever law an accelerating force acts from a centre on a body moving freely, the radius vector will always sweep out equal areas in equal lengths of time."

Nothing is assumed except the law of inertia and a little elementary mathematics, namely, the theorem that triangles on the same base and of the same altitude are equal in area. The form in which this theorem occurs in Newton's simple drawing is certainly astonishing. One feels that there in a few strokes a cosmic problem is solved ; the impression is ineffaceable.

This theorem together with its proof is contained in Newton's chief work, *Philosophiæ naturalis principia mathematica*. The interfusion of philosophy and mathematics furnished him with the natural principles of knowledge.*

Einstein made some illuminating remarks about Newton's famous phrase: " Hypotheses non fingo." I had said that Newton must have been aware that it is impossible to build up a science entirely free from hypotheses. Even geometry itself has arrived at that critical stage at which Gauss and Riemann discovered its hypothetical foundations.

Einstein replied : " Accentuate the words correctly and the true sense will reveal itself ! " It is the last word that is to be stressed and not the first. Newton did not want to feel himself free from hypotheses, but rather from the assumption that he invented them, except when this was absolutely necessary. Newton, then, wished to express that he did not go further back in his analysis of causes than was absolutely inevitable.

Perhaps, I allowed myself to interject, a more violent suspicion against the word " hypotheses " was prevalent with scholars in Newton's time than now. Newton's emphatic defence would then appear a shade more intelligible   Or did he cherish the belief that his world-law was the only possible one in Nature ?

Einstein again referred to the universality of Newton's genius, saying that Newton was doubtless aware of the range within which his law was valid : this law applies to the realm of observation and experience, but is not given *a priori*, no more than Galilei's Law of Inertia. It is certainly conceivable that beyond the domain of human experience there may be an undiscoverable universe in which a different fundamental law holds, and one which, nevertheless, does not contradict the principle of sufficient reason.

The antithesis : Simplicity—Complexity, led the conversation into a short bypath ; it arose out of an example which I quoted and that I shall repeat here even if it may seem irrelevant.

One might well expect that just as for attraction there must be a general law for resistance or repulsion. And if attraction occurs according to the inverse square of the distance, then it would be an extremely interesting parallel if a similar law were to hold for repulsion except that the proportionality were direct instead of inverse. There have actually been physicists who have proclaimed a direct square law of repulsion ; I have heard it in lectures myself. The action of a resisting medium, as, for example, the resistance of the air to the flight of a cannon-ball, is stated to be proportional to the square of the velocity of the projectile.

This theorem is wrong. If it were correct, and verified by experiment, we should have to regard it as being presumably the only possible and directly evident form of the law of repulsion or resistance. There would, at least, be no logical reason for contradicting it.

But here we have a mixed relationship, as Einstein calls it— that is, we are unable to express an exact connexion between the velocity of a body in flight and the air resistance.

This fallacious assumption by no means proceeded from illogical reasoning, and it seemed to rest on a sound physical basis. For, so it was argued, if the velocity is doubled, there is twice as much air to be displaced, so that the resistance will be four times as great. But this was contradicted outright by experimental evidence. One cannot even call it an approximate law, except for very low speeds. For greater speeds we find, instead of a quadratic relation, a cubical one, or one of a more complex nature. Photographs have demonstrated that the resistance experienced by a projectile in flight is due to the excitation of a powerful central wave, to the friction between the air and the surface of the projectile, and to eddies produced behind the projectile—that is, to various conjoined factors, each of which follows a different law, and such that the combined effect cannot be expressed by a simple formula at all. This phenomenon is thus very complicated and offers almost insuperable difficulties to analysis. A beautiful remark was once made, which characterizes such events in Nature.

During a conversation with Laplace, Fresnel said that Nature does not worry about analytical difficulties. There is nothing simpler than Newton's Law in spite of the complicated nature of planetary motions. "Nature here despises our analytical difficulties," said Fresnel; "she applies simple means, and then by combining them produces an almost inextricable net of confusion. Simplicity lies concealed in this chaos, and it is only for us to discover it!" But this simplicity when it is discovered is not always found to be expressible in simple formulæ, not must it be forgotten that even the ultimate discoverable simplicity points to certain hypothetical assumptions.

"Hypotheses non fingo!" This phrase of Newton's remains true, if we maintain Einstein's interpretation: "He did not wish to go further back in his analysis of causes than was absolutely inevitable." It interested me to pursue this line of thought suggested by Einstein still further, and I discovered that these words of Newton had actually been falsely accentuated and hence misinterpreted by many authorities on science. Even Mill and the great scholar, William Whewell, succumbed to this misunderstanding. Credit must be given to a more modern scholar, Professor Vaihinger of Halle, for being sufficiently keen of hearing to detect the true accentuation; and now that Einstein has corroborated fully this explanation, doubts as to the true sense of the words are no longer to be feared.

The trend of our talk brought us to a discussion of the

conception, "law of nature." Einstein recalled Mach's remarks, and indicated that the point was to determine how much we read out of Nature ; and these observations made at least one thing clear, namely, that every law signifies some limitation ; in the case of human laws, expressed in the civil and penal code, the limitation affects the will, and possible actions, whereas natural laws signify the limitations which we, taught by experience, prescribe to our expectations. Nevertheless, the conception remains elastic, for the question will always intrude itself : What does prescription mean ? Who prescribes ? Kant has assigned to Man the foremost position inasmuch as it is he who is regarded by Kant as prescribing laws to Nature. Bacon of Verulam emphasizes the ambiguous point of view by asserting: "Natura non vincitur nisi parendo," Man conquers Nature only by obeying her, that is, by conforming to her immanent norms. Thus the laws exist without us, and we have only to discover them. When they have been found, Man can react by applying them to subdue Nature. Man becomes the dictator and dictates to Nature the laws according to which she for her part has to subjugate mankind. Whether we adopt the one view or the other, there is a vicious circle, from which there is no escape. A law is a creation of intellect, and Mephisto's words remain true : " In the end we depend on the creatures of our own making ! "

In Newton's soul obedience and the wish to obey must have been pre-eminent traits. Is he not reputed to have been pious and strong of faith ?

Einstein confirmed this, and, raising his voice, he generalized from it, saying : " In every true searcher of Nature there is a kind of religious reverence ; for he finds it impossible to imagine that he is the first to have thought out the exceedingly delicate threads that connect his perceptions. The aspect of knowledge which has not yet been laid bare gives the investigator a feeling akin to that experienced by a child who seeks to grasp the masterly way in which elders manipulate things."

This explanation implied a personal confession. For he had spoken of the childlike longing felt by all, and had interpreted the subtle intricacies of the scientist's ideas in particular as springing from a religious source. Not all have confessed this ; we know, indeed, that the convictions of many a one were not so. Let us cling to the fact that the greatest in the realm of science—Newton, Descartes, Gauss, and Helmholtz—were pious, although their faith varied in degree. And let us not forget that the most bitter opponent of this attitude of mind, the originator of " Ecrasez l'infame," finally had a temple built bearing the inscription : " Deo erexit Voltaire."

In Newton positivism found its most faithful disciple, and his research was directly affected by his religious attitude. He, himself, was the author of that beautiful thought : " A limited measure of knowledge takes us away from God ; an increased measure of knowledge takes us back to Him." It was he who considered that the world-machine that he had disclosed was not sufficiently stabilized by his mathematical law, and so he enlisted the intermittent help of an assistant for the Creator, Concursus Dei, to attend to the functioning of the machine. Finally, he slipped from the path of naïve faith on to theological bypaths and wrote devout essays on apocalyptic matters. On the other hand, Descartes' piety, which was genuine at root, exhibited suspicious offshoots, and one cannot shake off the feeling that he was smiling up his sleeve when he was making some of his solemn declarations. He was a master of compromise, and gave due expression to its spirit, which F. A. Lange bluntly stated was merely a veil for " Cowardice towards the Church." Voltaire, an apostle of Newton's system of natural philosophy, went so far in his condemnation of Descartes' confession of faith that he affirmed : " The Cartesian doctrine has been mainly instrumental in persuading many not to recognize a God."

As Einstein had called special attention to the childlike nature of the scientist's root-impulse, I quoted a remark of Newton that seemed to me at the moment to be a confirmation of Einstein's attitude :

" I do not know what I may appear to the world, but to myself I seem to have been only like a boy playing on the seashore, and diverting myself in now and then finding a smoother pebble or a prettier shell than ordinary, whilst the great ocean of truth lay all undiscovered before me."

Are we not to regard this analogy of Newton's as being intended to convey a religious meaning ?

" There is no objection to this," said Einstein, " although it seems to me more probable that, in saying this, Newton set down the view only of the pure investigator. The essential purpose of his remarks was to express how small is the range of the attainable compared with the infinite expanse offered for research."

Through some unexpected phrase that was dropped, the conversation took a new turn at this point, which I should not like to withhold, inasmuch as it gave rise to a noteworthy observation of Einstein about the nature of genius. We were talking about the "possibility of genius for science being inherited " and about the comparative rareness with which it occurs. There seems to have been only one case of a real dynasty of great minds, that of the ten Bernoullis who were descended of a line of mathematicians, and all of them achieved important results, some of them making extraordinary discoveries. Why is this exception unique ? In other examples we do not get beyond three or four names in the same family, even if we take Science and Art conjointly. There were two Plinys, two Galileis, two Herschels, two Humboldts, two Lippis, two Dumas, several Bachs, Pisanos, Robbias, and Holbeins—the net result is very poor, even if we count similar names, disregarding the fact of relationship ; there is no recognizable dynasty except in the case of the ten Bernoullis.*

" And so," I continued, " the conclusion seems justified that Nature has nothing to do with a genealogy of talents, and that, if we happen to notice manifestations of talent in one and the same family, this is a mere play of chance."

Einstein, however, contradicted this emphatically : " Inherited talent certainly occurs in many cases, where we do not observe it, for genius in itself and the possibility of genius being apprehended are certainly far from always appearing in conjunction. There are only insignificant differences between the genius that expresses itself in remarkable achievements and

* The Roman family Cosmati (of the thirteenth century), which gave us seven splendid representatives of architecture and mosaic work, hardly comes into consideration, since not one of them is regarded in the history of art as a real genius.

the genius that is latent. At a certain instant, perhaps, only some impulse was wanting for the latent genius to burst forth with all clearness and brilliance ; or, perhaps, it required only an unusual situation in the development of science to call into action his special talents, and thus it remained dormant, whereas a very slight change of circumstances would have caused them to assert themselves in definite results.

" In passing I should like to remark that you just now mentioned the two Humboldts ; it seems to me that Alexander von Humboldt, at least, is not to be counted as a genius. It has struck me repeatedly that you pronounced his name with particular reverence——"

" And I have observed equally often, Professor, that you made a sign of disapproval. For this reason slight doubts have gradually been rising in me. But it is difficult to get free from the orders of greatness that one has recognized for decades. In my youth people spoke of ' a Humboldt ' just as we speak of ' a Cæsar ' or ' a Michelangelo,' to denote some pinnacle of unrivalled height. To me at that time Humboldt's Kosmos was the Bible of Natural Science, and probably such memories have a certain after-effect."

" That is easy to understand," said Einstein. " But we must make it clear to ourselves that for us of the present day Humboldt scarcely comes into consideration when we direct our gaze on to the great seers. Or, let us say more clearly, he does not belong to this category. I certainly grant him his immense knowledge and his admirable faculty of getting into touch with the unity of Nature, which reminds us of Goethe."

" Yes ; this feeling for the uniformity of the cosmos had probably persuaded me in his favour," I answered, " and I am glad that you draw a parallel with Goethe in this respect. It reminds me of Heine's story : If God had created the whole world, except the trees and the birds, and had said to Goethe : ' My dear Goethe, I leave it to you to complete this work,' Goethe would have solved the problem correctly and in a godlike manner—that is, he would have painted the trees green and given the birds feathers.

" Humboldt could equally well have been entrusted with this task. But various objections may be raised against such reflections of a playful poetic character . . . one objection being that Goethe's own knowledge of ornithology was exceedingly limited. Even when nearly eighty he could not distinguish a lark from a yellow-hammer or a sparrow ! Is that a fact ? ''

" Fully confirmed : Eckermann gives a detailed report of it in a conversation which took place in 1827. As I happened to come across the passage only yesterday, I can quote the exact words if you will allow me : ' Great and good man,' thought Eckermann, ' who hast explored Nature as few have ever done, in ornithology thou seemest still a child ! ' ''

For a speculative philosopher, it may here be interposed, this might well serve as the starting-point of an attractive investigation. Goethe, on the one hand, cannot recognize a lark, but would have been able to grasp the Platonic idea of the feathered species, even if there had been no such things as birds : Humboldt, on the other hand, would perhaps have been able to create the revolving planets, if Heaven had commanded it ; but he would never have succeeded in becoming the author of what we call an astronomical achievement, such as that of Copernicus or of Kepler.

And with reference to certain other men I elicited from Einstein utterances that reduced somewhat my estimate of their importance.

We were speaking of Leonardo da Vinci, omitting all reference to his significance in the world of Art—that is, only of Leonardo the Scholar and the Searcher. Einstein is far from disputing his place in the Valhalla of great minds, but it was clear that he wished to recommend a re-numbering of my list, so that the Italian master would not occupy a position in just the first rank.

The problem of Leonardo excited great interest in me, and it deserves the consideration of every one. The further the examination of his writings advances, the more does this problem resolve itself into the question : How much altogether does modern science owe to Leonardo ? Nowadays it is declared in all earnestness that he was a painter and a sculptor only by the way, that his chief profession was that of an engineer, and that he was the greatest engineer of all times. This has in turn given rise to the opinion that, as a scientist, he is the light of all ages, and in the abundance of his discoveries he has never been surpassed before or after his own time.

As this question had arisen once before, I had come equipped with a little table of facts, hastily drawn from special works to which I had access. According to my scheme, Leonardo was the true discoverer and author of the following things :

Law of Conservation of Momentum.

Law of Virtual Velocities (before Ubaldi and Galilei).

Wave Theory (before Newton).

Discovery of the Circulation of the Blood (before Harvey).

Laws of Friction (before Coulomb).

Law of Pressure for connected Tubes containing Fluid (before Pascal).

Action of Pressure on Fluids (before Stevin and Galilei).

Laws of Falling Bodies (before Galilei).

True interpretation of the twinkling of stars (before Kepler, who, moreover, did not succeed in finding the real explanation).

Explanation of the reflected light of the moon (before Kepler).

Principle of Least Action (before Galilei).

Introduction of the plus and the minus signs into calculations.

Definition of kinetic energy from mass and velocity.

Theory of Combustion (before Bacon).

Explanation of the motion of the sea (before Maury).

Explanation of the ascent of fluids in plants (before Hales).

Theory of Fossilization (before Palissy).

Added to these there are a great number of inventions, in particular those connected with problems of aviation, such as the parachute (before Lenormand), and so forth.

This list aroused great distrust in Einstein : he regarded it as the outcome of an inquisitive search for sources, excusable historically, but leading to misrepresentation. We are falsely led to regard slightly related beginnings, vague tracks, hazy indications, which are found, as evidences of a real insight, which disposes us to " elevate one above all others." Hence a mythological process results, comparable to that which, in former times, thrust all conceivable feats of strength on to one Hercules.

I learned that recently a strong reaction has asserted itself in scientific circles against this one-sided hero-worship ; its purpose is to reduce Leonardo's merits to their proper measure. Einstein made it quite clear that he was certainly not to be found on the side of the ultra-Leonardists.

It cannot be denied that the latter have valuable arguments to support their case, and that these arguments become multiplied in proportion as the publication of Leonardo's writings (in the *Codex Atlanticus*, etc.), which are so difficult to decipher, proceeds. The partisans of Leonardo derive considerable support in many points from recognized authorities, as in the case of Cantor, the author of the monumental history of mathematics. We there read : " The greatest Italian painter of the fifteenth century was not less great as a scientist. In the history of science his name is famous and his achievements are extolled, particularly those which give him a claim to be regarded as one of the founders of Optics." He is placed on a level with Regiomantus as one of the chief builders of mathematics of that time. Nevertheless, Cantor raises certain doubts by remarking that the results of investigations made up to the present do not prove Leonardo to be a great mathematician. On another page he is proclaimed simultaneously with Archimedes and Pappus as a pioneer of the doctrines of the centre of gravity.

With regard to the main points, Leonardo's priority in the case of the Laws of Falling Bodies, the Theory of Wave-motion, and the other fundamental principles of physics, Einstein has the conviction that the partisans of Leonardo are either mistaken in the facts or that they overlook forerunners. In the case of these principles, above all, there is always *some* predecessor, and it is almost impossible to trace the line of discoveries back to the first source. Just as writers have wished to deprive Galilei, Kepler, and Newton of their laurels in favour of Leonardo, so the same might be done with Copernicus.

This has actually been attempted. The real Copernicus,

so one reads, was Hipparchus of Nicæa, and if we go back still further, a hundred years earlier, two thousand years ago, we find that Aristarchus of Samos taught that the world rotated about its own axis and revolved round the sun.

And we need not even stop there, in Einstein's opinion. For it is open to conjecture that Aristarchus in his turn has drawn on Egyptian sources. This retrogressive investigation may excite the interest of archæologists, and in particular cases perhaps lead to the discovery of a primary claim to authorship, but it cannot fail to excite suspicion against the conscious intention of conferring all the honours of science on an individual discoverer. Leonardo's superlative constructive genius is not attacked in these remarks, and there seems no reason for objecting if anyone wishes to call him the most ingenious engineer of all times.

All the pressures and tensions occurring in Nature seemed to be repeated in him as " inner virtues," an expression borrowed from Helmholtz, who used it with reference to himself. This analogy might be extended by saying that, in the works of both, Man himself with his organic functions and requirements plays an important rôle. For them the abstract was a means of arriving at what was perceptual, physiologically useful, and stimulating in its effect on life. Leonardo started out from Art, and throughout the realm of mechanics and machines he remained an artist in method. Helmholtz set out from the medical side of physiology and transferred the valuations of beauty derived from the senses to his pictures of mechanical relationships. The life-work of each has an æsthetic colouring, Leonardo's being of a gloomy hue, that of Helmholtz exhibiting brighter and happier tints. Common to both is an almost inconceivable versatility and an inexhaustible productivity.

Whenever Einstein talks of Helmholtz he begins in warm terms of appreciation, which tend to become cooler in the course of the conversation. I cannot quote his exact words, and as I cannot thus give a complete account for which full responsibility may be taken, it may be allowable to offer a few important fragments that I have gathered.

Judged by the average of his accomplishments, Helmholtz is regarded by Einstein as an imposing figure whose fame in later times is assured ; Helmholtz himself tasted of this immortality while still alive. But when efforts are made to rank him with great thinkers of the calibre of Newton, Einstein considers that this estimate cannot be fully borne out. In spite of all the excellence, subtlety, and effectiveness of Helmholtz's astoundingly varied inspirations, Einstein seems to fail to discover in him the source of a really great intellectual achievement.

At a Science Congress held in Paris in 1867, at which Helmholtz was present, a colleague of his was greeted with unanimous applause when he toasted him with the words : " L'ophthalmologie était dans les ténèbres,—Dieu parla, que Helmholtz naquît—Et la lumière était faite ! " It was an almost exact paraphrase of the homage which Pope once addressed to Newton. At that time the words of the toast were re-echoed throughout the world ; ophthalmology was enlarged to science generally, and the apotheosis was applied universally. Du Bois-Reymond declared that no other nation had in its scientific literature a book that could be compared with Helmholtz's works on Physiological Optics and on Sensations of Tone. Helmholtz was regarded as a god, and there are not a few to whom he still appears crowned with this divine halo.

A shrill voice pierced the serene atmosphere, attacking one of his main achievements. The dissentient was Eugen Dühring, to whose essay on the Principles of Mechanics a coveted prize was awarded, a fact which seemed to stamp him as being specially authorized to be a judge of pre-eminent achievements in this sphere. Dühring's aim was to dislodge one of the fundamental supports of Helmholtz's reputation by attacking his " Law of the Conservation of Energy." If this assault proved successful, the god would lie shattered at his own pedestal.

Dühring, indeed, used every means to bespatter his fair name in science ; and it is hardly necessary to remark that Einstein abhors this kind of polemic. What is more, he regards it as a pathological symptom, and has only a smile of disdain for many of Dühring's pithy sayings. He regards them as documents of unconscious humour to be preserved in the archives of science as warnings against future repetitions of such methods.

Dühring belonged also to those who wished to exalt one above all others. He raised an altar to Robert Mayer, and offered up sanguinary sacrifices. Accustomed to doing his work thoroughly, he did not stop at Helmholtz in choosing his victims. No hecatomb seemed to him too great to do honour to the discoverer of the Mechanical Equivalent of Heat, and so his next prey was Gauss and Riemann.

Gauss and Riemann! Each was a giant in Einstein's opinion. He knew well that this raging Ajax had also made an assault against them, but he had no longer a clear recollection of the detailed circumstances ; as the references were near at hand, he allowed me to repeat a few lines of this tragi-comedy.

Helmholtz, according to Dühring (who also calls him " Helmklotz "), has done no more than distort Mayer's fundamental mechanical idea, and interpret it falsely. By "philosophizing " over it, he has completely spoilt it, and rendered it absurd. It was the greatest of all humiliations practised on Mayer that his name had been coupled with that of one whom he had easily out-distanced, and whose clumsy attempts at being a physicist were even worse than those by which he sought to establish himself as a philosopher.

The offences of Gauss and Riemann against Mayer are shrouded in darkness. But there was another would-be scientist, Justus von Liebig, who, being opposed to Mayer, aroused the suspicions of Dühring, particularly as he had used his " brazen-tongue " to defend the two renowned mathematicians. After he, and Clausius too, had been brought to earth, Dühring launched out against the giants of Göttingen. In the chapter on Gauss and "Gauss-worship," we read : " His megalomania rendered it impossible for him to take exception to any tricks that the deficient parts of his own brain played on him, particularly in the realm of geometry. Thus he arrived at a pretentiously mystical denial of Euclid's axioms and theorems, and proceeded to set up the foundations of an apocalyptic geometry not only of nonsense but of absolute stupidity. . . . They are abortive products of the deranged mind of a mathematical professor, whose mania for greatness proclaims them as new and superhuman truths ! . . . The mathematical delusions and deranged ideas in question are the fruits of a veritable *paranoia geometrica*."

After Herostratus had burnt to ashes the consecrated temple, the Ionian cities issued a proclamation that his name was to be condemned to perpetual oblivion ! The iconoclast Dühring is immortalized, for, apart from the charge of arson, he is notable in himself. In his case we found ourselves confronted with unfathomable problems of a scholar's complex nature, problems which even a searcher like Einstein failed to solve. The simplest solution would be to turn the tables and to apply the term " paranoia " as a criticism to the book on Robert Mayer, and thus demolish it. But this will not do, for if we merely pass over the pages of distorted thought, we are still left with a considerable quantity of valuable material.

Does Dühring, after all, himself deserve a place in our Valhalla ? The question seems monstrous, and yet cannot be directly answered in the negative. The individual is to be judged according to his greatest achievement, and not according to his aberrations. The works of Aristotle teem with nonsensical utterances, and Leonardo's *Bestiarius* is an orgy of abstruse concoctions. If Dühring had written nothing beyond his studies of personalities ranging from Archimedes to Lagrange, the portals would yet have been open to him. Even in his eulogy of Robert Mayer, which is besmirched with unseemly remarks, he displays at least the courage of his convictions.

The attempt at a comparison between Robert Mayer and Helmholtz is doomed to failure even when considered dispassionately, inasmuch as the disturbing factor of priority here intrudes itself. The definite fixing of the Law of Energy is certainly to the credit of Helmholtz, but perhaps he would have gained by laying more stress on the discovery of it five years earlier by the doctor in Heilbronn. And again, this would not have been final, for the invariance of the sum of energy during mechanical actions was known even by Huyghens. The Heilbronn doctor performed one act of genius in his life, whereas Helmholtz during his whole life moved asymptotically to the line of genius without ever reaching it. If my interpretation of Einstein's opinion is correct, Helmholtz is to be credited with having the splendour of an overpowering gift for research predominant in his nature, but is not necessarily

to be given a seat among the most illustrious of his branch of
science.   Einstein wishes to preserve a certain line of demarcation between this type and not only the Titans of the past,
but also those of the present.   When he speaks of the latter,
his tone becomes warmer.   He does not need circuitous
expressions, each syllable rings with praise.   He has in
mind, above all, Hendrik Antoon Lorentz in Leyden, Max
Planck, and Niels Bohr ; we then see that he feels Valhalla
about him.

. . . .

The reason that I have tried to maintain the metaphor of
a Temple of Fame is due to an echo of Einstein's own words
at a celebration held in honour of the sixtieth birthday of
the physicist Planck in the May of 1918.   This speech created
the impression of a happy harmony resulting from a fusion
of two melodies, one springing from the intellect, the other
rising from the heart.   We were standing as at the Propylons
with a new Heraclitus uttering the cry : Introite, nam et hic
dii sunt !

I should like to give the gist of this beautiful address in
an extract uninterrupted by commentaries.

" The Temple of Science "—so Einstein began—" is a
complex structure of many parts.   Not only are the inmates
diverse in nature, but so also are the inner forces that they
have introduced into the temple.   Many a one among them
is engaged in Science with a happy feeling of a superior mind,
and finds Science the sport which is congenial to him, and
which is to give him an outlet for his strong life-forces, and to
bring him the realization of his ambitions.   There are, indeed,
many, too, who offer up their sacrifice of brain-matter only
in the cause of useful achievements.   If now an angel of heaven
were to come and expel all from the temple who belonged to
these two categories, a considerable reduction would result,
but there would still remain within the temple men of present
and former times : among these we count our Planck, and
that is why he has our warm affection.

" I know full well that, in doing this, we have light-heartedly
caused many to be driven out who contributed much to the
building of the temple ; in many cases our angel would find
a decision difficult. . . .   But let us fix our gaze on those

who find full favour with him ! Most of them are peculiar, reserved, and lonely men, who, in spite of what they have in common, are really less alike than those who have been expelled. What led them into the temple ? . . . In the first place, I agree with Schopenhauer that one of the most powerful motives that attract people to Science and Art is the longing to escape from everyday life with its painful coarseness and unconsoling barrenness, and to break the fetters of their own ever-changing desires. It drives those of keener sensibility out of their personal existence into the world of objective perception and understanding. This motive force is similar to the longing which makes the city-dweller leave his noisy, confused surroundings and draws him with irresistible force to restful Alpine heights, where his gaze covers the wide expanse lying peacefully before him on all sides, and softly passes over the motionless outlines that seem created for all eternity. Associated with this negative motive is a positive one, by virtue of which Man seeks to form a simplified synoptical view of the world in a manner conformable to his own nature, in order to overcome the world of experience by replacing it, to a certain degree, by this picture. This is what the painter does, as also the poet, the speculative philosopher, and the research scientist, each in his own way. He transfers the centre of his emotional existence into this picture, in order to find a sure haven of peace, one such as is not offered in the narrow limits of turbulent personal experience.

" What position does the world-picture of the theoretical physicist occupy among all those that are possible ? He demands the greatest rigour and accuracy in his representation, such as can be gained only by using the language of mathematics. But for this very reason the physicist has to be more modest than others in his choice of material, and must confine himself to the simplest events of the empirical world, since all the more complex events cannot be traced by the human mind with that refined exactness and logical sequence which the physicist demands. . . . Is the result of such a restricted effort worthy of the proud name ' world-picture ' ?

" I believe this distinction is well deserved, for the most general laws on which the system of ideas set up by theoretical physics is founded claim to be valid for every kind of natural phenomenon. From them it should be possible by means of pure deduction to find the picture, that is, the theory, of every natural process, including those of living organism, provided that this process of deduction does not exceed the powers of human thought. Thus there is no fundamental reason why the physical picture of the world should fall short of perfection. . . .

" Evolution has shown that among all conceivable theoretical constructions there is at each period one which shows itself to be superior to all others, and that the world of perception determines in practice the theoretical system, although there is no logical road from perception to the axioms of the theory, but rather that we are led towards the latter by our intuition, which· establishes contact with experience. . . .

'' The longing to discover the *pre-established harmony* recognized by Leibniz is the source of the inexhaustible patience with which we see Planck devoting himself to the general problems of our science, refusing to allow himself to be distracted by more grateful and more easily attainable objects. . . . The emotional condition which fits him for his task is akin to that of a devotee or a lover ; his daily striving is not the result of a definite purpose or a programme of action, but of a direct need. . . . May his love for Science grace his future course of life, and lead him to a solution of that all-important problem of the day which he himself propounded, and to an understanding of which he has contributed so much ! May he succeed in combining the Quantum Theory with Electrodynamics and Mechanics in a logically complete system ! "

. . . .

" What grips me most in your address," I said, " is that it simultaneously surveys the whole horizon of science in every direction, and traces back the longing for knowledge to its root in emotion. When your speech was concluded, I regretted only one thing—that it had ended so soon. Fortunate is he who may study the text."

" Do you attach any importance to it ? " asked Einstein ; " then accept this manuscript." It is due to this act of generosity that I have been able to adorn the foregoing description of the excursion into Valhalla with such a valuable supplement.

.   .   .   .

The conversation had begun with the brilliant constellation Galilei-Newton, and near the end inclined again towards the consideration of a double-star : the names of Faraday and Maxwell presented themselves.

" Both pairs," Einstein declared, " are of the same magnitude. I regard them as fundamentally equal in their services in the onward march of knowledge."

" Should we not have to add Heinrich Hertz as a third in this bond ?   This assistant of Helmholtz is surely regarded as one of the founders of the Electromagnetic Theory of Light, and we often hear their names coupled, as in the case of the Maxwell-Hertz equations."

" Doubtless," replied Einstein, " Hertz, who is often mentioned together with Maxwell, has an important rank and must be placed very high in the world of experimental physics, yet, as regards the influence of his scientific personality, he cannot be classed with the others we have named. Let us, then, confine ourselves to the twin geniuses Faraday and Maxwell, whose intellectual achievement may be summarized in a few words. Classical mechanics referred all phenomena, electrical as well as mechanical, to the direct action of particles on one another, irrespective of their distances from one another.   The simplest law of this kind is Newton's expression : ' Attraction equals Mass times Mass divided by the square of the distance.'   In contradistinction to this, Faraday and Maxwell have introduced an entirely new kind of physical realities, namely, *fields of force.*   The introduction of these new realities gives us the enormous advantage that, in the first place, the conception of action at a distance, which is contrary to our everyday experience, is made unnecessary, inasmuch as the fields are superimposed in space from point to point without a break ; in the second place, the laws for the field, especially in the case of electricity, assume a much simpler form than if no field be assumed, and only masses and motions be regarded as realities."

He enlarged still further on the subject of fields, and while he was describing the technical details, I saw him metaphorically enveloped in a magnetic field of force. Here, too, an influence, transmitted through space from point to point, made itself felt, and there could be no question of action " at a distance " inasmuch as the effective source was so near at hand. His gaze, as if drawn magnetically, passed along the wall of the room and fixed affectionately on Maxwell and Faraday.

CHAPTER IV

EDUCATION

School Curricula and Reform of Teaching.—Value of Language Study.
—Economy of Time.—Practice in Manual Work.—Picturesque Illustrations.
—Art of Lecturing.—Selection of Talents by Means of Examinations.—
Women Students.—Social Difficulties.—Necessity as Instructress.

OUR conversation turned towards a series of pædagogic
questions, in which Einstein is deeply interested.
For he himself is actively engaged in teaching, and
never disguises the pleasure which he derives from imparting
instruction. Without doubt he has a gift of making his spoken
words react on wide circles anxious to be instructed, composed
not only of University students, but of many others quite outside
this category. When, recently, popular lectures on a large
scale were instituted, he was one of the first to offer his services
in this sound undertaking. He lectured to people of the
working class, who could not be assumed to have any preliminary information on the subject, and he succeeded in
presenting his lectures so that even the less trained minds could
easily follow his argument.

His attitude towards general questions of school education
is, of course, conditioned by his own personality and his own
work in the past. His first care is that a young person should
get an insight into the relationship underlying natural phenomena, that is, that the curricula should be mapped out so that
a knowledge of facts is the predominating aim.

" My wish," Einstein declared to me, " is far removed from
the desire to eliminate altogether the fundamental features of
the old grammar schools, with their preference for Latin, by
making over-hasty reforms, but I am just as little inclined
to wax enthusiastic about the so-called humanistic schools.
Certain recollections of my own school life suffice to prevent
this, and still more, a certain presentiment of the educational
problems of the future."—" To speak quite candidly," he

said, " in my opinion the educative value of languages is, in general, much over-estimated."

I took the liberty of quoting a saying that is still regarded as irrefutable by certain scholars. It was Charles V who said : " Each additional acquired language represents an additional personality " ; and to suggest the root of language formation he said it in Latin : " Quot linguas quis callet, tot homines valet." This saying has been handed down through the ages in German in the form : " Soviel Sprachen, soviel Sinnen " (An added language means an added sense).

Einstein replied : " I doubt whether this aphorism is generally valid, for I believe that it would at no time have stood a real test. All experience contradicts it. Otherwise we should be compelled to assign the highest positions among intellectual beings to linguistic athletes like Mithridates, Mezzofanti, and similar persons. The exact opposite, indeed, may be proved, namely, that in the case of the strongest personalities, and of those who have contributed most to progress, the multiplicity of their senses in no wise depended on a comprehensive knowledge of languages, but rather that they avoided burdening their minds with things that made excessive claims on their memories."

" Certainly," said I, " it may be admitted that this gives rise to exaggeration in some cases, and that the linguistic sort of sport practised by many a scholar degenerates to a mere display of knowledge. An intellectual achievement of lasting merit has very rarely or never been the result of a superabundance of acquired linguistic knowledge. An instance occurs to me at this moment. Nietzsche became a philosopher of far-reaching influence only after he had passed the stage of the philologist. As far as our present discussion is concerned, the question is narrowed down considerably : it reduces itself to inquiring whether we do sufficient, too little, or too much Greek and Latin. I must remark at the very outset that, formerly, school requirements went much further in this respect than nowadays, when we scarcely meet with a scholar even in the upper classes who knows Latin and Greek perfectly."

It is just this fact that Einstein regards as a sign of improvement and a result of examining the true aims of a school. He continued : " Man must be educated to ' react delicately ' ;

he is to acquire and develop 'intellectual muscles'! And the methods of language drill are much less suited to this purpose than those of a more general training that gives greatest weight to a sharpening of one's own powers of reflection. Naturally, the inclination of the pupil for a particular profession must not be neglected, especially in view of the circumstance that such inclination usually asserts itself at an early age, being occasioned by personal gifts, by examples of other members of the family, and by various circumstances that affect the choice of his future life-work. That is why I support the introduction into schools, particularly schools devoted to classics, of a division into two branches at, say, the fourth form, so that at this stage the young pupil has to decide in favour of one or other of the courses. The elementary foundation to the fourth form may be made uniform for all, as they are concerned with factors on education that are scarcely open to the danger of being exaggerated in any one direction. If the pupil finds that he has a special interest in what are called *humaniora* by the educationist, let him by all means continue along the road of Latin and Greek, and, indeed, without being burdened by tasks that, owing to his disposition, oppress or alarm him."

"You are referring," I interposed, "to the distress which pupils feel in the time allotted to mathematics. There are actually people of considerable intelligence who seem to be smitten with absolute stupidity when confronted with mathematics, and whose school-life becomes poisoned owing to the torment caused by this subject. There are many cases of living surgeons, lawyers, historians, and litterateurs, who, till late in life, are visited by dreams of their earlier mathematical ordeals. Their horror has a very real foundation, for, whereas the pupil who is bad at Latin yet manages to get an idea of the language, and he who is weak in history has at least a notion of what is being discussed, the one who is unmathematical by nature has to worry his way through numberless lessons in a subject which is entirely incomprehensible to him, as if belonging to another world and being presented to him in a totally strange tongue. He is expected to answer questions, the sense of which he cannot even guess, and to solve problems, every word and every figure of which glares at him like a sphinx of evil omen. Sitting on each side of him are pupils to whom this is merely play, and some of whom could complete the whole of school mathematics within a few months at express rate. This leads to a contrast between the pupils, which may press with tragical force on the unfortunate member throughout his whole school existence. That is why a reform is to be welcomed that sifts out in time those who should be separated from the rest, and which adapts the school curriculum as closely as possible to individual talents."

Einstein called my attention to the fact that this division had already been made in many schools in foreign countries, as in France and in Denmark, although not so exclusively as suggested by him. " Moreover," he added, " I am by no means decided whether the torments that you mentioned are founded primarily on absence of talent in the pupil. I feel much more inclined to throw the responsibility in most cases on the absence of talent in the teacher. Most teachers waste their time by asking questions which are intended to discover what a pupil does *not* know, whereas the true art of questioning has for its purpose to discover what the pupil knows or is capable of knowing. Whenever sins of this sort are committed—and they occur in all branches of knowledge—the personality of the teacher is mostly at fault. The results of the class furnish an index for the quality of the preceptor. All things being taken into consideration, the average of ability in the class moves, with only slight fluctuations, about mean values, with which tolerably satisfactory results may be obtained. If the progress of the class is not up to this standard, we must not speak of a bad year but rather of an inefficient instructor. It may be assumed that, as a rule, the teacher understands the subject with which he is entrusted, and has mastered its content, but not that he knows how to impart his information in an interesting manner. This is almost always the source of the trouble. If the teacher generates an atmosphere of boredom, the progress is stunted in the suffocating surroundings. To know how to teach is to be able to make the subject of instruction interesting, to present it, even if it happens to be abstract, so that the soul of the pupil resonates in sympathy with that of his instructor, and so that the curiosity of the pupil is never allowed to wane."

" That is in itself an ideal postulate. If we assume it to be fulfilled, how do you wish to see the subjects distributed in the curriculum ? "

" We must leave the detailed discussion of this question for another occasion. One of the main points would be the economy of time ; all that is superfluous, vexatious, and only intended as a drill must be dropped. At present the aim of the whole course is the leaving certificate. This test must be given up ! "

" Is that serious, Professor ? Do you wish to do away with the examination for matriculation ? "

" Exactly. For it is like some fearful monster guarding our exit from school, throwing its shadow far ahead, and compelling teacher and pupil to work incessantly towards an artificial show of knowledge. This examination has been elevated by forcible means to a level which the violently drilled candidates can keep only for a few hours, and is then lost to sight for ever. If it is eliminated, it will carry away with it this painful drilling of the memory ; it will no longer be necessary to hammer in for years what will be entirely forgotten within a few months, and what deserves to be forgotten. Let us return to Nature, which upholds the principle of getting the maximum amount of effect from the minimum of effort, whereas the matriculation test does exactly the opposite."

" Yes, but who is then to be allowed to enter the university ? "

" Every one who has shown himself to be capable not only in a crucial test of an accidental kind, but in his whole behaviour. The teacher will be the judge of this, and if he does not know who is qualified, he again is to be blamed. He will find it so much the easier to decide who is sufficiently advanced to obtain a leaving certificate, in proportion as the curriculum has weighed less on the minds of the young people. Six hours a day should be ample—four at school and two for home-work ; that should be the maximum. If this should appear too little to you, I must ask you to bear in mind that a young mind is being subjected to strain even in leisure hours, as it has to receive a whole world of perceptions. And if you ask how the steadily increasing curriculum is to be covered in this very moderate number of hours, my answer is : Throw all that is unnecessary overboard ! I count as unnecessary the major part of the subject that is called ' Universal History,' and which is, as a rule, nothing more than a blurred mass of history compressed into dry tables of names and dates. This subject should be brought within the narrowest possible limits, and should be presented only in broad outline, without dates having to be crammed. Leave as many gaps as you like, especially in ancient history ; they will not make themselves felt in our ordinary existences. In nowise can I regard it as a mis-fortune if the pupil learns nothing of Alexander the Great, and of the dozens of other conquerors whose documentary remains burden his memory like so much useless ballast. If he is to get a glimpse of the grey dawn of time, let him be spared from Cyrus, Artaxerxes, and Vercingetorix, but rather tell him something of the pioneers of civilization, Archimedes, Ptolemy, Hero, Appolonius, and of inventors and discoverers, so that the course does not resolve into a series of adventures and massacres."

" Would it not be expedient," I interrupted, " to take some of the history time to branch off into an elementary treatment of the real evolution of the state, including sociology and the legal code ? "

Einstein does not consider this desirable, although he him-self is deeply interested in all manifestations of public life. He does not favour an elementary political training received at school, presumably above all owing to the fact that in this branch the instruction cannot be removed from official in-fluences, and because political questions require the attention of a mature mind. His picture of how a youth is to meet the requirements of modern life is something quite different, far removed from all theories. His whole efforts are directed at finding a means of counteracting the tendency to overburden one side of the youthful mind. " I should demand the intro-duction of compulsory practical work. Every pupil must learn some *handicraft*. He should be able to choose for him-self which it is to be, but I should allow no one to grow up without having gained some technique, either as a joiner, bookbinder, locksmith, or member of any other trade, and without having delivered some useful product of his trade."

" Do you attach greater importance to the technique itself or to the feeling of social relationship with the broad masses of the people which it engenders ? "

" Both factors are equally important to me," said Einstein, " and others become added to these which help to justify my wish in this respect. The handiwork need not be used as a means of earning money by the pupil of the secondary school, but it will enlarge and make more solid the foundation on which he will rest as an ethical being. In the first place, the school is not to produce future officials, scholars, lecturers, barristers, and authors, but human beings, not merely mental machines. Prometheus did not begin his education of mankind with astronomy, but by teaching the properties of fire and its practical uses. . . ."

" This brings to my mind another analogy," I continued, " namely, that of the old *Meistersinger*, who were, all of them, expert smiths, tinkers, or shoemakers, and yet succeeded in building a bridge to the arts. And at bottom, the sciences, too, belong to the category of free arts. Yet, a difficulty seems to me to arise. In demanding a compulsory handicraft, you lay stress on practical use, whereas in your other remarks you declared science in itself as being utterly independent of practice."

" I do this," replied Einstein, " only when I speak of the ultimate aims of pure research, that is, of aims that are visible to only a vanishing minority. It would be a complete misconception of life to uphold this point of view and to expect its regulative effectiveness in cases in which we are dealing only with the preliminaries of science. On the contrary, I maintain that science can be taught much more practically at schools than it is at present when bookwork has the upper hand. For example, to return to the question of mathematical teaching : it seems to me to be almost universally at fault, if only for the reason that it is not built up on what is *practically* interesting, what appeals directly to the senses, and what can be seized intuitively. Child-minds are fed with definitions instead of being presented with what they can grasp, and they are expected to be able to understand purely conceptual things, although they have had no opportunity given them of arriving at the abstract by way of concrete things. It is very easy to do the latter. The first beginnings should not be taught in the schoolroom at all, but in open Nature. A boy should be shown how a meadow is measured and compared with another. His attention must be directed to the height of a tower, to the length of his shadow at various times, to the corresponding altitude of the sun ; by this means he will grasp the mathematical relationships much more rapidly, more surely, and with greater zeal, than if words and chalk-marks are used to instil into him the conceptions of dimensions, of angles, or perchance of some trigonometrical function. What is the actual origin of such branches of science ? They are derived from practice, as, for example, when Thales first measured the height of the pyramids with the help of a short rod, which he set up at the ultimate point of the pyramid's shadow. Place a stick in the boy's hand and lead him on to make experiments with it by way of a game, and if he is not quite devoid of sense, he will discover the thing for himself. It will please him to have discovered the height of the tower without having climbed it, and this is the first thrill of the pleasure which he feels later when he learns the geometry of similar triangles and the proportionality of their sides."

" In the matter of physics," pursued Einstein, " the first lessons should contain nothing but what is experimental and interesting to see. A pretty experiment is in itself often more valuable than twenty formulæ extracted from our minds ; it is particularly important that a young mind that has yet to find its way about in the world of phenomena should be spared from formulæ altogether. In his physics they play exactly the same weird and fearful part as the figures of dates in Universal History. If the experimenter is ingenious and expert, this subject may be begun as early as in the middle forms, and one may then count on a responsiveness that is rarely observable during the hours of exercise in Latin grammar."

" This leads me," said Einstein, " to speak in this connexion of a means of education that has so far been used only by way of trial in class-teaching, but from an improved application of which I expect fruitful results later. I mean the school cinema. The triumphal march of the cinematograph will be continued into pedagogic regions, and here it will have a chance to make good its wrongs in thousands of picture shows in showing absurd, immoral, and melodramatic subjects. By means of the school-film, supplemented by a simple apparatus for projection, it would be possible firstly to infuse into certain subjects, such as geography, which is at present wound off organ-like in the form of dead descriptions, the pulsating life of a metropolis. And the lines on a map will gain an entirely new complexion in the eyes of the pupil, if he learns, as if during a voyage, what they actually include, and what is to be read between them. An abundance of information is imparted by the film, too, if it gives an accelerated or retarded view of such things as a plant growing, an animal's heart beating, or the wing of an insect moving. The cinema seems to me to have a still more important function in giving pupils an insight into the most important branches of technical industry, a knowledge of which should become common property. Very few hours would suffice to impress permanently on the schoolboy's mind how a power-station, a locomotive, a newspaper, a book, or a coloured illustration is produced, or what takes place in an electrical plant, a glass factory, or a gasworks. And, to return to natural science, many of the rather difficult experiments that cannot be shown by means of school apparatus may be shown with almost as great clearness on a film. Taken all in all, the redeeming word in school-teaching is, for me : an increased appeal to the senses. Wherever it is possible, learning must become living, and this principle will predominate in future reforms of school-teaching."

.   .   .   .

University study was only touched on lightly during this talk. It has become known that Einstein is a very strong supporter of the principle of free learning, and that he would prefer to dispense entirely with the regular documents of admission which qualify holders to attend lecture courses. This is to be interpreted as meaning that as soon as anyone desirous of furthering his studies has demonstrated his fitness to follow the lecturer's reasoning by showing his ability in class exercises or in the laboratory, he should be admitted immediately. Einstein would not demand the usual certificate of " general education," but only of fitness for the special subject, particularly as, in his own experience, he has frequently found the cleverest people and those with the most definite aims to

be prone to one-sidedness. According to this, even the intermediate schools should be authorized to bestow a certificate
of fitness to enter on a course in a single definite subject as
soon as the pupil has proved himself to have the necessary
ability. If he earlier spoke in favour of abolishing the matriculation examination, this is only an indication of his effort to
burst open the portals of higher education for every one.
Nevertheless, I remarked that, in the course of university work
itself, he is not in favour of giving up all regulation concerning
the ability of the student—at least, not in the case of those who
intend to devote themselves to instruction later. He does not
desire an intermediate examination (in the nature of the
tentamen physicum of doctors), but he considers it profitable
for the future schoolmaster to have an opportunity early in
his course to prove his fitness for teaching. In this matter,
too, Einstein reveals his affectionate interest in the younger
generation, whose development is threatened by nothing so
much as by incapable teachers : the sum of these considerations is that the pupil is examined as little as possible, but
the teacher so much the more closely. A candidate for the
teaching profession, who in the early stages of his academic
career fails to show his fitness, his individual *facultas docendi*,
should be removed from the university.

There can be no doubt but that Einstein has a claim to
be heard as an authority on these questions. There are few
in the realm of the learned in whose faces it is so clearly
manifest that they are called to excite a desire for knowledge
by means of the living word, and to satisfy this desire. If
great audiences assemble around him, if so many foreign
academies open their arms to him to make him their own,
these are not only signs of a magnetic influence that emanates
from the famous discoverer, but they are indications that he
is far famed as a teacher with a captivating personality.
Let us consider what this signifies in his profession. Philosophers, historians, lawyers, doctors, and theologians have at
their disposal innumerable words which they merely need to
pronounce to get into immediate contact with their audiences.
In Einstein's profession, theoretical physics, man disappears ;
it leaves no scope for the play of emotion ; its implement
mathematics—and what an instrument it is !—bristles with

formal difficulties, which can be overcome only by means of symbols and by using a language which has no means of displaying eloquence, being devoid of expression, emotion, and regular periods. Yet here we have a physicist, a mathematician, whose first word throws a charm over a great crowd of people, and who extracts from their minds, so to speak, what, in reality, he alone works out before them. He does not adhere closely to written pages, nor to a scheme which has been prepared beforehand in all its details ; he develops his subject freely, without the slightest attempt at rhetoric, but with an effect which comes of itself when the audience feels itself swept along by the current. He does not need to deliver his words passionately, as his passion for teaching is so manifest. Even in regions of thought in which usually only formulæ, like glaciers, give an indication of the height, he discovers similes and illustrations with a human appeal, by the aid of which he helps many a one to conquer the mountain sickness of mathematics. His lectures betray two factors that are rarely found present in investigators of abstract subjects ; they are temperament and geniality. He never talks as if in a monologue or as if addressing empty space. He always speaks like one who is weaving threads of some idea, and these become spun out in a fascinating way that robs the audience of the sense of time. We all know that no iron curtain marks the close of Einstein's lecture ; anyone who is tormented by some difficulty or doubt, or who desires illumination on some point, or has missed some part of the argument, is at liberty to question him. Moreover, Einstein stands firm through the storm of all questions. On the very day on which the above conversation took place he had come straight from a lecture on four-dimensional space, at the conclusion of which a tempest of questions had raged about him. He spoke of it not as of an ordeal that he had survived, but as of a refreshing shower. And such delights abound in his teaching career.

.   .   .   .

It was the last lecture before his departure for Leyden (in May 1920), where the famous faculty of science, under the auspices of the great physicist Lorentz, had invited him to accept an honorary professorship. This was not the first invitation of this kind, and will not be the last, for distinctions are being showered on him from all parts of the world. It is true that the universities who confer a degree on him *honoris causa* are conferring a distinction on themselves, but Einstein frankly acknowledges the value of these honours, which he regards as referring only to the question in hand, and not the person. It gives him pleasure on account of the principle involved being recognized, and he regards himself essentially only as one whom fate has ordained as the personal exponent of these principles.

What this life of hustle and bustle about a scientist signifies is perhaps more apparent to me, who have a modest share in these conversations, than to Einstein himself, for I am an old man who—unfortunately—have to think back a long way to my student days, and can set up comparisons which are out of reach of Einstein. Formerly, many years ago, but in my own time, there was an *auditorium maximum* which only one man could manage to fill with an audience, namely, Eugen Dühring, the noted scholar, who was doomed to remain a lecturer inasmuch as he went under in his quarrels with confrères of a higher rank. But before he made his onslaught against Helmholtz, he was regarded as a man of unrivalled magnetic power, for his philosophical and economical lectures gathered together over three hundred hearers, a record number in those times. Nowadays, in the case of Einstein, four times this number has been surpassed, a fact which has brought into circulation the playful saying : One can never miss his auditorium ; whither all are hastening, that is the goal ! To make just comparisons, we must take account of the faithfulness of the assembled crowd, as well as its number. Many an eminent scholar has in earlier times had reason to declare, like Faust : " I had the power to attract you, yet had no power to hold you." Helmholtz began regularly every term with a crowded lecture-hall, but in a short time he found himself deserted, and he himself was well aware that no magnetic teaching influence emanated from him. There is yet another case in university history of a brilliant personality who, from similar flights of ecstasy, was doomed to disappointment. I must mention his name, which, in this connexion, will probably cause great surprise, namely, Schiller ! He had fixed his first lecture in history at Jena, to which he was appointed, and had prepared for an audience of about a hundred students. But crowd upon crowd hustled along, and Schiller, who saw the oncoming stream from his window, was overcome with the impression that there was no end to it. The whole street took alarm, for at first it was imagined that a fire had broken out, and at the palace the watch was called out—yet, a little later in the course, there was a depressing ebb of the tide, after the first curiosity had been appeased; the audience gradually vanished into thin air, a proof of the fact that the nimbus of a name does not suffice to maintain the interest between the lecturer's desk and the audience.

I mentioned this example at the time when Einstein's gift for teaching had gradually increased the number of his hearers to the record figure of 1200, yet I did not on this occasion detect any inordinate joy in him about his success. I gained the impression that he had strained his voice in the vast hall. His mood betrayed in consequence a slight undercurrent of irritation. In an access of scepticism he murmured the words, "A mere matter of fashion." I cannot imagine that he was entirely in earnest. It goes without saying that I protested against the expression. But, even if there were a particle of truth in it, we might well be pleased to find such a fashion in intellectual matters, one that persists so long and promises to last. The world would recover its normal healthy state if fashions of this kind were to come into full swing. It is, of course, easy to understand on psychological grounds that Einstein himself takes up a sort of defensive position against his own renown, and that he occasionally tries to attack it by means of sarcasm, seeing that he cannot find serious arguments to oppose it.

.   .   .   .

Whether Einstein's ideas and proposals concerning educational reform will be capable of realization throughout is a question that time alone can answer. We must make it clear to ourselves that, if carried out along free-thinking lines, they will demand certain sacrifices, and it depends on the apportionment of these sacrifices as to what the next, or the following, generation will have to exhibit in the way of mental training.

An appreciable restriction will have to be imposed on the

time given to languages.   It is a matter of deciding how far this will affect the foundations that, under the collective term *humaniora*, have supported the whole system of classical schools for centuries.   The fundamental ideas of reform, which, owing to the redivision of school-hours and the economy of work, no longer claim precedence for languages, indicate that not much will be left of the original Latin and Greek basis.

We have noticed above that Einstein, although he does not, in principle, oppose the old classicism, no longer expects much good of it.   But nowadays the state of affairs is such that it is hardly a question of supporting or opposing its retention in fragmentary form.   Whoever does not support it with all his power strengthens indirectly the mighty chorus of those who are radically antagonistic to it.   And it is a remarkable fact that this chorus includes many would-be authorities on languages who have influence among us because they are champions of the cause of retaining languages.

They do not wish to rescue languages as such, but only the German tongue ; they point to the *humaniora* of classical schools, or to *Humanisterei*, as they call it, as the enemy and corrupter of their language.   In what sense they mean this is obvious from their articles of faith, of which I should like to cite a few in the original words of one of their party-leaders :

" Up to the time of the hazardous enterprise of Thomasius (who first announced lectures in the German language in 1687) German scholars as a body were the worst enemies of their own tongue.—Luther did not take his models for writing German from the humanistic mimics who aped the old Latins. In the case of many, including Lessing and Goethe, we observe them making a definite attempt to shake themselves free from the chaos of humanistic influences in Germany.—The inheritance of pseudo-learned concoctions of words stretches back to pretentious humanism as do most of essential vices of learned styles.—The far-reaching and lasting corruption of the German language by this poisonous Latin has its beginnings in the humanism of the sixteenth century."

And, quite logically, these heralds extend their attacks along the whole academic front.   For, according to their point of view, the whole army of professors is deeply immersed in the language slime of the traditional humanism of the Greeks and Latins. "The whole language evil of our times," so these leaders say, "is at bottom due to scientists, who, in the opinionated guise of a language caste, and without enriching our conceptions in the slightest, seek by tinkling empty words to give us the illusion of a new and particularly mysterious occult science, an impression which is unfortunately often produced on ignorant minds. . . . However many muddy outlets official institutions and language associations may purge and block up, ditch-water from ever new quagmires and drains pours unceasingly into the stately stream of our language."

Thus the attack on the Latin and Greek language foundation in schools identifies itself with the struggle against the academic world as a whole, and a scholar who does defend the classical system of education with all his might finds himself unconsciously drifting into the ranks of the brotherhood which in the last instance is seeking his own extermination.

This danger must not be under-estimated. It is just this peril, so threatening to our civilization, that moves me to show my colours frankly here. I am not a supporter of bookworm drudgery in schools, but I feel myself impelled to use every effort in speech and writing to combat the anti-humanists whose password, "For *our* language," at root signifies "Enemies of Science!"

We must put no weapons into their hands, and the only means to avoid this is, in my opinion, to state our creed emphatically and openly after the manner of almost all our classical writers.

This creed, both as regards language and substance, is to be understood as being based on the efficacy of the old classical languages. It is the luminous centre of the life and work of the men who caused Bulwer to proclaim our country the country of poets and thinkers. The superabundance of these is so excessive that it is scarcely fair to mention only a few names such as Goethe, Lessing, Schiller, Wieland, Kant, and Schopenhauer. Our literature would be of a provincial standard and not a world possession if this creed had not asserted its sway at all times.

If the question is raised as to where our youth is to find time for learning ancient languages under the present conditions of crowded subjects, the answer is to be furnished by improved methods of instruction. My personal point of view is that even the older methods were not so bad. Goethe found himself in no wise embarrassed through lack of time in acquiring all sorts of knowledge and mental equipment, although even as a boy of eight years he could write in Latin in a way which, compared with the bungling efforts of the modern sixth-form boy, seems Ciceronian. Montaigne could express himself earlier in Latin than in French, and if he had not had this " Latin poison " injected into his blood he would never have become Montaigne.

It seems to me by no means impossible that the cultured world will one day in the distant future return to the once self-evident view of classical languages, and indeed just for reasons of economy of time, unless the universal language so ardently desired by Hebbel—not to be confused with the artificial patchwork called Esperanto—should become a reality. But even this language, at present Utopian, but one which will help to link together the nations, will disclose the model of the ancient languages in its structure. Scientific language of the present day shows where the route lies ; and this route will be made passable in spite of all the efforts of Teutonic language saints and assassins of humanism to block it.

The working out of ideas by research scientists leads to enrichment of language. And since, as is quite natural, they draw copiously on antique forms of expression, they are really the trustees of an instruction that makes these expressions intelligible not merely as components of an artificial language like Volapük but as organic growths. That is how they proceed when they carry on their research, or describe it and lecture on their own subject. But if they are to decide how the school is to map out its course in actual practice, the problem of time again becomes their chief consideration—that is, they feel in duty bound to give preference to what is most important. Hence there results the wish to reduce the hours apportioned to the language subjects as much as possible.

On this matter we have a detailed essay by the distinguished Ernst Mach mentioned earlier, who exposes the actual dilemma with the greatest clearness. He treats this exceedingly important question in all its phases, and arrives at almost the same conclusion as Einstein. At the outset he certainly chants a Latin psalm almost in the manner of Schopenhauer. Its lower tones represent an elegy lamenting that Latin is no longer the universal language among educated people, as it was from the fifteenth to the eighteenth century. Its fitness for this purpose is quite indisputable, for it can be adapted to express every conception however modern or subtle it may be.

What a profusion of new conceptions was introduced into science by Sir Isaac Newton, to all of which he succeeded in giving correct and precise Latin names ! The natural inference suggests itself to us that young people should learn the ancient classical tongues—and yet a different result is coming about ; the modern child is to be content with understanding words with a world-wide currency, without knowing their philological origin.

It is not necessary to be a schoolmaster to feel the inadequacy of this proceeding. It is true that without knowing Arabic we can grasp the sense and meaning of the word " Algebra," and in the same way we can extract the essence of a number of Greek and Latin expressions without digging at their etymological roots. But these expressions are to be counted in hundreds and thousands, and are increasing daily, so that we are put before the question whether, merely from the point of view of time, it is practicable to learn them as individual foreign terms or as natural products of a root language with which we have once and for all become familiar.

It is scarcely necessary for me to point out that Einstein himself is not sparing in the use of these technical expressions, even when he is using popular language. He assumes or introduces terms of which the following are a few examples : continuum, co-ordinate system, dimensional, electrodynamics, kinetic theory, transformation, covariant, heuristic, parabola, translation, principle of equivalence, and he is quite justified in assuming that every one is fully acquainted with such generally accepted expressions as : gravitation, spectral analysis, ballistic, phoronomy, infinitesimal, diagonal, component, periphery, hydrostatics, centrifugal, and numberless others which are diffused through educated popular language in all directions. Taken all together these represent a foreign realm in which the entrant can always succeed in orientating himself when he receives explanations, examples, or translations, whereas with a little preliminary knowledge of the ancient languages he immediately feels himself at home with them ; in this we have not even taken into consideration the general cultural value of this training in view of the access it gives to the old literature and to Hellenic culture.

Perhaps I am going too far in adopting the attitude of a *laudator temporis acti* towards Einstein's very advanced opinion. We are here dealing with a question in which nothing can be proved, and in which everything depends on disposition and personal experiences. In my own case this experience includes the fact that at a very early age, in spite of the very discouraging school methods, I enjoyed the study of Latin and Greek, and that I learned Horatian odes by heart, not because I had to, but because they appealed to me, and finally that Homer opened up a new world to me. When Einstein expresses his abhorrence of drill, I agree with him ; but these languages need not be taught as if we are on parade. We see thus that it is a question of method and not of the subject involved. Einstein gives the subject its due by recommending a double series of classes. He allows the paths to diverge, giving his special blessing to the group along the one without setting up obstacles to prevent the other pilgrims from attaining happiness in their own way.

.   .   .   .

We spoke of higher education for women, and Einstein expressed his views which, as was to be expected, were tolerant, and yet did not suggest those of a champion of the cause. It was impossible to overlook the fact that in spite of his approval he had certain reservations of a theoretical nature.

" As in all other directions," he said, " so in that of science the way should be made easy for women. Yet it must not be taken amiss if I regard the possible results with a certain amount of scepticism. I am referring to certain obstacles in woman's organization which we must regard as given by Nature, and which forbid us from applying the same standard of expectation to women as to men."

" You believe, then, Professor, that high achievements cannot be accomplished by women ? To keep our attention on science, can one not quote Madame Curie as a proof to the contrary ? "

" Surely only as one proof of brilliant exceptions, more of which may occur without refuting the statute of sexual organization."

" Perhaps this will be possible after all if a sufficient time for development be allowed. There may be much fewer geniuses among the other sex, but there has certainly been a concentration of talent. Or, in other words, totally ignorant women have become much rarer. You, Professor, are fortunate in not being in a position to compare young women of to-day with those of forty or more years ago. This I can do, and just as once I found it natural that there should be swarms of little geese and peacocks, I never recover from my astonishment nowadays at the amount of knowledge acquired by young womanhood. It requires a considerable effort on my part very often to avoid being completely overshadowed by a partner at dinner. The more this stratum of talent increases, the more we have reason to expect a greater number of geniuses from them in the future."

" You are given to prognostication," said Einstein, " and calculate with probabilities which sometimes are lacking in foundation. Increased education and even an increase of talents are quantitative assumptions that make an inference regarding higher quality reaching to genius appear very bold."
—A passing look of ominous portent flashed over his face, and I noticed that he was preparing to launch a sarcastic aphorism. So it was, for the next words were : " It is conceivable that Nature may have created a sex without brains ! "

I grasped the sense of this grotesque remark, which was in no way to be taken literally. It was intended as an amusing exaggeration of what he had earlier called the reason for his failing expectation : the organic difference which, being rooted in the physical constitution, had somewhere to express itself on the mental plane, too. The soul of woman strong in impulse shows a refinement of feeling of which we men are not susceptible, whereas the greatest achievements of reason probably depend on a preponderance of brain substance. It is this plus beyond the normal amount that gives promise of great discoveries, inventions, and creations. We can just as little imagine a female Galilei, Kepler, and Descartes, as a female Michelangelo or Sebastian Bach. But when we think of these extreme cases, let us also recall the balance on the other side : although a woman could not create the differential calculus, it was she that created Leibniz ; similarly she produced Kant if not the Critique of Pure Reason. Woman, as the author of all great minds, has at least a right of access to all means of education and to all advancement that is proffered by universities. And in this connexion Einstein expressed his wish clearly enough.

. . . .

One of the most discussed themes in matters touching school education is at the present time : " the selection of gifted pupils." It has developed into a principle that is generally recognized by the great majority, the only point of disagreement being in respect to the number that is to be selected.

The idea running through it is that derived from Darwin's theory of selection : man completes the method of selection practised by Nature. He sifts and chooses, and allows those that are more talented to come to the fore more rapidly and more decidedly ; he favours their advancement and makes easy their ascent.

This principle has really always been in existence. It started with the distribution of prizes in ancient Olympia and reaches to the present-day examinations that are clearly intended as a means of selecting talents. A greater discrimination based on a systematic search for talents was reserved for our own day.

It was scarcely a matter of doubt to me what attitude Einstein would take up towards this matter. I had already heard him say hard words about the system of examinations, and knew his leaning towards allowing each mind to develop its power freely and naturally.

In effect, Einstein declared to me that he would hear nothing of a breeding of talents in a sort of sporting way. The dangers of the methods of sport would creep in and lead to results that had only the appearance of truth. From the results so far obtained it was impossible to come to a final decision about it. Yet it was conceivable that a selective process conducted along reasonable lines would in general prove of advantage in education, particularly in the respect that many a talent that would ordinarily become stunted owing to its being kept in darkness would now have an opportunity of coming to light.

This resolved itself into a talk bearing on many questions, and of which I should like to state the main issue here. It was specially intended to make clear the gambling method that Einstein repudiates, and the danger of which seems still more threatening to me than to him.

If certain pedagogues, whose creed is force, were to have their way, the " most gifted " pupils would be able, or would be compelled, to rush through school at hurricane speed, and, at an age at which their fellows were still spending weary hours at their desks, they would have to clamber to the topmost branches of the academic tree. All things are possible, and history even furnishes cases of such forced marches. Luther's friend Melanchthon qualified at the age of thirteen to enter the University of Heidelberg, and at the age of seventeen he became a professor at Tübingen, where he gave lectures on the most difficult problems of philosophy, as well on the Roman and Greek writers of classical antiquity. This single instance need only be generalized, and we have the new ideal rising up before our astonished gaze : a race of professorial striplings whose upper lips are scarcely darkened with the down of youth ! It is a mere matter of making an early discovery of the most gifted, and then raising the scaffolding up which the precocious know-alls can climb as easily as possible.

[Interposed query : Where are these discoverers of talent, and how do they prove their own talent ? There was a good opportunity for them in a case which I must here mention. Einstein told me in another connexion that, as early as 1907, that is, when he was still very young in years, he had not only succeeded in successfully representing the Principle of Equivalence, one of the main supports of the General Principle of Relativity, but had even published it ; yet it made not the slightest impression on the learned world. No one suspected the far-reaching consequences, and no one pointed out this flaming up of a new talent of the highest order. And just as this was able to remain concealed from the learned Areopagus of the world at that time, so a similar lack of understanding may easily be possible on a smaller scale at school. We know actually that among the recognized great men of science, there were many who did only moderately well at school ; as, for example, Humphry Davy, Robert Mayer, Justus Liebig, and many others. Wilhelm Ostwald goes so far as to affirm : " Boys ordained to be discoverers later in life have, almost without exception, been bad at school ! It is just the most gifted young people who have resisted most strongly the form of intellectual development prescribed by the school ! Schools never cease to show themselves to be the bitter, unrelenting enemies of genius ! "—in spite of all efforts at selection which have always been in vogue in the guise of advancement into higher forms.]

But the new mode of selection is intended to prevent mistakes and oversights. Is this possible ? Do not the traces of previous attempts inspire distrust ? There was once a very ideal selection that had to stand the test of one of the most eminent bodies in existence, the French Academy. Its duty was to discover geniuses on an incomparably higher plane. It, however, repudiated or overlooked : Molière, Descartes, Pascal, Diderot, the two Rousseaus, Beaumarchais, Balzac, Béranger, the Goncourts, Daudet, Emile Zola, and many other extremely gifted people, whom it should really have been able to find.

The only true, and at the same time necessary as well as sufficient, breeding is carried out by Nature herself in conjunction with social conventions, which promise the more success the less they assume the character of incubators and breeding establishments. If you wish to apply tests to discover pupils of genius in any class, examine as much as you like, excite interest and ambition, distribute prizes even, but not for the purpose of separating at short intervals the shrewd and needle-witted heads from the rest ; and do not lose sight of the fact that among those who appear as the sheep as a result of these systematized tests to discover ingenuity there are many who, ten or twenty years later, will take up their positions as men of eminent talent.

There is no essential difference between the forced promotion of such pupils and the breeding of super-men according to Nietzsche's recipe as exemplified by his Zarathustra.

Assuming that super-men are justified in existing at all, they will come about of themselves, but cannot simply be manufactured. Workmen, taken as a class, represent super-men more definitely than an individual such as Napoleon or Cæsar Borgia. So the " super-scholar " exists perhaps already to-day, not as an individual phenomenon, but as a whole, representing his class. Whoever has had experience in these things will know that nowadays there are difficult subjects in which it is possible to apply to pupils of fifteen years of age tests that are far above the plane of comprehension of pupils of the same age in former times, provided that the average is considered, that no accidental or artificial separation has occurred, that no pretentiously witty questions have had to be answered, and that there has been no systematic and inquisitive search for talent.

Let us rest satisfied if we find that the sum-total of talent is continually on the increase. On the other hand, it is by no means proved that we are doing civilization a service by persisting in the impossible project of abolishing from the world the struggle for existence prescribed by Nature. It is an elementary fact, and one that is easy to understand, that many talents perish unnoticed. On the other hand, observe the long list of eminent men who fought their way upwards out of the lowest stages of existence only to recognize that the difficulties that have been overcome are mostly necessary accompaniments of talent, that is, that Nature's way of selection is to oppose obstacles and raise difficulties in order to test their powers. In the case of the poor lens-grinder Spinoza and many others ranging to Béranger, who was a waiter, what a chain of desperate experiences, yet what triumphs ! Herschel, the astronomer, was too poor to buy a refracting telescope, and it was just this dispensation of poverty that made him succeed in constructing a reflecting type composed of a mirror. Faraday, the son of a blacksmith without means, made his way for years as a bookbinder's apprentice. Joule, one of the founders of the mechanical theory of heat, started as a beer-brewer. Kepler, the discoverer of the planetary laws, was descended from a poverty-stricken innkeeper. Of the members in Goethe's circle, Jung-Stilling, of whom Nietzsche was so fond, was a tailor's apprentice; Eckermann, Goethe's intimate associate, was a swine-herd, and Zelter was a mason. We could add many recent names to this list, and very many more if we continue the line backwards to Euripides, whose father was a publican and whose mother was a vendor of vegetables. This might serve as a basis for many reflections about the " upward course of the talented," and about its less favourable reverse side. For one might put the apparently paradoxical question whether a soaring career for many or all talents is a necessity for our civilization, or whether it would not be better to have a sub-stratum interspersed with talent, to cultivate a mossy under-growth which is to serve as nourishment for the blooming plants of the upper layer.

Maximum is not equivalent to optimum, and we learned elsewhere that Einstein is far removed from identifying them. In the previous case it was a question of the problem of popu-lation; and in the course of the discussion he mentioned that we are subject to an old error of calculation when we regard it as a desirable aim to have a maximum number of human beings on the earth. It seems, indeed, that this false con-clusion is already in process of being corrected. A beginning is being made with new and very active organizations and unions whose programme is to reduce the number so that an optimum may be attainable by those left.

If we extend this line of reasoning still further, we arrive at the depressing question whether too much might not be done for talent, not only as regards breeding it, but also in favouring the greatest number. It is quite possible that in doing so, we might overlook, or take insufficient account of the harm that might be done to the lower stratum, in that we should be depriving it of forces which, according to the economy of Nature, should remain and act in concealment.

This fear, as here expressed, is not shared by Einstein. However brusquely he repudiates breeding, he speaks in favour of smoothing the way for talent. " I believe," he said, " that a sensible fostering of gifts is of advantage to humanity generally and prevents injustice being done to the individual. In great cities which give such lavish opportunities of educa-tion, this injustice manifests itself less often; but it occurs so much the more in rural districts, where there are certainly many cases of gifted youths who, if recognized as such at the right age, would attain to an important position, but who, together with their gifts, become stunted, nay, go to ruin, if the principle of selection does not penetrate to their circle."

This brings us to the most difficult and most dangerous point. The spectre of responsibility is rapping at the portals of society, and is reminding us insistently that it is our duty to see that no injustice be done to any talent that may be among us. And this duty is but little removed from the demand that it should be disburdened of the worries of daily life, for, so the moral argument runs, talent will ripen the more surely the less it has to combat these ceaseless disturbances of ordinary life.

But this thesis, so evident on moral grounds, will never be proved empirically. On the contrary, we have good reason to suppose that necessity, the mother of invention on the broader scale, will often in the case of the individual talent prove to be the mother of its best results. Goethe required for his development an unchallenged life of ease, whereas Schiller, who never emerged from his life of misery, and who, up to the time when he wrote *Don Carlos*, had not been able to earn sufficient with his pen to buy a writing-desk, required distress to make his genius burst into flower. Jean Paul recognized this blessing of gloomy circumstances when he glorified poverty in his novels. Hebbel followed him along this path by saying that it is more fruitful to refuse the most talented person the necessities of life than to grant them to the least gifted. For among a hundred who have been chosen by the method of sifting, there will be only one on the average who will receive the certificate of excellence in the test of future generations, for the latter use entirely different methods of sifting from that practised by a committee of examiners who expect ready answers to prepared questions.

This projects us on to the horns of a severe dilemma that scarcely allows of escape. The consciousness of duty towards the optimum expresses itself only in a maximum of assistance, and overhears the whispered objection of reason that Nature has also coarser means at her disposal to attain her ends; in her own cruelty of selection she often enough proves the truth of Menander's saying, which, freely translated, says: to be tormented is also part of man's education. The fact that Einstein—with certain reservations—favours the giving of help to the selected few, it is for me a proof, among many others, of his love towards his fellow-men, which fills his heart absolutely, all questions of relativity notwithstanding.

THE DISCOVERER

NEXT time—so one of our talks ended—next time, as you insist on it, we shall talk of discovery in general. This was a promise of special import for me, for it meant that I was to draw near to a fountain-head of instruction, and to have an opportunity of hearing the pronouncements of one whose authority could scarcely be transcended.

We are precluded from questioning Galilei personally about the foundations of Mechanics, or Columbus about the inner feelings of a navigator who discovers new lands, or Sebastian Bach about the merits of Counterpoint, but a great discoverer lives among our contemporaries who is to give us a clue to the nature of discovery. Was it not natural that I should feel the importance of his acceptance of my proposal?

Before meeting him again I was overwhelmed with ideas that arose in me at the slightest echo of the word " discovery " in my mind. Nothing, it seemed to me, could be higher: man's position in the sphere of creation and the sum of his knowledge can be deduced from the sum of his discoveries which find their climax in the conceptions civilization and philosophy, just as they are partly conditioned by the philosophy of the time. We might be tempted to ask: which of these two precedes, and which follows? And perhaps the ambiguous nature of this question would furnish us with the key to the answer. For, ultimately, these two elements cannot at all be resolved into the relationship of cause and effect, antecedent and consequent.

Neither is primary, and neither secondary: they are intimately interwoven with one another, and are only different aspects of one and the same process. At the root of this process is our axiomatic belief that the world can be comprehended, and the indomitable will of all thinking men, acting as an elementary instinct, to bring the perceptual events in the universe into harmony with the inner processes of thought. This impulse is eternal; it is only the form of these attempts to make the world fully intelligible that alters and is subject to the change of time. This form finds expression in the current philosophy which brings each discovery to fruition, just as philosophy bears in itself constituents of the ripe discovery.

It seemed to me that even at this stage of my reflections I was somewhere near interpreting Einstein's intellectual achievement. For his principle of relativity is tantamount to a regulative world-principle that has left a mighty mark in the thought of our times. We have lived to see the death of absolutism; the relativity of the constituents of political power, and their mutability according to view-point and current tendencies, become manifest to us with a clearness unapproached by any experience of earlier historical epochs. The world was far enough advanced in its views for a final achievement of thought which would demolish the absolute also from the mathematico-physical aspect. This is how Einstein's discovery appeared as inevitable.

Yet a shadow of doubt crossed my mind. Einstein's discoveries came to light in the year 1905—that is, at a time when hardly a cloud was visible to forewarn us of the storms which were to uproot absolutism in the world. But what if a different kind of necessity had imposed itself on world-history, and hence on the world-view? Nowadays we know from authentic accounts, which no one doubts, that all that we have experienced during the war and the revolution has hung upon the activities of one frail human being of quite insignificant exterior, a bureaucrat of the Wilhelm-Strasse, a choleric eccentric who succeeded in frustrating the Anglo-German alliance which was unceasingly being pressed upon us for six long years after the beginning of the century.

Amid the noisy progress of universal evolution the secret

and insignificant nibbling of a mole cannot be regarded as of momentous importance for history, and yet if we eliminate it from the complete picture of events we find as a result that all our experiences have been inverted. Absolutism would not have been thrown overboard, but would probably have kept the helm with greater mastery than ever as the exponent of an Anglo-German hegemony of the world, and a political outlook fundamentally different in tendency would now have been prevailing on the earth.

But Einstein's Theory of Relativity would not have taken the slightest heed of this. It would have arisen independently of the current forms of political conceptions, simply because we had reached that point in our intellectual development and because Einstein was living and spinning his webs of thought. And the question whether his theory will also have crushed absolutism for the non-physicist cannot be answered.

It may indeed be doubted whether its time had already come. In the case of many important events in the history of thought their moment of birth can be fixed to within about ten years, as for example the Theory of Evolution, which had been conceived in several minds at the same time and had of necessity to come to life in one of them, even if it had failed in the case of the others. I venture to say that without Einstein, the Theory of Relativity in its widest sense, that is, including the new doctrine of gravitation, would perhaps have had to wait another two hundred years before being born.

This contradiction is cleared up if we use sufficiently great time intervals. History does not adapt itself to the time measures of politics and of journalism, and philosophies are not to be calculated in terms of days. The philosophy of Aristotle held sway right through the Middle Ages, and that of Epicurus will gain its full force only in the coming generation. But if we make our unit a hundred years the connexion between philosophies and great discoveries remains true.

Whoever undertakes to explore the necessity of this connexion cannot evade the fact that the lines of the result had been marked out in the region of pure thought, as can be proved, before even the great discovery or invention was able to present it in a fully intelligible form. Even the achievement of Copernicus would follow this general rule of development : it was the last consequence of the belief in the Sun Myth which had never been forsaken by man in spite of the violent efforts of the Church and of man himself to force the geocentric view. Copernicus concentrated what had survived of the wisdom of the earliest priests—which includes also the germ of our modern ideas of energy and electricity—of the teachings of Anaxagoras and the Eleatics which had remained latent in our consciousness: his discovery was the transformation of a myth into science. Mankind, whose wandering fancy first feels presentiments, then thinks and wishes to know, is a large edition of the individual thinker. The latter sees further only because he, so to speak, stands on the shoulders of a sum-total of beings with a world-view.

Let us turn our attention to an example from the most recent history of philosophy and discovery. The absolute continuity of events was one of the generally accepted canons of thought, and is even nowadays taught by serious philosophers as an incontrovertible element in our knowledge. The old quotation *Natura non facit saltus*, popularized by Linné, is one of the formulæ of this apparently invincible truth. But deep down in the consciousness of man there has always been an opposition to it, and when the French philosopher Henri Bergson set out to break up this line of continuity by metaphysical means in ascribing to human knowledge an intermittent, cinematographic character, he was proclaiming in an audible and eloquent form only what had lain latent in a new but as yet incomplete philosophy. Bergson made no new " discovery," he felt his way intuitively into a new field of knowledge and recognized that the time was ripe for the real discovery. This was actually presented to us in our day by the eminent physicist Max Planck, the winner of the Nobel Prize for Physics in 1919, in the form of his " Quantum Theory." This is not to be taken as meaning that a revolutionary philosophy and a triumph of scientific research now become coincident, but only that a discontinuous, intermittent sequence, an atomistic structure, was proved by means of the weapons of exact science, to be true of energies which, according to current belief, were expected to be radiated regularly and connectedly. This was probably not a case of the accidental coincidence of a new philosophical view with the results of reasoning from physical grounds, but a demand of time, exacting that the claims of a new principle of thought be recognized.

As above suggested, it is more difficult to find a link between Einstein's discoveries and antecedent presentiments of relativity. For a mere reference to the downfall of absolutism in the world of human events will not suffice. In the case of Einstein, we see such a tremendous rush of thought in one being that we almost feel compelled to recognize an analogy with the Quantum Theory and believe in a discontinuity in the course of intellectual history. Yet there are certainly threads that connect Einstein's achievement with a prophetic insight. In this case, however, we must spread out over centuries what in the case of other discoveries extends, in comparison, only over decades. That doubt of Faust, which troubles the spirit of every thinker : " whether in yonder spheres there is also an Above and a Below," and which goes back as far as Pyrrhon and Protagoras, is itself relativistic ; it expresses doubt whether the co-ordinate system passing through our own lives as centres is valid. It is ultimately a matter of point of view, and the mathematico-physical consequences of the endless series of questions, and the relation, which arises from the couple, Above-Below, probably leads to a new mode of comprehending the constitution of the world, for which Einstein's creative work found the adequate expression in abstract terms. And from this point onwards, in accordance with the principle of reciprocal action, a new stream of knowledge will pour itself into the hazy stretches of philosophy. A fundamental and radical reform of our philosophy seems inevitable, particularly with respect to our conceptions of Space and Time, perhaps, too, even with respect to Infinity and Causality. Much dross will have to be sifted out of our old categories of thought and out of our world wisdom, which once served as material for fine structures. What will the finer ones look like that are to take their places in obedience to the command of physics ? Who would care to take it upon himself to form an estimate ?

Much will be uprooted, and it is possible that even the defiant " ignorabimus," the antipole of the search for truth from Pyrrhon to Dubois, will again take up the cudgel. For in the face of despairing uncertainty there is the one certainty : what cannot be comprehended is being encircled more and more by the great discoverers! And even if the absolute point of convergence can never be reached, there is within our reach at least another point which is a haven of rest in the passing stream of philosophies, namely, a moral centre around which eddies of happiness circle. At the heart of this world-view there is the uplifting belief in an advance of knowledge in spite of all, and a belief in the vanishing of age-long problems and difficulties under the flood of discoveries. And even if afterwards and concurrently ever new problems and difficulties arise, these do not suppress our feeling of triumph. Every achievement in this field gives us a sense of enfranchisement from prejudices, not the least of which is narrowness of national outlook. Not only do discoverers construct bridges of thought that stretch to astronomical distances, but, what is more difficult, they build bridges for our feelings, that surmount political obstacles. Every thinking being who plays a part in the making of some great discovery and who, with deepened vision, bows before a new achievement of mind, gradually becomes a disciple of the religion of universal politics, the creed of which is faith in the brotherhood of thought. The nucleus of a philosophy that belongs to the future is the recognition that differing national view must be compounded into a unity, and that every great discovery means a step towards attaining this end.

Even if we accept Pascal's wonderful dictum that human knowledge is represented by a sphere which is continually growing and increasing its points of contact with the unknown, we must not interpret it as a sign of despair. It is not the enlargement of the unknown, but only that of knowledge that stirs our feelings with ethical forces. The positive calls up in us a living force by inspiring in us the feeling that the sphere of knowledge is destined to grow, and that there can be no higher duty for all the energies of mind than to obey the call for combined action towards this growth which will bring the world into harmony.

Full of such reflections I entered the home of the great discoverer, whose activities unceasingly hovered before my vision as ideal examples of creative effort. I discovered him, as almost always, seated before loose sheets of paper which his hand had covered with mathematical symbols, with hieroglyphics of that universal language in which, according to Galilei, the great book of Nature is written.

What a very different picture many an outsider draws of the manner in which a seeker in the heavens works ! He is imagined like Tycho Brahe to be surrounded by unusual pieces of apparatus, spying through the ocular of a long range refractor into the universe, seeking to unravel its ultimate secrets. The true picture does not correspond to this fancy in the slightest. Nothing in the make-up of the room reminds one of super-earthly sublimity, no abundance of instruments or books is to be seen, and one soon becomes aware that here a thinker reigns whose only requirement for his work, which encompasses the world, is his own mind, plus a sheet of paper and a pencil. All that acts on the observatories outside, that gives rise to great scientific expeditions, that, indeed, ultimately regulates the relationship of mankind to the constitution of the universe, the revolution in the knowledge of things connecting heaven and earth, all this is here concentrated in the simple figure of a still youthful scholar, who spins out endless threads from the fabric of his mind : the words of a poet are recalled to our memory, which, addressed to all of us, have been fulfilled to the last degree by one living among us :—

" Whereso thou roamest in space, thy Zenith and Nadir unite thee—
This to the heavenly height, that to the pole of the world,—
Whatsoever thou do, let thy will mount up into Heaven—
But let the pole of the world still o'er thine actions preside."
(SCHILLER : *Translation by Merivale.*)

And this one helped to fulfil this aim and I must break off his thread of thought to put the question : What is Discovery, and what does it signify ?

It is a purely abstract question that may appear to many to be devoid of content. Such will repeat to themselves, as best they can, the list of discoveries and think a man makes a discovery when he finds out something important, such as the Laws of Falling Bodies, the formation of Rainbows, or the Origin of Species : a general denomination may be found for it perhaps only by ascribing to Discovery something requiring a powerful mind, a creative genius.

At first it staggered me to hear Einstein say : " The use of the word ' Discovery ' in itself is to be deprecated. For discovery is equivalent to becoming aware of a thing which is already formed ; this links up with proof, which no longer bears the character of ' discovery ' but, in the last instance, of the means that leads to discovery." He then stated at first in blunt terms, which he afterwards elaborated by giving detailed illustrations : " Discovery is really not a creative act ! "

Arguments for and against this view flashed through my mind, and I thought involuntarily of a great master of music who, when he was asked : " What is Genius ? " answered : " A genius is one to whom ideas occur." This parallel might be carried still further, for I have repeatedly heard Einstein call " ideas " what we would regard as wonderful thoughts. Does not the philosopher Fritz Mauthner speak of the discovery of gravitation as being an " aperçu " of Newton ; yes, in the sense of *aperçus* as applied in ancient Greek philosophy, and which included almost everything that was left by Pythagoras, Heraclitus, etc., as a token of their genius. On the other hand, we are all possessed of the desire to differentiate clearly between an idea and a creative act of thought, as occurs in Grillparzer's aphorism : " An idea is not a thought ; a thought knows its bounds, whereas the idea leaps over them and succeeds in accomplishing nothing ! "

Here, then, we must revise our view. We know, for example, how much Einstein's " ideas," felt by him to be such and named so accordingly, accomplished. Let us hear how he characterizes in a few words his own " idea " which shook the world :

" The underlying thought of relativity," he said, in connexion with this question, " is that there is physically no unique (specially favoured) state of motion. Or, more exactly, among all states of motion there is none that is favoured in the sense that, in contradistinction to the others, it may be said to be a state of rest. Rest and Motion are not only by formal definition but also by their intrinsic physical meaning *relative conceptions*."

" Well, then," I interposed, " surely this was a creative act ! This first flashed across *your* mind, Professor ; it represents *your* discovery, so that we may well let the word retain the meaning usually associated with it ! "

" By no means," answered Einstein, " for it is not true that this fundamental principle occurred to me as the primary thought. If this had been so perhaps it would be justifiable to call it a " discovery." But the suddenness with which you assume it to have occurred to me must be denied. Actually, I was lead to it by *steps* arising from the *individual* laws derived from experience."

Einstein supplemented this by emphasizing the conception " invention," and ascribed a considerable importance to it : " Invention occurs here as a constructive act. This does not, therefore, constitute what is essentially original in the matter, but the creation of a method of thought to arrive at a logically coherent system . . . the really valuable factor is *intuition* ! "

I had thought, long and intently, about these theses to discover as nearly as possible what distinguished their content from the usual view. The fundamental differences suggest an abundance of ideas whose importance grows in value as we apply them to various cases as illustrations. And I feel convinced that we shall yet have to occupy ourselves with these words of Einstein, which present themselves as a confession, as with the famous " hypotheses non fingo " that Newton set up as the idea underlying his work.

The latter as well as the former implies something negative : it denies something. In Einstein's words there is apparently a repudiation of the really creative act in discovery ; he lays stress on the gradual, methodical constructive factors, not omitting to emphasize intuition. There is no other course open to us but to seek indirectly a synthesis of these conceptions, and to eliminate what is apparently contradictory in them.

I consider this possible if we decide to subdivide the discovery into a series of individual acts in which succession takes the place of instantaneous suddenness The creative factor may then remain intact ; indeed, it attains a still higher degree of importance if we imagine to ourselves that a *series* of creative ideas must be linked together to make possible a single important discovery.

The original idea never springs fully equipped and armed like Minerva out of the head of its creator. And it is wise to bear in mind that even Jupiter had to suffer in his head a period of pregnancy accompanied with great pain. It is only in the after-picture that Pallas Athene appears with the attribute of suddenness. It is the nature of our myth-building imagination to leap over the actual act of birth so as to give a more brilliant form to the finished creation.

We feel great satisfaction when we learn that Gauss, the Prince of Mathematicians, declared in one of his valuable flashes of insight : " I have the result, only I do not yet know how to get to it." For in this utterance we see above all that he emphasizes a lightning-like intuition. He has possession of a thing, which is, however, not yet his own, and which can only become his own when he has found the way to it. Is this contradictory ? From the point of view of elementary logic, certainly ; but methodologically, by no means. Here it is a question of : *Erwirb es um es zu besitzen !* This makes necessary a series of further intuitions along the road of invention, and of construction.

This is, then, where that phase commences, which Einstein denotes by the word " gradual," or " by steps." The first intuition must be present ; its presence as a rule usually guarantees that further intuition will follow in logical sequence

This does not always happen. In passing, we discussed several special cases from which particular inferences may be drawn. The powerful mathematician Pierre Fermat has presented the world with a theorem of extremely simple form which he discovered, a proof of which is being sought even nowadays, two and a half centuries after he stated it. In easy language, it is this : the sum of two squares may again be a square, for example, $5^2 + 12^2 = 13^2$, since $25 + 144 = 169$; but the sum of two cubes can *never* be a cube, and, more generally, as soon as the exponent, the power index n, is greater than 2, the equation $x^n + y^n = z^n$ can never be satisfied by whole number values for x, y, and z ; it is impossible to find three whole numbers for x, y, and z, which, when substituted in the equation, give a correct result.

This is certainly true ; it is an intuitive discovery. But Fermat's assertion that he possessed a " wonderful proof," is for very good reasons open to contradiction. No one doubts the absolute truth of the theorem. But the later inspiration, the next step after the intuition, has occurred neither to Fermat nor to anyone else. It cannot be established whether his remark about the proof was due to a subjective error, or was baseless. In any case it seems probable that Fermat had arrived at the result *per intuitionem* without knowing the way to it. His creative act stopped short ; it was only a first flare of a conflagration, and did not fulfil the condition that Einstein associates with the conception of a logically complete method.

We may, indeed, pursue this case of Fermat still further. He had enunciated another theorem, again *per intuitionem*, namely, that it was possible to construct prime numbers of any magnitude by a formula he gave. Euler later showed by a definite example that the theorem was false. It was stated in a letter to Pascal written in 1654 in the words : the result of squaring 2 continuously and then adding 1 must in each case be a prime number, that is, $2^{2^k}+1$ must always be a prime no matter what value k may have. Fermat added : " This is a property for the truth of which I answer." Euler chanced to try $k=5$, and found that $2^{32}+1=4,294,967,297$, which may be represented as the product of 641 and 6,700,417, and hence is not a prime.

It is conceivable that no Euler might have lived, and that no one else might have discovered this contradiction. What would then have been the position of this " discovery " of Fermat ?

We should certainly not have disputed its creative character, for we should have said that it corresponds to a fact which is fully formed, but cannot be proved. But now that we know that the fact does not exist at all, the thing assumes a different colour. It was not a discovery at all, but an erroneous conjecture. But one would never be able to arrive at an erroneous conclusion of this sort without being a mathe- matical genius, and having the inspiration of the moment. And from this again it follows that to make a discovery in the full sense of the word the intuition of the moment does not suffice, but must be supported by a series of intuitions, and this is the condition that it become a permanent com- ponent of universal truth.

The fact that Einstein refers to the action of " inventing " in his explanation, gives support, it seems to me, to the view that, strictly speaking, discovering and inventing are never to be regarded as being separable. In discovering, what has to be constructed persists, and in inventing, it is a question of finding the path along which there is the promise of success, be it by a method, a proof, or by some general work. We spoke of works of art, and I was delighted to see that Einstein was by no means disinclined to claim certain works of pure thought, which are usually placed in the category of scientific discovery, as works of art. In the latter, however, the pure process of invention plays the prominent part, for in them something is represented that did not exist at all before ; this has repeatedly led to the artist's achievement being given the higher rank, as being properly and exclusively creative. The argument runs somewhat along these lines : the infinitesimal calculus would certainly have been discovered even if there had been no Newton and no Leibniz, but without Beethoven we should never have had a C Minor Symphony, and never in the future would it have appeared, for it was a subjective, absolutely personal, and unique product of its creator.

I believe this may be admitted, and that we may nevertheless retain the view that in the work of art, too, the act of discovering is to be found. Let us consider for a moment the elementary substance of the first movement of this fifth symphony, a colossal movement of 500 bars, which expresses itself quite definitely in four notes, of which one is repeated three times. " Thus Destiny thunders at the gates " is Beethoven's motto for this section ; it is expressed tonally in a succession of notes which through all eternity existed among the possible permutative arrangements of these sounds.

Beethoven, so it is expressed, invented it. But it is just as correct to say—in Einstein's words—" he became aware of what was already formed "—that is, he " discovered " the fundamental theme, and afterwards " proved it " in terms of musical logic unheard-of beauty in a methodical elaboration. We may, indeed, go further still. This *motif* of four tones was not only extant as an abstractum, as a possible mathematical arrangement, but also as something natural. Czerny, a pupil of Beethoven, to whom the master confided many a remark about the origin of his compositions, reports that a bird, the yellow-hammer, had sung this theme to Beethoven in the woods. But neither the bird nor any other living creature had invented it ; rather what could not be created, because it had always been in existence, became objectified in the medium of sound. Beethoven found it ; it was *res nullius* when he found it and when he discovered simultaneously with the succession of tones that they were appropriate for a powerful musical representation of sombre Destiny. Every theme, be it of Beethoven, Bach, Wagner, or anyone else, may be represented graphically by a curve (in the case of Bach's fugal themes this has, in fact, been done for special purposes), and just as it is certain that every elliptic-arc existed before all geometry, so it may be affirmed with equal certainty that everything musical was in existence before the advent of composition, and was merely waiting for a discoverer whom we designate the inventor, the creative organ.

But may not some of this glory be reflected on to scientific discovery ? When we are in an ecstasy of admiration, we talk of a creative act as of something divine ; may we not also grant to the scientist this tribute which, owing to a slight confusion of conceptions, we shower on the artists ? And I believe that Einstein's definition does not set up an insuperable barrier in this respect to our admiration, which exerts every effort to pass beyond, refuses to come to a standstill before the rigid fact that the discoverer reveals only what is pre-formed ; our emotions prove to be stronger than our minds with their objective valuation. In the last instance, we opine, the scientific discoverer, too, creates something new, namely, a piece of knowledge that was previously not in existence. And we obey the impulse of hero-worship, when we call a definite first discoverer a creator.

This silences opposition certainly only for a time, without vanquishing it. For this knowledge, too, lay ready before the first discoverer appeared : he did not create it, but merely drew back the veil that enveloped it. So that, ultimately, we get back to " intuition " in its literal sense, a becoming aware of things, an exact consideration of things, states, and relationships ; and this intensive consideration, full of wonderment, has always been a privilege of a very few chosen men.

It might be asked : Was there any knowledge of Pythagoras'

Theorems before Pythagoras gave us his proof ? We should have to answer : It was in existence at least in the still dark field of vision of Pythagoras, which became illumined one day when he took such a view of the number-ratios 3—4—5 that an exact intuition could actually come about. It is erroneous to assume that a creative act suddenly called up before his soul as if by magic the figure with the three squares drawn externally on the sides of a triangle. Rather, he " took his stride " (as we know from Vitruvius) by considering a triangle whose sides were of a definite length ; and the well-known proof, which is linked indissolubly in our minds with his work, is not his at all, but Euclid's. Yet our annals grow musty, centuries pass by, and the credit of being the creator rests with the man who first succeeded in getting a clear picture of such a triangle.

It seems natural to test discoveries by experiments. The first result of doing this is a very remarkable increase in the rate at which the intuitive process has developed. In ancient times, intuition, it seems, scarcely felt the need of proving things by experiment ; all that was discovered by Archimedes in mechanics, by the Pythagoreans in acoustics, by Euclid in optics, may be reduced practically to the formula " heureka," and it is probably scarcely an exaggeration to say that more and more fruitful experiments are performed in one week nowadays than in the whole of the classical age taken together.*

* Recently certain precisians in definition have been seeking to establish a fundamental difference between physicists of reality, experimental physicists, and " blackboard-physicists." The last term is given jeeringly to theoretical physicists because they, in the opinion of these critics, wish to found Nature entirely on formulæ argued out on the blackboard. The history of science does recognize this distinction, although it is, of course, quite possible for a physicist to arrive at important discoveries without making any experiments.

One might be more justified in asserting that the great theorist need not necessarily be a great experimenter and vice versa. But I can quote no example of a physicist who confined himself obstinately to blackboard discussion, and on principle disowned all experimental work.

I must add that Einstein himself is fond of experimenting, and has had much success in experimental work. The amount of advice and encouragement that he has given, and still gives, to many workers in this field is very considerable. But he does not practise experimental work regularly, and remarked that he is obliged to appeal to outside help for certain practical tests. There are specific experimental geniuses, whose activity assumes the happiest and most fruitful form when it supplements that of the theorist and fertilizes it.

Experiments have become, if not the sole, yet the most definite, test of intuition. I need only recall the observations of the solar eclipse of 1919, which were of an experimental character inasmuch as they used apparatus to question Nature. To the world generally, they gave the irrefutable confirmation of Einstein's Theory of Gravitation, but not to Einstein himself, whose intuition felt itself so certain that the confirmation was a mere matter of course.

But this is not the average case ; in many cases the intuition of the discoverer appeals to experiment as a judge of great authority, who is to confirm, reject, or correct.

Let us take some examples of cases in which the intensity and the value of intuition were measured by the experimental results. Benjamin Franklin's Kite Experiment may be taken as a classical instance. Here is a man in whose head the idea takes root that lightning and electricity are one and the same thing. Innumerable persons before and after his time might have hit on the same idea, which is now the common knowledge of children. Yet, a single man had to appear who became aware of this pre-formed fact and who simultaneously thought out a method of putting it to proof. In 1752 he constructed a kite, sent it up into the clouds during a storm, and caught up sparks on the ground by a metallic contrivance, and, as d'Alembert so aptly described it to the French Academy :

" Eripuit coelo fulmen . . ."

He wrested the lightning from the heavens. Jupiter tonans illuminated a great discovery, a mighty intuition which had entered like a lightning stroke into the brain of a discoverer.

This case would be classical, were it not that nine-tenths of it is based on legend. Franklin was by no means the first who had this intuition, and his experimental test was so full of faults that it was within an ace of failing. Franklin used a dry thread of hemp, which he thought to be a conductor, but which became a conductor only after it had been made wet by rain. Till that moment the exhibition of sparks on the ground had been poor enough, and little was wanting for Franklin to give up his attempt and confess that he had been inspired, not with an intuition, but with a hallucination.

But to whom then is the glory of this discovery due ? This

is a difficult point to decide.   As early as 1746, that is, six years
before Franklin's kite made its ascent in Philadelphia, Professor
Winkler of Leipzig had asserted in a dissertation that the two
phenomena were identical, and had proved this theoretically ;
and three years earlier still Abbé Nollet had declared the
storm clouds to be the conductors of an electrical induction
machine.   Almost simultaneously with Franklin, Dalibard,
Delor, Buffon, Le Monnier, Canton, Bevis, and Wilson made
experiments on an elaborate scale, which far exceeded that of
Franklin in their results.   To this must be added that the
experiment was conducted with evident success only in 1753,
when de Romas of Nerac in South France wove a real conductor
of thin annealed wire into the kite-string, and succeeded in
bringing down a regular thunderstorm with flashes of lightning
ten feet long, accompanied by a deafening uproar.   It was only
then that the track of the inspiration was traced back through
time to the Roman Kings, Numa Pompilius and Tullus Hosti-
lius, as the first experimenters with lightning.   And then the
physicist Lichtenberg sought to furnish a proof that the old
Hebrew ark of the Covenant, together with the tabernacle, were
nothing other than great pieces of electrical apparatus highly
charged with electricity derived from the air ; thus the first
intuition, and the priority of discovery, would have to be
ascribed to Moses or Aaron !   And connected with this was
the fact, supported by substantial proof, that the Temple of
Solomon was protected by lightning-conductors.

I must not omit to mention that Einstein regards this
whole chain of proofs stretching back to early times as by no
means established, although besides Lichtenberg, other important scholars, such as Bendavid in Berlin and Michaelis in
Göttingen, have vouched for their truth.   And as it is a matter
of electrical relationships, Einstein's doubts cannot be passed
over.   As far as I recollect, they were not directed against
the rough facts in themselves, but against the sense that is
construed into them—that is to say, in the case of both the
ancient Roman and the Biblical data, the conception of discovery must be excluded, and must be awarded rather to those
intellectual efforts which have led to the creation of a method
of thought.   None the less, we may uphold our statement that
in this case, presumed to be classical, neither Franklin nor any-

one else is to be claimed as the discoverer or as the central figure in a creative act.

The experimental case of spectral analysis is incomparably simpler and less open to dispute. It is without doubt a discovery of fundamental importance bearing all the characteristics of originality, for no predecessors are discernible. I have always felt a little dissatisfied with the fact that it required two men to think it out, that a duo of minds was necessary for one act of thought which appears quite uniform, elementary and inseparable from the intuition of a single mind. But it seems possible that tradition has not handed the facts down to us faithfully, and that the two men, with a unanimity arising from their partnership in work, combined their results, which were not, at the beginning, of a dual character. This possibility became clear to me from a remark of Einstein which made it plain to me that the conjunction Kirchhoff and Bunsen is to be taken as denoting Kirchhoff and then, after a pause, Bunsen in the next breath ! But if we discard this question of unity or duality, we are left with the fact that the idea of a spectral analysis occurred to some one (as a result of preceding optical experiments with Fraunhofer lines), and was fully confirmed by later experiments. Only fully confirmed ? No, the classic rank of this case manifested itself in a much more triumphant manner, for it is impossible that the intuition of Kirchhoff and Bunsen could have grasped the whole significance and range of their discovery even after they had made it their own.

Every discovery encloses a germ of hope. However great this may have been in the case of Kirchhoff, it could not by any stretch of imagination approach the degree of its fulfilment. The fundamental theoretical idea that " a vapour absorbs from the ray-complex of white light only those wave-lengths which it can emit " gave rise to a process, the ingenuity, delicacy, and certainty of which is almost inconceivable. When rays of light emitted by incandescent vapour were separated by a prism, there were discovered fine coloured lines that betrayed some unknown mystery. The spectroscopic experiments proved, in a succession of results, that the author of the above idea had made not only one discovery, but a whole host of them. For example, it was observed that, in burning minute residues obtained by evaporating certain mineral waters, a red line and a blue line that had never been seen before appeared in the spectrum. One knew immediately that an element, hitherto undiscovered, was proclaiming its presence. In this way in quick succession the element Cæsium was discovered, then Rubidium, Thallium, Indium, Argon, Helium, Neon, Krypton, Xenon—certainly things that were already pre-formed in Nature, just as the idea of a bridge from Optics to Chemistry lay all ready in the heart of Nature ; but no blame can be given to the astonished contemporaries who regarded this fundamental discovery of spectroscopic analysis as a creative achievement of the intellect.

This ray of hope gave a glimpse of the degree of accuracy attainable. In this connexion the experiment confirmed infinitely more than the boldest imagination could ever have dreamed. A yellow line was detected in the spectrum of sodium. And it was found experimentally that the three-millionth part of a thousandth of a gramme of a sodium salt is sufficient to produce this sodium line in the spectrum of a Bunsen burner. There commenced a dizzying passage in the Calculus of Probabilities for, since it was found that in the sun's atmosphere hydrogen, carbon, iron, aluminium, calcium, sodium, nickel, chromium, zinc, and copper were present, the question arose as to how great was the possibility of an error in this observation. Kirchhoff calculated it as a chance of a trillion to one that these substances are actually present in the sun !

Never before had an experiment verified to such an extreme degree a discoverer's idea. It seems appropriate at this stage to deal with a doctrine which seeks to shed light into the deepest recesses of the connexion between experiment and discovery. It teaches that an *experimentum crucis*, an experiment that verifies absolutely, is *impossible* in physics. That is to say, every idea of a discoverer involves a hypothesis, and, however the experiment that follows may turn out, there still remains the possibility that this hypothesis was false, and may later have to make way for another essentially contradictory hypothesis which will be valid again only for a limited time.

The chief exponent of this theory is the eminent scholar, Pierre Duhem, Membre de l'Institut. He draws a parallel between experiment and mathematical proof, particularly with the indirect, apagogic form which has been so successfully applied in Euclidean geometry. In this method it is assumed that a certain statement is erroneous ; it is then shown that it leads to an obvious contradiction ; consequently the statement was correct provided that a certain doubt be excluded. Thus in the domain of mathematics we have a real *experimentum crucis*.

In accordance with this, Duhem tests the validity of two physical theories, both of which were put forward and claimed as discoveries. Newton had discovered the nature of light to consist in " emission " ; to him, as well as to Laplace and Biot, light consists of projectiles that are emitted with very great velocity. The discovery of Huyghens, supported by Young and Fresnel, substitutes wave-motion in place of corpuscular emission. Hence, according to Duhem, we have, or we had, here two hypotheses which appear to be the only ones possible. Experiment was to pronounce a judgment, and at first it decided irrefutably in favour of the wave-theory. Therefore, the discovery of Huyghens is alone true, and that of Newton is shown to be an error ; there is no third outlet, and so we have quite certainly an *experimentum crucis* before us.

The term itself originates in Bacon's *Novum Organum*. Contrary to Duhem's assumption, it does not refer to a signpost at cross-roads giving various routes, nor is it connected with *croix ou pile*, heads or tails. *Experimentum crucis* denotes rather a divine judgment at the cross, that is a test that is absolutely decisive and beyond further appeal. But no ! adds Duhem, there is no room for a third judgment in the case of two contradictory statements in geometry, but there is between two contradictory statements in physics. And, in fact, this third possibility has manifested itself in the discovery of Maxwell, who has shown that the nature of light is founded on a process of periodic electromagnetic disturbances. Hence, so concludes Duhem, experiment can *never* decide whether a certain theory is alone valid. The physicist is never certain that he has exhausted all conceivable possibilities of thought. The truth of a physical statement, the validity of a discovery, cannot be confirmed by any *experimentum crucis*.

According to this argument, therefore, it is also possible

that the scientific grounds of spectral analysis do not conform to truth. A contradictory hypothesis may, indeed, be set up, with the result that the same experiments that had led Kirchhoff's discovery from one triumph to another would have to be interpreted in a totally different sense.

I must frankly confess that I cannot subscribe to such an extreme eventuality, since, in my opinion, Duhem's analogy with mathematics excludes this possibility. For if a certain probability is expressed by a trillion to one, then I venture to state that even in the case of mathematical truths certainty reaches no higher degree of probability. From the history of mathematics we know of theorems which were enunciated and provided with complete proofs, and yet did not succeed in establishing themselves ; hence we see that, however evident a mathematical theorem may be, it is still only a matter of very great probability.

If, following our usual habits of thought, we take this for absolute certainty, then we may also consider the sum-total of experiments in the realm of spectral analysis to be a great *experimentum crucis* for the correctness of the theory itself.

Far removed from it, and yet connected with it, there is the " Periodic System of the Elements," the discovery of Mendelejew and Lothar Meyer. It, too, offered prophetic glances into the future, foretold the unknown, hinted at things that were present only in imagination in a scheme of thought that assigned definite places of existence to undiscovered things. The Periodic System is represented by a table containing vertical and horizontal rows, in the squares of which the elements are entered according to certain rules depending on their atomic weights. The discovery consisted theoretically in stating that the physical and chemical properties of each element is the arithmetic mean between the properties of its horizontal and vertical neighbours. This gave rise to pre-dictions concerning the unoccupied squares. These gaps, these blank spaces in the table, seem to say prophetically : There are elements missing here that must be discoverable. The neighbours will betray them, and the empty space itself shows by what means they are to be found. With the shrewd-ness of a detective, Mendelejew was able to say : There must be elements of the atomic weights 44, 70, and 72 ; we do not know them yet, but we are in a position to determine the properties of these foundlings of the future, and, what is more, the properties of their compounds with other elements. Later researches, which led to the discovery of the elements, Scandium, Gallium, and Germanium, have actually confirmed all these predicted properties.

The metal Gallium was discovered in 1875 by spectroscopic means. Its properties are the mean of those of Aluminium and Indium, and this places it in a position which had already been assigned to it in the periodic table before its discovery; for, owing to a gap in the system, Mendelejew had asserted its existence five years previously, although he then knew nothing of its characteristic spectral signs, namely, two beautiful violet lines. Radium, too, which was discovered in 1900 and was found to have the atomic weight 226, completely satisfied this test and fitted exactly into the place which this number reserved for it in the table. Thus prediction and confirmatory discovery were fully congruent in this case; the experiment followed on the visionary insight just as a Euclidean proof follows on a mathematical assertion, and we have every reason to say that the system of Mendelejew and Lothar Meyer has stood the crucial test. Future hypotheses will perhaps supplement the system or enlarge our knowledge of it, but will certainly not reduce it *ad absurdum*.

.   .   .   .

Apart from these cases, there are achievements by men who may be called *lucky* discoverers, although they displayed no genius for finding nor for creating. The philosopher-physicist, Ernst Mach, has devoted a lecture to such intellects, which seems to me very valuable, if only for the reason that he traces back the conceptions of discovery and invention to one common root of knowledge, and explains their difference as being due only to a difference in the application of this discovery.

But when Ernst Mach in this lecture, " On the Influence of Accidental Circumstances on the Development of Inventions and Discoveries," extends the influence of chance to include accidental circumstances that can only enter when the discoverer is closely attentive, it seems to me that certain limitations are advisable. Otherwise, if we pursue Mach's line of thought to its extreme, we could declare every discovery to be due to chance, and this would be the end of the intuitive-creative idea. This assertion would ultimately mean that genius owes its achievements to the accidental arrangement of the molecules in the brain-cells of its associated body. This would be just as wrong as saying that chess is a game of chance because we lose a game when, by chance, we come up against a better player.

Huyghens, the great discoverer and inventor, says, in his *Dioptrica*, that he would have to consider anyone who invented the telescope without the favourable intervention of chance to be a superhuman genius. Why should he choose just the telescope ? To many the invention of the Differential Calculus will appear grander and due to a higher degree of ingenuity. And since it was produced quite methodically, and since chance was excluded, we may follow Huyghens and with good reason proclaim its authors superhuman geniuses.

.   .   .   .

Many a true inspiration is dependent on some impulse from without. Who discovered Electromagnetism ? The world-echo answers, " Oersted," with the same confidence that it couples together the names America and Columbus. This shows how enormously important was the achievement. Next to steam-power nothing has exerted such a revolutionary influence in all branches as electromagnetism. Without it, the world of to-day would present a totally different aspect. Without it, we should have no dynamos, no electric trams, no telegraphy, no electric-power stations, all of which are due to the work of Arago, Gay-Lussac, Ampère, Faraday, Gramme, and Siemens. Without it, there would be none of the abundance of brilliant discoveries that are associated with the names of Maxwell, Hertz, and Einstein. The fact that physics used to be divided into three parts—Mechanics, Optics, Electrodynamics—and that, since then, the coherent unity of the physical picture of the world has been developed, shows us a picture in the background of which we see the illuminating figure of Hans Christian Oersted. It must not be overlooked, however, that in the case of his great discovery, too, chance played a definite part. It occurred one day when Oersted was holding a lecture in the winter of 1819–20 ; a magnetic needle situated near his Volta-battery began to vibrate irregularly. This apparently unimportant trembling of the metal points contained the key to a fact, the whole consequences of which could in no conceivable way have entered the mind of this observer of a hundred years ago, in spite of the genius of the Danish scientist, which is documented in the classical and far-famed dissertation, " Experimenta circa effectum conflictus electrici in Acum magneticam," which appeared in July 1820. It cleared the way for intuitions that were equally as fruitful for theory as for practice. Thirteen years after this initial discovery the world saw the first very important consequence in Gauss' and Weber's electric telegraph, and a little later the eminent discoverer Fechner, in Leipzig, proclaimed it as his conviction that, within two years, electromagnetism would entirely reform the world of machines, and would entirely supersede steam- and water-power. Of course, his time estimate fell far short of the mark. It has been reserved for the present generation to realize that we live in an electromagnetic world, and that we have, theoretically and practically, to spend our life electromagnetically. The first indication of this knowledge hung upon the quivering point of a magnetic needle, and from it there evolved the electromagnetic ideas that we are so fond of picturing as our handmaids, but which, in reality, are sovereign over us all.

. . . .

A great deal of the history of discovery must be revised and corrected. The Spiral of Archimedes is not due to Archimedes, nor Marriotte's Law to Marriotte, nor Cardan's formula to Cardan, nor Crookes' Tube to Crookes, and Galvanism is only related to Galvani by the following anecdote. It arose from an accidental experience of Madame Galvani in the kitchen : a half-skinned frog that was to be fried for the evening meal happened to rest between a scalpel and a tin plate, which brought it into metallic contact with an accidental discharge of electricity ; the frog twitched ; the head of the house gave a very naïve interpretation to the phenomenon ; and it was under such auspices that Galvanism made its entry into the world. It would be a futile task to endeavour to trace the connexion between experiment and the underlying idea, which, in this case, first came to life in Alexander Volta. What would have remained a mere frog-dance if left to Galvani now acquired the rank of a discovery through the work of a thinking physicist, who set up a " Voltaic series " ; this discovery then assumed power and dignity in the hands of Nicholson, Davy, Thomson, Helmholtz, and Nernst. The words Galvanic Electricity should be made to give way entirely to Voltaic Electricity,* as in the case of many another expression for which chance and insufficient thought have stood sponsor.

It often happens that experiment acts as a corrective of the underlying idea, neither confirming nor contradicting, but nursing it, as it were, strengthening, and purging it of errors. Such experiments, partly in conjunction with chance, play an important, sometimes a decisive, rôle in the works of Dufay, Bradley, Foucault, Fresnel, Fraunhofer, and Röntgen. Faraday, who was incapable of observing otherwise than intensively, found himself compelled, whilst studying induction phenomena, to alter his initial view, and it is just this correction by experiment that constitutes Faraday's real discovery. In many cases the initial idea is corrected, nay surpassed, by te result. Columbus worked methodically when he set out to reach the East Indies by travelling westwards ; but what he discovered was not a confirmation of his nautical idea only, but something much greater, which certainly did not lie in his calculation. Thus he became the archetype of all searchers, who had thought out and anticipated essentially different conditions from those that were afterwards discovered to be prevalent. Among these are to be counted Priestley and Cavendish, who clung to the erroneous notion of phlogiston, even when they had the evidence to the contrary in the elements they had themselves discovered, namely, oxygen and hydrogen. Graham Bell, the inventor, was seeking something quite different from what he later hit on : as a teacher of the deaf and dumb he was trying to give a visual picture of sounds, in order to make clear the formation of sounds to his pupils ; this led him to construct an electrical apparatus, which finally led to the discovery of the telephone.

The truest and sharpest contrast with the *experimentum crucis* is furnished by experiment when it shows the exact

* The usual term in England is Voltaic Electricity, or, simply, Current Electricity.—H. L. B.

opposite of what the explorer was expecting. But since an absolute No entails a very decisive Yes—namely, in this case, the affirmation of a relationship that was previously held to be impossible—a negative experiment of this kind, when it occurs, will be followed by momentous consequences ; these will be the more important in proportion as the question, the affirmation of which was expected by the physicist, is of a fundamental character.

The experiments of Michelson and Morley, directed at proving the existence of the ether, are to be regarded as the true classical instances of these experiments answering with an overwhelming negative. Their first effect was to produce a sense of helplessness, a check to thought, a void in the chamber of ideas. And to fill this void there arose new views of the world in which we nowadays recognize the true thought-pictures of the universe. The great names—Lorentz, Min-kowski, Albert Einstein—shone out !

As there are forerunners for almost every important event, so also in the case of the *experimentum crucis* of Michelson and Morley. Henri Poincaré, the famous mathematician, whilst still a student of the École Polytechnique, had initiated experiments with his fellow-student Favé, which followed the same object. The Michelson-Morley experiment was at least a hundred times more accurate. In each case the con-clusion was that the laws of optics are not disturbed by a motion of translation, such as that of the earth through space this is, however, contrary to what the old physical ideas lead us to expect.

If we assume the existence of a space-filling ether, the earth, owing to its own velocity of nineteen miles per second, would have to pass through a hurricane just as in the case of travellers sitting in an open train rushing along at very great speed. If we send out light rays in all directions simultane-ously from any point on the earth's surface, some will travel in the teeth of the ether-storm, others will experience only a part of the storm's power ; so that of two light-rays travelling in exactly opposite directions the retardation of the one should be equal to the acceleration of the other ; and yet they are not quite equal, for a simple calculation shows that in every case the retardation is slightly more than the acceleration.

This may be made clear by means of a model of easy construction, or, better still, by considering a ship that is subject to a constant current and, simultaneously, to a pressure of the wind. The time taken by the boat in making a trip up and down stream can never be the same for the cases when the wind is in the direction of the current, and vice versa.

In the case of the ray of light, which is sent backwards and forwards by means of a contrivance of mirrors, this fact should be clearly demonstrated by means of the interference-fringes, which are able to show much smaller effects than the experiment demands. The experimental oracle was to speak, but it remained silent. This portentous silence signified : no interference-effect, no action of the ether-current, no influence due to translation—nothing !

This " nothing " compelled a decision of a very startling kind, for the result of this experiment was in direct contradiction to another famous experiment. Fizeau had proved that the ether is practically rigid and remains fixed in interstellar space. A decision had to be taken in favour of Fizeau or Michelson and Morley. Yet this was impossible, for both had operated with unsurpassable accuracy. It was impossible to reconcile both views as they were diametrically opposed. This contradiction remains, even if we assume a different hypothesis, not involving the ether, for Fizeau's experiment. A solution was impossible without undertaking revolutionary changes in the whole of physical thought.

This radical change was effected by Einstein ; and this mysterious contradiction disappeared in the resulting revolution of thought. Einstein supplanted the absolute time-conception by a new relative conception, and thus the perplexing problem disappeared. Two great principles arose as regulative factors in thought, and wherever these were applied, they achieved wonders : one was the new conception of time that deprived the earth of her unique position as the sovereign of time by the introduction of the principle that the rate at which time elapses is different in media moving at different speeds ; the other is the principle of the constancy of the velocity of light. One feels a temptation to apply a mythical allegory : just as the world, according to the Biblical story, originated from nothing, so there arose from the " nothing " of the Michelson-Morley experiment a new world, a world of knowledge, a cosmos of thought, in which perfect harmony reigns.

Its truth was contained in itself before the experimental proof was furnished.   And this realization of truth has become a fact in the *experimentum crucis* for which the sun and stars formed the material.   This will be discussed in another part of the book.

" The really important factor is ultimately intuition," Einstein had said to me.   It made me think of Huyghens' remark about the genius who would have been able to create the telescope without the help of chance.   Was not this intellect, imagined by Huyghens, sitting opposite me at that moment ?   An inner voice answered in the affirmative, for Einstein's thought-complex seemed to me at that moment a kind of telescope for the human mind, a telescope that had arisen out of pure intuition, and whose range stretched to the limits of the universe

CHAPTER VI

OF DIFFERENT WORLDS

Imaginary Experiment with " Lumen."—Impossibilities.—A Destroyed Illusion.—Is the World Infinite ?—Surface Creatures and Shadow Rambles: —What is the Beyond ?—Action at a Distance.—Ideas of Multi-dimensional Regions.—Hypnotism.—Recollections of Zöllner.—Science and Dogma.—The Trial of Galilei.

A CONVERSATION held during April 1920 destroyed an illusion which had become dear to me.

It concerned the fantastic figure, " Lumen," conceived as an actual human being, imagined as endowed with an extraordinary power of motion and keenness of sight. Mr. Lumen is supposed to be the invention of the astronomer Flammarion, who produced him in the retort of fancy, as Faust produced Homunculus, to use him to prove the possibility of very remarkable happenings, in particular, the reversal of Time.

Einstein declared outright : " Firstly, Lumen is not due to Flammarion, who has derived him from other sources ; and secondly, Lumen can in no way be used as a means of proving things."

Moszkowski : " It is at least very interesting to operate with him. Lumen is supposed to have a velocity greater than that of light. Let us assume this as given, then the rest follows quite logically. If, for example, he leaves the earth on the day of a great event, such as the battle of Waterloo, and—— May I trace out this example, at the risk of tiring you ? "

Einstein : Do repeat it, and act as if you were telling something entirely new. It is clear that the Lumen-story gives you great amusement, so please talk quite freely. But I cannot forgo the privilege of showing later how the whole adventure and its consequences must be demolished.

M. : Well then, the person, Lumen, sets off at the end of the battle of Waterloo to make an excursion into space with a speed of 250,000 miles per second. He thus catches up all the light-rays that left the field of battle and moved in his direction. After an hour he will already have attained a lead of about twenty minutes. This lead will be gradually increased, so that at the end of the second day he will no longer be seeing the end of the battle, but the beginning. What has Lumen been seeing in the meantime ? Clearly he has been observing events happening in the reverse direction, as in the case of a cinematograph which is exhibiting pictures backwards. He saw the projectiles leaving the objects they had struck, and returning into the mouths of the cannon. He saw the dead come to life, arise, and arrange themselves into battalion order. He would thus arrive at an exactly opposite view of the passing of time, for what he observes is as much his experience as what we observe is ours. If he had seen all the battles of history and, in fact, all events happening in the reverse order, then in his mind " before " and " after " would be interchanged. That is, he would experience time backwards ; what are causes to us would be effects to him, and our effects would be his causes ; antecedents and consequents would change places, and he would arrive at a causality diametrically opposite to our own. He would be quite as justified in adopting his view of the happening of things, according to his experiences, and of the causal nexus as it appears to him, as we are justified in adopting ours.

EINSTEIN : And the whole story is mere humbug, absurd, and based on false premises, leading to entirely false conclusions.

M. : But it is only to be taken as an imaginary experiment that plays with fantastic impossibilities to direct our ideas on to the relativity of time by a striking illustration. Did not Henri Poincaré adduce this extreme example to discuss the " reversal " of time ?

EINSTEIN : You may rest assured that Poincaré, even if he used this example as an entertaining digression in his lectures, took the same view of Lumen as I do. It is not an imaginary experiment : it is a farce, or, to express it more bluntly, it is a mere swindle ! These experiences and topsy-turvy perceptions have just as little to do with the relativity of time, such as it is taught by the new machanics, as have the personal sensations of a man, to whom time seems long or short according as he experiences pain or pleasure, amusement or boredom. For, in this case, at least the subjective sensation is a reality, whereas Lumen cannot have reality because his existence is based on nonsense. Lumen is to have a speed greater than that of light. This is not only an impossible, but a foolish assumption, because the theory of relativity has shown that the velocity of light cannot be exceeded. However great the accelerating force may be, and for however long it may act, it cannot cause this limit to be transcended. Lumen is supposed to be equipped with the organ of sight, that is, he is supposed to have a corporal existence. But the mass of a body becomes infinitely great when it reaches the velocity of light, so that it is quite absurd to go beyond this stage. It is admissible to operate with impossibilities in imagination, that is, with things that contradict our practical experience, but not with absolute nonsense. That is why the other adventure of Lumen, in which he jumps to the moon, is also an absurdity. In this, he is supposed to leap with a speed greater than light, and, when he reaches the moon, to turn round instantaneously, with the result that he sees himself jumping from the moon to the earth backwards ! This jump is logically meaningless ; and if we try to make deductions of an optical nature from such a nonsensical assumption, we deceive ourselves.

M. : Nevertheless, I should claim extenuating circumstances for this case on the ground that I am enlisting the help of the conception of impossibility. A journey even at a speed of only 1000 miles per second is impossible for a man or a homunculus.

EINSTEIN : Yes, according to our experience, if we measure it against facts. We cannot state definitely that a journey into the universe at an enormous yet limited velocity is absolutely impossible. Within the indicated bounds every play of thought that is argued correctly is allowable.

M. : Now, suppose that I strip Lumen of all bodily organs and take him as being a pure creature of thought, entirely without substance. A velocity greater than that of light can be imagined, even if it cannot be realized physically. If, for example, we think of a lighthouse with a revolving light, and consider a beam of light about 600 miles long, which rotates

200 times per second. Then we could represent to ourselves that the light at the circumference of this beam travels with a speed of nearly 760,000 miles per second.

EINSTEIN : As for that, I can give you a much better example of the same thing. We need only imagine that the earth is poised in space, motionless, and non-rotating. This is physically admissible. Then the most distant stars, as judged by us, would describe their paths with almost unlimited velocities. But this projects us right out of the world of reality into a pure fiction of thought, which, if followed to its conclusion, leads to the most degenerate form of imagination, namely, to pathological individualism. It is in these realms of thought that such perversities as the reversal of time and causality occur.

M. : Dreams, too, are confined to the individual. Reality constrains all human beings to exist in one and the same world, whereas, in dreams, each one has his own world with a different kind of causality. Nevertheless, dreams are a positive experience, and signify a reality for the dreamer. Even for waking reality it would be easy to construct cases in which the causal relationship is shattered. Suppose a person who has grown up in a confined retreat, such as Kaspar Hauser, looks in a mirror for the first time in his life. As he knows nothing of the phenomena of optical reflexion, he sees in it a new, objective world that gives a shock to, or even subverts, his own idea of causality in so far as it may have become developed in him. Lumen sees himself jump backwards, whereas Kaspar Hauser sees himself performing gestures on the wrong side of his body ; should it not be possible to draw a reasonable parallel between these two cases ?

EINSTEIN : Quite impossible. However you set about it, your Lumen will inevitably come to grief on the conception of time. Time, denoted in physical expressions by the symbol " t," may, indeed, be given a negative value in these equations, so that an event may be calculated in the reverse direction. But then we are dealing with pure matters of calculation, and in this case we must not allow ourselves to be drawn into the erroneous belief that time itself may travel negatively, that is, retrogressively. This is the root of the misapprehension : that what is allowable and indeed necessary in calculations is confused with what may be thought possible in Reality.* Whoever seeks to derive new knowledge from the excursions of a creature like Lumen into space, confuses the time of an experience with the time of the objective event ; but the former can have a definite meaning only if it is founded on a proper causal relation of space and time. In the above imaginary experiment the order of the experiences in time is the reverse of that of the events. And as far as causality is concerned, it is a scientific conception that relates only to events ordered in space and time, and not to experiences. In brief, the experiments with Lumen are swindles.

M. : I must resign myself to giving up these illusions. I must frankly confess that I do so with a certain sadness, for such bold flights of constructive fancy exert a powerful attraction on me. At one time I was near outdoing Lumen by assuming a Super-Lumen, who was to traverse all worlds at once with infinite velocity. He would then be in a position to take a survey of the whole of universal history at a single glance. From the nearest star, Alpha Centauri, he would see the earth as it was four years ago ; from the Pole Star, as it was forty years ago ; and from the boundary of the Milky Way, as it was four thousand years ago. At the same moment he could choose a point of observation that would enable him to see the First Crusade, the Siege of Troy, the Flood, and also the events of the present day simultaneously.

EINSTEIN : And this flight of thought, which, by the way, has been indulged in repeatedly by others too, has much more sense in it than the former one, because you may make an abstraction which disregards speed altogether. It is only a limiting case of reflection.

M. : I should like to touch on other limiting cases, in particular two that I find it impossible to interpret. Lotze mentions them in his Logic. The first concerns the infinitely long lever whose fulcrum, or turning-point, is at the confines of the universe. According to the Laws of Levers, a mass of

---

* Perhaps an analogy will serve to make this clear. Suppose that a certain quantity of some foodstuff is consumed by $\frac{1}{10}$ head of population. The false inference would be that a population is possible which has $\frac{1}{10}$ heads ! In the same way the statistics may be quite correct in arriving at the figure $\frac{1}{5}$ suicides, but if we leave the realms of calculation, then the $\frac{1}{5}$ suicide loses its meaning entirely.

magnitude zero will suffice to keep in equilibrium at the end of the other lever-arm any weight, no matter whether it is a million times heavier than the earth. Our imaginations cannot even picture this. Yet I cannot feel satisfied with the mere explanation that it is an exceptional case, an extension of a general law to a case in which it is no longer applicable. The second example is still more perplexing because it does not require a journey into other worlds, but leads us into inconceivable consequences even if we remain on the earth. Lotze considers this second limiting case easier ; to me it seems more difficult. It is this : The force that a wedge exerts is inversely proportional to its thickness. If it is infinitely thin, this formula gives an infinitely great result, whereas, actually, the force exerted is nil. This very thin wedge, transformed finally into a geometrical plane, should be able to split in twain any wooden or even steel block. And now, consider a special arrangement of this wedge in which it is resting with its extremely sharp edge vertically downwards, whereas at the top it broadens to a little ledge which supports a weight. We then get the incredible result that this wedge, which can be imagined concretely, should be able to cut through the whole earth with its extremely fine edge, if placed on some base. Where is the fallacy in this case ?

EINSTEIN : The mechanical facts have not been taken sufficiently into consideration.—He illustrated his further remarks by drawing a few strokes with his pen, and proved from his diagram that a wedge of this sort would be able to perform what I assumed, only if the base on which it is placed is composed of separate laminæ. Otherwise the assumption that the force is infinitely great would be erroneous.

.   .   .   .

After this digression to a limiting case on the earth we returned to more general problems, and the question of the finitude or infinitude of the universe. Shortly before, Einstein had given an address to the Berlin Academy on this point, involving difficult calculations, and I hoped to hear from him an easy explanation at least in general terms.

It is one of the ultimate problems. Whoever talks of the limits of the world endeavours also to mark off the bounds of the understanding. The average person, at first sight, almost always decides in favour of an infinite universe, on the ground that a finite world is inconceivable. He argues that, if it were considered finite, we should immediately be confronted with the question : What lies *beyond* the finite boundary ? Something must be present, even if it is only empty space. This brings us into an inevitable conflict with the first of Kant's " antinomies," with the thesis and antithesis, from which there is no escape. What is the meaning of the fact that the apprehensive understanding seeks refuge in " Infinity " ? It signifies that he gets entangled in the folds of a negative conception, that furnishes him with no explanation at all, and expresses merely that his first assumption of finitude cannot be thought out to its conclusion.

Besides this, a second disturbing question arises. Is there a finite or infinite number of stellar bodies ? If this question refers to an assumed infinite space, even if such space is inconceivable, then there are two possible answers. For it would be possible to imagine a finite number of stars even if no limit could be found for space.

Whereas the general question of space in the universe belongs exclusively to speculative philosophy, the star-question is not purely metaphysical, but is physical, too, and has accordingly been treated by physicists. The great astronomer Herschel imagined he could solve it by means of optical principles, and he arrived at the conclusion that the number of heavenly bodies must be finite, as otherwise the aspect of the starry firmament, from the point of view of illumination, would be entirely different. But this proof did not establish itself among scientists, for the number of stars of the type of the sun might be finite, whilst there was an infinite number of *dark* stars.

A further question presented itself : Would it be possible for a definite part of the heavens (say, that north of the ecliptic) to contain an infinite number of stars, whilst other parts contained only a finite number ? At first this sounds very extraordinary, but it is by no means unreasonable, as a concrete example will show : If, on a scale of temperature, we count the degrees of heat from a certain point, then they stretch apparently to infinity in one direction, whereas they extend only to $-273°$ (Centigrade) in the other direction, that is, to the absolute zero. Thus we can imagine an arrangement which stretches to infinity only in one direction.

To get an insight into the discussion by Einstein which is about to follow, we must first dispose of a certain arbitrariness of language, lying in the customary indiscriminate use of the terms, infinite, immeasurable, and unbounded. Suppose we have a globe about one foot in diameter, the surface of which is inhabited by extremely small, ultramicroscopic creatures that can move about freely and can think. The surface of the sphere constitutes the world of the micro-men, and he has a very good reason for considering it infinite, for, however far and in whatever direction he may move, he never encounters a boundary. But we, who live in our space, look on to this spherical surface, and recognize that his judgment is erroneous. To us his spherical world seems decidedly finite and quite measurable, although it has no determinable beginning and no end, and thus must appear unbounded to the micro-man. In fact, we ourselves may regard it as boundless, if we can succeed in forming an abstraction that leaves out of account its limitations in our own space.

Now, it might occur to a particularly intelligent microbeing to undertake a voyage for the purpose of making measurements. He carefully marks his point of departure, walks straight ahead in a certain direction, describing a circle on his sphere—a circle which he will necessarily regard as a straight line. He continues ever onwards in the firm conviction that he is getting farther and farther away from his starting-point. Suddenly, he discovers that he has reached it again. He discovers, by the mark he made, that he has not been describing a straight line, but a line that merges into itself.

The micro-professor would be compelled to declare : Our world, the only one known to me, is not infinite, although in a certain sense boundless. Moreover, it is not immeasurable, since it can be measured in at least one direction by the number of steps I have walked. From this we may infer that our former geometrical view was either wrong or incomplete, and that, in order to understand our world properly, we must build up a new geometry.

We may assume that the majority of the remaining microinhabitants would at first protest strongly against this decision.

The idea that a line, which appears to them to be pointing always in the same direction, is curved, seems to them inconceivable and absurd. They would only gradually overcome their scruples of thought by getting an insight into a newly developed geometry that makes clear to them for the first time the conception of a sphere.

In our world of space, which includes all stars, we are the micro-inhabitants. We have been born with, or have inherited, the idea of a straight and ever-advancing path in space, and we become filled with the utmost astonishment if some one asks us to believe that if we undertake a voyage in one direction out into the universe, beyond Sirius and a million times farther, we should finally arrive at our starting-point again, although we had not changed our direction. But the macro-being, who belongs to a universe of higher dimensions and who looks on our world as we looked on the above spherical world one foot in diameter, sees the narrowness of our view. We, too, are in a position to rise above this narrow view by means of a theory founded on our experience, which will lead us to an extended world-geometry, just as the micro-professor used his experience to extend his theory of the circle to include the conception of a sphere.

After these preliminary remarks we shall endeavour to get an insight into Einstein's reasoning, not in the form in which it was originally presented (in the Report of the Proceedings of the Berlin Academy of Science of 8th February 1917), but in a very easy description which was given to me during a conversation. Here, too, I shall try to preserve the sense of Einstein's remarks without binding myself strictly to his words. For although I am indebted to him for his efforts to avoid difficult points, yet the aim of this book is, if possible, to make the explanation still easier. Any lack of accuracy arising from this last simplification is to be debited to me. The new form of representing the argument, which is as important as it is fascinating, is, of course, due to Einstein.

The final result stated by Einstein was : The universe, both as regards extent and mass, has finite limits and can be measured. If anyone asks whether this can be pictured, I shall not deprive him of the hope. All that is required is a power of imagination that is great enough to follow a pictorial description and that can take up the right attitude towards a sort of figurative representation.

Let us again imagine a sphere of modest dimensions with its two-dimensional surface. We are concerned only with the latter, and not with the cubical content. The sphere is to be considered as resting on an absolutely plane white table of unlimited extent in all directions. The sphere touches the table at a single point which we shall call its South Pole ; on the top side directly opposite, we have the North Pole. To simplify matters we may make a sketch on paper of a vertical section through the centre of the sphere. This profile-picture will show us the sphere as a circle, and the white table as a straight line ; the line joining the two poles is the axis of the globe, and the sectional circle is a meridian.

Let us further suppose a creature (resembling, say, a lady-bird in shape) having length and breadth, but no thickness, to crawl along this meridian. Although it has no thickness, we shall imagine it to have one property of a solid body, that of being opaque, so that it can throw a shadow if properly illuminated. We assume the globe itself to be transparent. At the North Pole we suppose a very strong point-source of light, a little electric lamp, that sends out rays freely in all directions.

The insect begins its journey at the South Pole and sets out along the meridian to reach the North Pole. It is illuminated by the lamp all the way, so that it continually throws a shadow on the white table. The shadow moves along the table farther and farther from the South Pole, in proportion as the insect moves up the meridian, with the difference that while the insect is describing an arc of a circle, its shadow moves along a straight line. The position of the shadow can be determined at any moment by drawing the straight line connecting the lamp to the insect, and producing it to meet the white surface of the table ; the point of intersection is the projection of the insect on the plane.

At the beginning of the excursion the shadow is exactly as large as the flat insect itself, if we assume that its dimensions are negligible compared with the surface of the sphere, for it will then coincide with its own shadow. But when the insect crawls upwards, its shadow will increase, because of the shortened distance between the insect and the lamp, and because the points of projection on the table separate more and more as their distances from their corresponding points on the sphere become greater. There is thus a twofold increase. The shadows move away more and more rapidly, and at the same time increase in size.

When the insect gets very near the North Pole, its shadow, now of enormous dimensions, has moved to a very great distance; and when finally it reaches the Pole, its shadow becomes infinitely great and thus stretches to infinity.

But let the insect wander on along the meridian, past the North Pole, down towards the South. At the moment when it passes the upper Pole its shadow jumps from the right side to the left. Its shadow now emerges from an infinite distance to the left, and, instead of being infinite size, again becomes finite in dimensions as it approaches. It contracts as it approaches, and, in short, the same process as occurred during the first half of the journey now occurs in the reverse order.

[If we fix on the critical moment of the jump from the right to the left, that is, from plus infinity to minus infinity, we may encounter difficulties. For the surface-creature pursues its way without interruption and continuously, and we experience a wish to ascribe to it a shadow-path that is also unbroken and continuous. This is possible only if we assume the two points at infinity to be connected, that is, if we consider them identical. This assumption will seem more natural if we reason as follows. In the profile-picture the table is represented as a straight line, and it is along this line that the shadow travels. We may regard this line as an infinitely great circle, for an infinitely great circle has zero curvature, just as the straight line, from which it is therefore indistinguishable. The infinitely great circle has, however, only one point situated at an infinite distance, that is, it associates together the two apparent points at infinity of the straight line with which we identify it. Accordingly, we preserve the continuity of the shadow-journey, too. Einstein considers it allowable to say that the right and the left portion each represent a half of the infinite projection, which becomes complete only when the two ends are joined.]

Now we must be prepared for an effort of thought which

will need considerable help from our imaginations. Firstly, instead of one surface-creature, we shall suppose several crawling about on different meridians, so that a series of shadows will be moving about along straight lines radiating from the South Pole. Next, let us imagine the whole picture to have its dimensions increased by one, that is, we transform the plane-picture into a space model. The phenomena are to remain the same, except that they are to be strengthened by one dimension, surface conditions becoming space conditions, and surfaces becoming solids.

What we now see are actual insects with round bodies (if we retain our original type of creatures), or, since there is no restriction as to their size—the shadows have assumed all possible sizes—we may assume any solid bodies whatsoever, stars or even star-systems. Their motions take place in exactly the same way as those of the shadows previously thrown by the flat bodies.

This means that, if a stellar body moves, its size increases until it reaches the spherical boundary of space, where it becomes infinitely great, and, at the same moment, passes from plus infinity to minus infinity, that is, it enters the universe from the opposite direction; then, if it continues moving in its original direction (as it has been doing all along), it gradually becomes smaller in size until, finally, it reaches its original position and its original size. If we suppose the body to be endowed with the power of sensation, it would not be able to observe its own changes of size, since all its scale-measures would be altered in the same proportion. This whole complex of phenomena would still be taking place in an infinite world of space, but, according to the General Theory of Relativity, the geometry that is valid in this world would no longer be that of Euclid; it is replaced by a system of laws that arise from physics as a geometric necessity. In this new geometry, a circle described with unit radius is a little smaller than it would be in Euclidean geometry, with the result that the greatest conceivable circle in this world cannot assume an infinite size.

Thus we have to imagine that our solid bodies, say stars, arrive at a point in their travels which we may term only "enormously distant." If we call the directions right and left instead of positive and negative, then the process reduces itself to this : the moving body reaches the point, which is enormously distant on the right, and which is identical with the point enormously distant on the left ; this means that the body never moves out of the space continuum of this world, but returns to its initial point of departure even when it moves ever onward in what is apparently a straight line. It moves in a " warped " space.

Einstein has succeeded in finding an approximate value for this non-infinite universe, from the fact that there is a determinable gravitational constant. In the constitution of the universe it denotes the same for the mass-relationships of the earth as the gravitational constant of the earth denotes for us, namely, the quantity from which we can calculate the final velocity attained by a freely falling body during a unit of time. He also assumes a probable average for the density of distribution of matter in the universe, by supposing that it is about the same as that of the Milky Way. On this basis Einstein has arrived at the following result by calculation :

The whole universe has a diameter of 100 million light-years, in round numbers. That amounts to about 700 trillion miles.

M. : Does this follow from the discussion you entered on just now ?

EINSTEIN : It follows from the mathematical calculations which I presented in " Cosmological Considerations arising from the General Theory of Relativity," in which the figure I have just quoted is not given. The exact figure is a minor question. What is important is to recognize that the universe may be regarded as a closed continuum as far as distance-measurements are concerned. Another point, too, must not be forgotten. If, in deference to your wish, I used an easy illustration, this must not be regarded otherwise than as an improvised bridge to assist the imagination.

M. : Nevertheless, it will be very welcome to many, who are unable to grasp the difficult Cosmological Considerations. The number that you mention is overwhelming in the extreme. Indeed, it seems to me that a diameter of 100 million light-years suggests an infinitely great distance more than the word " infinity " itself, mentioned *per definitionem*, which conveys nothing to the ordinary mind. It calls up a regular carnival of numbers, particularly in those to whom the immense number alone gives a certain pleasure. But you were going to give me the number expressing the mass, too ? "

And then I learned that the weight of the whole universe, expressed in grammes, was 10 multiplied by itself 54 times, that is 10^{54} (453 grammes $= 1$ lb., roughly). This seems rather disappointing at first, but assumes a different aspect when we represent to ourselves what this figure signifies. It means that the weight of the universe in kilogrammes is high in the octillions. The earth itself weighs six quadrillion kilogrammes, hence the weight of the Einstein universe bears the same relation to the weight of the whole earth as the latter bears to a kilogramme. Again, the earth's weight to that of the sun is as 1 is to 324,000. Hence we should have to take at least a trillion, that is, a milliard times a milliard, suns to get the weight of the universe. And as far as the linear extent is concerned, let us consider the most distant stars of the Milky Way, which are at an inconceivable distance, expressible only in light-years. If we place 10,000 such Milky Ways end to end we shall arrive at this diameter of the universe, which, accordingly, will have a cubical content a thousand milliard times greater than the region accessible to astronomical observation.

Thus we have a very spacious universe. Yet it is not spacious enough to satisfy all the demands that a mathematician interested in permutations and combinations might make. One of such combinations is exemplified in the so-called *Universal Book*, that originated in an imaginary experiment of Leibniz. If we picture to ourselves the sum-total of all books that can be printed by making all possible arrangements and successions of our letters, each book differing from any other even if only in one symbol, then, together, they must contain all that can be expressed in sense and non-sense, and everything that is ever realizable actually or in dreams. Hence, among other things, they would include all world-history, all literature, and all science, even from the beginning of the world to the end. If we agree to the convention of operating with 100 different printed signs (letters, figures, stops, spacings, etc.), and of allowing each such book a million paces for signs, so that each book will still be of a handy size, then the number of these books would amount to exactly 10 to the two-millionth power, or, in figures, *i.e.* $10^{2,000,000}$. This fully exhaustive universal library containing all wisdom would consist of so many volumes that it could not be contained in a case of the size of the entire stellar universe. And, unhappily, it must be added that the closed universe, just described by Einstein and having a diameter of a hundred million light-years would be much too small to contain this library.

" Nevertheless," said I, " your universe pictures something inconceivably great ; one might call it an infinity expressed in figures. For in your world there still remains one property of infinity, namely, that it imposes no limitations on motion of any kind. On the other hand, the figures proclaim a limited measure in the mathematical sense, however great this measure may be. This calls up the old restlessness of mind, due to the persistent question : What lies beyond ? The absolute Nothing ? Or is it a something which yet does not occupy space ? Descartes and many other great thinkers have never overcome this difficulty, and have always affirmed that a closed world is impossible. How, then, is the average person to reconcile himself with the dimensions you have established ? "

Einstein gave an answer which, it seemed to me, offered a last escape to apprehensive minds. " It is possible," so he said, " that other universes exist independently of our own."

That is to say, it will never be possible to trace a connexion between them. Even after an eternity of observation, calculation, and theoretical investigation, no glimpse or knowledge of any of these ultra-worlds will ever enter our consciousness. " Imagine human creatures to be two-dimensional surface-creatures," he added, " and that they live on a plane of indefinite extent. Suppose that they have organs, instruments, and mental attitude adapted strictly to this two-dimensional existence. Then, at most, they would be able to find out all the phenomena and relationships that objectify themselves in this plane. They would then have an absolutely perfect science of two dimensions, the fullest knowledge of their cosmos. Independent of this, there might be another cosmic plane with other phenomena and relationships, that is, a second analogous universe. There would then be no means of constructing a connexion between these two worlds, or even of suspecting such a connexion. We are in just the same position as these plane-inhabitants except that we have one dimension more. It is possible, in fact, to a certain degree probable, that we shall by means of astronomy discover new worlds far beyond the limits of the region so far investigated, but no discovery can ever lead us beyond the continuum described above, just as little as a discoverer of the plane-world would ever succeed in making discoveries beyond his own world. Thus we must reckon with the finitude of our universe, and the question of regions beyond it can be discussed no further, for it leads only to imaginary possibilities for which science has not the slightest use."

. . . .

Einstein left me for a while to the tumult of ideas that he had roused up in me. After I had overcome the first shock, I sought to gain a haven in the idea that arose out of the first shadow-argument, in which the spherical bodies occurred that seek to escape towards infinity on the right but reappear, instead, at enormous distances on the left. Has anyone ever had presentiments of this kind of world? Perhaps something of the sort is to be found in earlier books of science? If so, they have escaped my notice. Yet, a passage of a poet occurs to me. It is to be found in a volume by Heinrich von Kleist ; it is a volume dealing only with earthly matter and bare of astronomical ideas. Imagine a book the subject of which is a puppet-show, containing, in the middle of it, a section foreshadowing Einstein's universe! Quite by chance Kleist comes to speak of " the intersection of two lines which, after passing through infinity, suddenly appear on the other side, like a picture in a concave mirror, which moves away to infinity and suddenly returns again and is quite close," and, quite in accordance with our new cosmology, he declares : " Paradise is locked and barred, and the cherub is behind us ; we must make a voyage round the world, and see whether we cannot discover an exit elsewhere at the other end perhaps."

Perhaps poets of the future will busy themselves with this universe, not lyrical poets, but descendants of Hesiod, Lucretius, or Rückert. They will express in verse that Einstein's world offers a source of consolation to tormented spirits which have sickened of Kant's antinomies. For in this still almost immeasurable world the fateful conception " infinite " has been made bearable for the first time. In a certain way it relieves us from what is quite inconceivable, yet into which we are usually driven, and forms a bridge between the thesis " finite " and the antithesis infinite. We are brought to a common stream, in which both conceptions peacefully flow together. There was no mention of this in our talk, and I had good reason for being cautious about following out the theme along these lines. I must not allow any doubts to arise on this point : Einstein, himself, clings with unerring logic to the strict mathematically defined conception of infinity, and allows no compromise with the non-infinite.

When I, on some previous occasion, sought to lead him on to a compromise, involving a transition-boundary, it availed me nothing that I quoted Helmholtz to support the possibility of such an operation : my effort came to an abrupt end.

.　　.　　.　　.　　.　　.　　.　　.

In pursuing these considerations about the universe, we arrived at things which, in ordinary language, are usually called " occult." In connexion with this, these remarks ensued : " I am, of course, far from trying to trace out a connexion between the four-dimensionality that you establish, Professor, and the four-dimensionality of certain spiritistic pseudo-philosophers, yet it suggests itself to me that in such occult circles efforts will be made to derive advantage from the fact that the same word is used in both cases. This is more than a conjecture, indeed, for there are no misgivings among the ignorant, and so we actually find the name Einstein quoted in connexion with mediumistic experiments that are flavoured with four-dimensionality."

" It will not be expected of me," said Einstein, " to enter into discussion with ignoramuses and misinterpreters. Discarding them, then, let us confine ourselves to a brief consideration of the conception ' occult,' as this has played a part in serious science. The chief example of this in history is gravitation. Huyghens and Leibniz refused to accept gravitation, for, so they said, according to Newton's view, it is an action at a distance and hence belongs to the realm of the occult. Like everything occult, it contradicts the causal order in Nature. We must not regard Huyghens' and Leibniz's contradiction as being due to lack of perspicacity ; rather, they objected on grounds which, as investigators, they had every right to uphold. For, as far as our everyday experience is concerned, every mutual influence of things in Nature occurs only by direct contact, as by pressure or impact, or by chemical action, as when a flame is lit. The fact that sound and light apparently form exceptions is not usually felt as a contradiction to the postulate of contact. The case of a magnet appears much more striking because its effect asserts itself as a direct manifestation of force. I must mention that when I, as a child, made my first acquaintance with a compass—and this was before I had ever seen a magnet—it created a sensation in me, which I consider to have been a dominant factor in my life up to the very present. There is, indeed, a fundamental difference between pressure and impact on the one hand, and what we hear and see on the other, even in everyday experience. In the case of light and sound, something must be ' happening ' continually, if the effect is to occur and continue. . . ."

" Yet another difference seems to enter here," I interposed. " Is it possible to give a full explanation of gravitation by using only the conceptions pressure and impact ? Perhaps ' pressure at a distance ' would not have seemed to contemporaries of Newton as unintelligible as a ' tension or pull at a distance.' It seems to me that it is particularly difficult to imagine a pull or an attraction towards a distant object."

Einstein does not consider this difference considerable, and regards it as possible to overcome it even in a manner which can be directly pictured. " If the force is exerted by a corpuscular transmission," he explained, " we may imagine a ' forceshadow ' into which the bombarding corpuscles cannot penetrate. Thus if an obstacle, which produces such a shadow, becomes interposed between a body A and a body B, then there will be a lesser pressure on the side of B facing A, and hence B will experience a greater corpuscular pressure on the other side, with the result that B will be forced in the direction of A, and the observer would gain the impression of a pull from B to A. Nowadays, when the theory of ' fields of force ' dominates our physical views, we need trouble just as little about using corpuscular pressures and impacts as about the vortices which Descartes once considered as the ultimate causes of the motions of the heavenly bodies. The efforts of certain reformers to reintroduce these vortices and whirlpools as explanations must be regarded as futile."

" Nevertheless," I answered, " it seems admissible to say that, ultimately, there is always an occult element in every physical explanation, an absolutely final and elementary something which we recognize as a principle, without concealing from ourselves that we have reached the limit of explanation, and our knowledge avails no further. This brings me to another question the discussion of which, as I clearly perceive, leads us on to dangerous ground."

EINSTEIN : Don't hesitate to say what is troubling you. I cannot yet see what you are aiming at.

M. : I am referring to certain phenomena which are also called " occult "—with the object of discrediting them. They may at times degenerate to hocus-pocus and fall into the category of dubious arts. It seems to me, however, that scientists have not always drawn the line with sufficient care, and that they have been disposed to reject as humbug, without examination, everything inexplicable that dares to present itself in the form of open display.

EINSTEIN : In general, they will be in the right, for investigators cannot be expected to occupy themselves with things bolstered up by advertisement, and which are supposed to be connected with some fabulous, occult regions.

M. : Nevertheless, in my opinion even among such displays there sometimes occur phenomena which scientists should not pass over with contempt. I, myself, have experienced such cases, and have said to myself : There are stranger happenings here——

EINSTEIN : —than are dreamt of in your philosophy, you were about to say ?

M. : Exactly. These are things that in the guise of sensationalism often hide a physical truth well worthy of study.

EINSTEIN : But you must not overlook the fact that in such cases you have mostly played the part of an onlooker, and hence were exposed to all possible manner of deception. You are baffled on all sides by undiscoverable tricks and by other persons, whose collusion you do not suspect. This renders an objective criticism impossible.

M. : This presumes that the performing artist is not entirely isolated. It is possible to bring about conditions that positively eliminate all tricks from the very outset.

EINSTEIN : If you have experienced any such cases, relate them by all means.

M. : I shall be brief, and shall state only facts. . . .

EINSTEIN : Or, expressed more accurately, only things which seem to have been facts as far as you can trust to memory. Well then, you think that you have grounds for saying that you caught a glimpse of a mysterious world at that time.

M. : It is certainly long ago, more than thirty years. Hansen, the freak, one of the most eminent of his profession, was showing hypnotic and telepathic experiments that were partly identical with experiments that the celebrated scientist Charcot at Paris was performing for purposes of pathology.

EINSTEIN : Well, then, why did you hesitate before ? These experiments come under the head of science, and require no occult veil to appear in the open.

M. : This touches the main issue. Hansen did not work in the interests of science, but wished, above all, to earn money. Nevertheless he had in his own way produced marvellous results that were used later for scientific work. Unfortunately in his case, owing to the fact that he cloaked it in occultism at the outset, he was brusquely repudiated by scientists. The result was that Hansen was condemned to a long period of imprisonment in Dresden, thanks to the recommendation of scientists who declared that the experiments were only possible if deception was practised, and hence that Hansen was an impostor who should be made harmless by being incarcerated.

EINSTEIN : And how did you yourself seek to discover whether his experiments were genuine ?

M. : Very easily and with absolute certainty. One of my acquaintances, the wealthy race-horse owner, von Oelschläger, had induced him by means of a high fee to experiment at his country house, at some distance from Berlin, in the presence of persons, not one of whom Hansen knew, and in the case of whom there could be no question of secret collaboration. I can assure you that everything succeeded without exception. A single second was sufficient for him to communicate his will to each subject of experiment. He operated like a supernatural being on those present.

EINSTEIN : I should like to hear examples.

M. : Herr von Oelschläger introduced four jockeys, and suggested a race in the great salon. Hansen placed them astride over chairs, hypnotized them on the spot, described the shape of the course, giving distances in kilometres, curves, and even the value of the prizes. He then gave the signal for starting. The jockeys immediately began treating their chairs as race-horses, exhibiting all the signs of extreme strain which accompany the actual ride.

EINSTEIN : This is not yet a positive proof. The subjects of experiment may have become cognizant of the fact that they were to serve some eccentric display. Their acquiescence in a prescribed part need by no means signify that they were subjectively convinced of the genuineness of the affair.

M. : There could be not the slightest doubt on this point. After a few seconds perspiration was streaming over their faces as a result of the exertion, a symptom that exhibits itself only when the participants are convinced of the absolute earnestness of their undertaking. All that gazed on this baffling ride made the acquaintance of a grotesque reality, and were looking into a strange world of dreams, which transformed wooden chairs into living thoroughbreds. In the course of his following experiments in the transference of his will-power, Hansen experimented with an actress who was famous at that time, and with whom he had no more acquaintance than with the others. He again produced deep hypnosis, and gave the order : I shall ask you various questions, all of which you will be able to answer correctly, with one exception : you will have forgotten your name. And so it happened. In her trance the actress gave correct answers, until, when the question, " What is your name ? " was asked, her own name, Helene Odilon, had vanished from her memory. And immediately afterwards, she told me herself that, in spite of her state of coma, she had retained full consciousness, had understood everything, and had been possessed of her memory until it came to the critical moment when, in spite of extreme

efforts, she could not recollect the words Helene Odilon.
But Hansen did not stop at dictating his thoughts to others,
he also transformed corporate things. By a single motion
of his hand he converted a stable-boy into a rigid block,
devoid of sensation. Never would I have thought such an
intense state of cramp possible. He placed the boy with
his feet and head alone resting on two supports, so that the
body itself was poised in space. He then stood on the body
with his whole weight, without the rigid body of the boy
bending even an inch.

EINSTEIN : How did he, in all these cases, restore the
normal state ?

M. : Always by a single gesture, which, like everything
that he did, worked at lightning speed. I must admit that
his display became a little monotonous after a while, and
that his programme did not seem capable of much variation.
Things were different, however, in the case of a man who,
some years previously, had toured the world as an exponent
of occult phenomena, and to whom scientists will some time
in the future look back with regret. When he appeared,
most academicians took only sufficient notice of him to reject
him without having given him a trial. It was Henry Slade,
the American, who is not to be confused with other Slades
who appropriated his name in order to dupe people whose
insatiable curiosity was aroused.

EINSTEIN : One might almost suppose that your genuine
Henry Slade served as a model for them.

M. : For certain reasons I regard this as out of the question,
mainly because the true Slade gave " demonstrations " only
occasionally, his chief object being to interest scientists. He,
himself, repeatedly asserted that he did not understand his
own achievements, and he unceasingly requested the super-
vision of professional physicists and physiologists, to whom
the unusual phases in his nature were to serve as objects of
study. The result was that people like Dubois-Reymond,
Helmholtz, and Virchow refused to see him, not to mention
experiment with him.

EINSTEIN : These men cannot be reproached for acting in
this way. Slade was regarded as a representative of a four-
dimensional world in the spiritistic sense ; serious scientists

must avoid all humbug of this sort, since even slight interest in it can easily be misinterpreted by the ignorant public.

M. : Not every one was afraid of compromising himself. After closed doors had greeted Slade in Berlin, he went to Leipzig, where he became an object of study for one important scientist.

EINSTEIN : You are referring to Friedrich Zöllner, who undoubtedly had a reputation as an astrophysicist to preserve. But he would have served his reputation better if he had not entered into this adventure with the American spiritist.

M. : Perhaps there will some day be cause for a revision of opinion on this point. The documents are extant, even if, half forgotten, they are reposing in various libraries. A renewed investigation of Zöllner's *Scientific Dissertations*, dating from 1878 to 1891, might lead to the judgment that his ghostly interpretations are to be regarded as occult in the worst sense, and yet one would marvel that a great scientist, such as he was, should have felt himself at a complete loss with his knowledge, so that he was forced to resort to abstruse methods in order to escape from the mental confusion into which Slade had plunged him.

EINSTEIN : That merely shows that Slade, as a cunning practician, surpassed him, and that Zöllner did not succeed in seeing through his machinations.

M. : This would lead one to assume that Slade knew more physics than the Leipzig professor. For in a great number of experiments Zöllner himself had prescribed the conditions, including all contrivances which made deception so much the more unlikely, since Slade himself could not know what Zöllner's intentions were. It was a question of Electricity, Magnetism, Optics including prepared conditions of polarization, involved Mechanics, in short, things that Zöllner as a professional physicist understood thoroughly, and which, moreover, were controlled by others of his profession. Among the latter was the celebrated professor of Electricity, Wilhelm Weber, who, like Zöllner, found himself faced by phenomena that were utterly incomprehensible to him. It would be a profitable undertaking to bring these dissertations to light again, and it would easily be recognized that the things described actually deal with scientific problems and have not the remotest connexion with tricks of magic. For example, there is an account of an incredible anatomical feat. On flour which had been placed carefully in a dish beforehand, there suddenly appeared the imprint of a naked human foot, whilst Slade was present at a certain distance, being fully clothed and subject to careful scrutiny. The footprint showed all the surface-details of the skin, as was confirmed by authorities, just as only a left foot could produce them, but not an artificial copy.

EINSTEIN : And from this Zöllner inferred the intervention of supernatural beings ? He would have done better to measure the dimensions of the foot.

M. : So he did—at once. A difference of four centimetres between the length of Slade's foot and the copy was disclosed. This riddle, like so many others, remained unexplained. I must repeat that I am not in the slightest degree disposed to assert that occult phenomena really occur, but am interested only in seeing that they are investigated carefully by qualified persons.

EINSTEIN : Your remarks show that Leipzig scientists did so at that time with no better result than that Zöllner's mental confusion became still greater.

M. : The conjecture remains that the Leipzig experiments, abundant as they were, did not suffice. Allow me to ask a direct question, Professor. Supposing another such agent of miracles should appear, would you yourself feel impelled to test him experimentally ?

EINSTEIN : Your question is misdirected. I explained above that I share the point of view taken up by Dubois-Reymond and his colleagues.

M. : The following case may be conceived. A certain man, X, might suddenly appear, who has control of a certain natural force that has never before been investigated ; like one who knew how to use electricity at a time when people had never experienced any electrical phenomenon. He would be able to give hundreds of demonstrations, all of which we should relegate to the realm of inexplicable magic. We should, for instance, be much astonished if he were to draw sparks from a living person. Now, suppose two professors express an opinion. Professor A declares the whole thing to be a farce, and refuses to look into it at all. Professor B is ready to investigate the achievements of X only if the latter subjects himself from the beginning to all the physical conditions that are to be determined beforehand. And suppose the professor arranges his conditions so that they make impossible the occurrence of electrical phenomena. If, now, all scientists were to behave like A and B, the consequences would be very depressing. For here was an important field of investigation, which is cut off owing to the distrust or obstinacy of scientists, who should have been the first to open it up. It is quite irrelevant whether X had the character of a charlatan or not, for behind his charlatanism there were facts which clamoured for investigation.

EINSTEIN : The most that I can grant is that your imagined case does not lie outside the scope of possibility. Yet the chance that there is such a " natural force " hitherto undiscovered by Man, that is, one that is a " secret force " as far as we are concerned, is so vanishingly small that it may be set down as equal to impossible. I should refuse to take part in any such practices, served up in the form of sensation, for one reason that I should regret the waste of time, as there are better things to do. It is a different matter if the mood takes me to visit a variety entertainment, in order to derive amusement from such mystifications. For example, only yesterday I was in a little theatre, in which, among diverse items, a thought-reading woman was performing. She correctly guessed the numbers 61 and 59 that I had in my mind. But let no one mention this as a case of telepathic actions at a distance or wireless communication between minds, for an intermediate person, the manager, was present, and I had to whisper the numbers to him. The distance to the stage was certainly too great to allow the sound to be conveyed directly to an audible degree. Hence there must have been a different, very cunningly arranged code of signals, which eluded the notice of people in the stalls. The process consists actually in an extraordinary refinement of observation, which does not, however, seem to me any more wonderful than the training of a reckoner who extracts cubic roots mentally, or than the practised muscles of a juggler all working in unison to enable him to perform feats with twelve plates simultaneously.

M. : It gives me enough satisfaction, Professor, that you conceded me before a certain limited chance of finding a last refuge in occultism. And even if you, yourself, as a representative of the most rigorous research of physical reality, refuse to consider it, yet the fact that many others are drawn irresistibly towards mysterious phenomena cannot be denied. Should one feel shame on this account ? I believe that, in this matter, we are touching on inner confessions that are quite independent of the standard of the mind in which they are embedded. Newton considered the key of the universe to be a personal God, whereas Laplace proclaimed : *Dieu—je n'avais pas besoin de cette hypothèse* : this contrast allows no inference to be drawn as to their relative keenness of mind. And probably the same may be said of the question whether there are other hidden universes besides the one in which we live. In any case, those who feel enthusiasm for such questions can quote in their support good names from the learned world. Immanuel Kant occupied himself seriously and intensively with the wonders of Swedenborg, Kepler practised Astrology, in which he had a firm belief, Roger Bacon, Cardanus, Agrippa, Nostradamus, van Helmont, Pascal, and, among the modern, Fechner, Wallace, Crookes, are to be counted among the mystics. No matter whether the views they held were theosophical, occult, four-dimensional in the spiritistic sense, or coloured by any other superstition ; they proclaimed that things that could be rigorously proved were, alone, insufficient for them. Out of presentiment and conjecture they constructed wings with which to fly into regions *extra naturam*. This is how it happened that, as the common folk could not find a place in science for many extraordinary achievements, they assigned their authors to the realm of magicians, as in the case of Paracelsus, Albertus Magnus, Raimundus Lullus, Sylvester II, who were regarded as sorcerers. And this coin is still current : to Edison, of our times, the term, " sorcerer of Menlo-Park," has become attached. In the minds of the populace discovery and invention, works of genius and supernatural phenomena, become confused and indistinguishable ; it may even happen to you, Professor, that your works will become invested with legend. I should not like to conjure up what your fate would have been if your theory of relativity had originated at the time of the

Inquisition. For the views put forward by Giordano Bruno are mere child's play compared with your theory of the universe as a quasi-spherical closed space of hyper-Euclidean character. The tribunal of the Inquisition would not have understood your differential equation, gravitational potentials, tensors, and equivalence theory; they would abruptly have declared the whole theory to be a magical formula or a manifestation of the devil, and would have honoured it and you with a funeral pyre.

EINSTEIN : This is clearly a slight exaggeration. Mathematico-physical and astronomical works have never been attacked by the Papal courts, but, on the contrary, have been much encouraged by them down to the present day. This is abundantly clear from the fact that we can set up a whole list of Brothers of Orders, particularly Jesuits, who have made eminent discoveries in natural science. From my personal knowledge of you, I foresee that you will one day sketch a fantastic trial, in which the new world-system will have to defend itself against the *Sanctum Officium*.

M. : This would be a very grateful task, judged from the literary point of view. What a splendid colouring could be obtained by bringing these two worlds of thought into conflict with one another, the Relative against the Absolute, which has been established in tradition and dogma. But we need not even call the historical fancy into action, for, actually, the theory of the structure of the world is even now still at variance with traditional ideas, that act with dogmatic violence. There is no need to deny the fact that every person of education, who makes the acquaintance of Lorentz's, Minkowski's, Einstein's ideas for the first time, feels excited to offer contradictions, and becomes involved in a tumult of pros and cons, and each one experiences in himself the excitement of an inquisitorial tribunal. The triumph of the new theory passes over the corpses of conceptions that lie at the cross-roads of thought and, long after, retain a ghostly existence. Only very few of us are aware of the further inner revolution that awaits us along the line of development of Einsteinian ideas ; we have only vague presentiments that whisper to us that the end of forms of thought once considered as irrefragable is drawing nigh. When once the principle of causality has been set on a relative base, and all

" properties " have been resolved into occurrence, and all that is three-dimensional has come to be recognized as an abstraction from the four-dimensional world that is alone valid, then the time will have come to arrange for the death procession of all the philosophies that once served as the main pillars of thought.

A retrospect of the trials of Giordano Bruno and of Galileo Galilei offers certain parallels other than those usually discovered by scholars. And if, to-day, we proclaim Einstein as the Galilei of the twentieth century, it must be added that in character he is fortunately a Bruno and not a Galilei. For it is not true that the latter came out of the persecution as a moral victor with an *eppur si muove*, rather, in spite of the protection of influential prelates and dignitaries, even of the entourage of the Pope, he lacked courage and bowed his head, betraying his science and denying himself as well as Copernicus. Are we to picture how Einstein would have acted under similar circumstances, even if they cannot recur again ?

Whoever has even an inkling of his character will entertain no doubts. At that time, three hundred years ago, the materials for a magnificent scene, " one world *versus* the other," lay ready. Only one condition was wanting, the moral courage of the hero. The lack of this one factor spoilt the final act for the history of that time. The fine ethical feelings of later generations have had to be propitiated by improvising a legend iridescent with beautiful colours.

CHAPTER VII

PROBLEMS

WE spoke of the objects and problems of science in general, and touched on certain recurrent questions with which reputed men of science are confronted from time to time, so that we may ascertain their opinions about immediate as well as more remote aims, and about worthy objects and those within reach. .

" Such stimuli," said Einstein, " may be quite interesting inasmuch as they sharpen the appetite of the public for the works of investigators, and give the latter the opportunity of making wider circles acquainted with their plans. Yet the value of their suggestions must not be overrated, when they are directed at giving trustworthy information about the future lines of development of science. Every scientist, in working out his own research, gravitates to particular points on the boundary which separates the known from the unknown, and becomes inclined to take his particular perspective from these points. It must not, however, be expected that these individual aspects will form a complete picture, and will indicate the only paths along which science can or will advance."

" May I suggest, Professor," I answered, " that we select certain answers that have been given to these recurrent questions for discussion ?   I have brought along a whole series of them ; it would be of value to know what attitude you take up towards some of the statements that have been made about future possibilities."

Einstein acquiesced, and so I read out a number of expressions of opinion, given by eminent authorities, particularly in natural science and mathematics. They came under

the heading, " The Future Revolution of Science." At the
outset we encountered arguments by Bailhaud, the director
of the Paris Observatory ; he dealt with the so-called " Problem
of Three Bodies," and with " The Finitude or Infinitude of the
Universe."

Einstein elucidated these questions as follows. The celebrated Problem of Three Bodies is a special case of the general
problem of Many Bodies, the object of which is to discover the
exact paths of the heavenly bodies. If we suppose that the
planets and the comets are subject only to the attraction of
the central body, the sun, then their paths would be exactly
those given by Kepler's Laws—that is, they would move about
the central body, or, more precisely, about the common centre
of gravity in perfectly elliptical orbits. The same result would
happen if we regard the orbit of a moon to depend solely on
its parent planet. But this assumption is not in agreement
with reality, since all the bodies of our system are also subject
to their mutual attraction depending on their masses and
distances. Consequently we have the so-called disturbances,
perturbations, and divergences from the ideal paths ; and the
problem of ascertaining these disturbances is essentially
identical with the Problem of Three Bodies. Regarded from
the point of view of pure mechanics, this problem may be
considered solved in so far as we are able to write down the
equations of motion. But, in addition to this purely
mechanical process, there is a mathematical problem which
has not been completely solved—that is to say, the integral
expressions that occur in it can be calculated only approximately. This makes no difference to the practical calculation,
since the degree of approximation, according to the present
methods, may be carried as far as we wish. The error may
be reduced to any desirable extent, so that it is probably wrong
to expect new revelations on this point from future upheavals
in physics. We read on and discovered that several of the
scientists mentioned did not stop at expecting all advances
of the future from pure theory. They had visions of an
optimum of happiness, to gain which the increase of knowledge alone did not suffice. Thus the celebrated Swedish astrophysicist Svante Arrhenius had summarized his judgment in
a few lines : " After the stupendous progress that has been

made in the physical and chemical sciences in recent times, it seems to me that the moment has come for attacking the most important problems of mankind with full success, namely, those of biology, and in particular of the art of healing, with the weapons that are furnished by the arsenal of the exact sciences." And the mathematician, Emile Picard, Membre de l'Académie, expressed himself in still more hopeful terms : " There is no doubt but that the discoveries which the human race is awaiting with impatience are those that are seeking to eliminate sickness and the decrepitude of old age. Injections giving immunity against all diseases, an elixir of life (*une eau de Jouvence*) for persons of advancing age—these are the discoveries that are longed for by every one. There are also sciences that are to be termed ' moral,' from which we are impatiently expecting that guidance which will diminish the hate which seems to be increasing from day to day among the nations. That would be a splendid discovery."

" These are, indeed, noble and inspiring words," said I. " It shows how deeply rooted is the demand for ethical values in human nature, when even a mathematician, whose intellectual interests are directed primarily towards exact results, ranks the discoveries of ethics above all others."

Einstein answered : " We must carefully distinguish between what we wish for in general and what we have to investigate as belonging to the world of knowledge. The question under consideration is not one of wishes and feelings, but was unmistakably aimed at the advances and revolutions in the realm of science. It does not come within the scope of science at all to make moral discoveries ! Its one aim is rather the Truth. Ethics is a science about moral values, but not a science to discover moral ' truths.' Ethics, conceived as a science in the usual way, can therefore serve to discover or to promote truth only indirectly. To illustrate my point of view I shall quote an example taken from a totally different field ; it is merely to serve as an analogy. Let us consider the game of chess. Its value and its meaning is not to be sought in scientific factors, but in something entirely different, in a struggle which takes place according to definite rules. But even chess, inasmuch as it sharpens the intellect, may exhibit an indirect value for promoting truth. It may, for instance, suggest examples in permutations, which may contain mathematical, that is, purely scientific, truths. I certainly do not deny that there is an ethical factor in all genuine sciences. For being occupied with things for the sake of truth alone emancipates and ennobles the mind."

" This ennobling effect," I interposed, " should surely show itself in a moderation of the passions which were mentioned in the above expression of opinion. With Picard we should expect above all things to see a diminution in the feelings of hate between peoples, the tragic consequences of which we have experienced."

Einstein smiled, and, with a touch of sarcasm, said, " Hate is presumably a privilege of the ' cultured,' who have the time and the energy for it, and who are not the slaves of care." His tone indicated clearly that he used the generic term " cultured " to denote the Philistines of culture, its snobbish satellites, but not those whose intensive work aimed at increasing and deepening the fields of culture. In general he maintained his view that it is an illusion to expect " discoveries " in the realm of ethics, since every real discovery belonged alone to the sphere of truth in which the division only into right and wrong, not that into good and evil, holds good.

This led us to the old question of Pilate : What is Truth ? In seeking an answer to this question Einstein first called special attention to the conception of " approximation," which plays a great part in the actual search for truth, inasmuch as every physical truth, expressed in measures and numbers, always leaves some remainder, that marks its distance from the unattainable truth of reality. This conception, which manifests itself so prominently in the relation of Einstein's own researches to the older, so-called classical, mechanics, will be developed here according to his line of thought as far as I can recollect from a number of conversations.

Let us suppose that we overhear two people arguing about the shape of the earth's surface. The one affirms that it is an unlimited plane, whilst the other maintains that it is a sphere. We should not hesitate a moment to say that the first is in error, and that the second gives the true answer. As long as the question was to be decided in favour of a " Plane or a Sphere," the sphere would represent the absolute truth. Yet it would be only relative, for these two statements are contradictory only between themselves, but will no longer be so if a third assertion is made which opposes a new alternative to " sphere."

If this alternative objection is actually raised, the third person would be quite justified in saying that the " sphere " explanation is wrong. For the conception " sphere " requires that all diameters be equal, whereas we know that they are not so, since the distance from pole to pole has been proved to be smaller than that between opposite points on the equator. The earth is an ellipsoid of rotation, and this truth is absolute in the face of the errors which are expressed by the terms, plane and sphere.

It would again have to be added that this absoluteness would stand only as long as this contradiction is regarded as being one between a definite sphere and a definite ellipsoid. If, as in the case of the earth, there are quite different diameters in the equatorial and the diametral planes, then there is complete contradiction between the two statements, and as the supporter of the ellipsoid is right, the one who supported the sphere must now give in, although he previously triumphed over his first opponent. His statement was true compared with the latter, but showed itself to be an error when compared with the statement of the third person.

This does not run counter to the laws of elementary logic. One of these, somewhat inadequately called the Law of Contradiction, states that two directly contrary statements—*e.g.* this figure is a circle, and this figure is not a circle—cannot both be true simultaneously. The truth of the one implies necessarily the falseness of the other. As this cannot be disputed, it follows in our case that we cannot have been confronted with contradictory judgments at all concerning the figure of the earth.

This is to be understood in a geometrical sense. The sphere does not entirely contradict the ellipsoid, since it is a limiting case of the latter : and the plane is likewise a limiting case of the sphere, as well as of the surface of ellipsoids.

But we are not concerned with purely geometrical considerations, for the earth is a definite body, and not a limiting configuration derived from abstraction. We are here dealing with measurable quantities, whose difference can be proved, and hence we must have one of the disputants proclaiming the absolute truth, whilst the other proclaims an absolute error. This, however, again is incompatible with our result that the second person is right in the one case and wrong in the other.

The logical Law of Contradiction overcomes the dilemma in the simplest way. None of these assertions contains the truth, hence none of these judgments allows the falseness of the others to be deduced. Only this may be said, that there is a fraction of truth in each judgment. The true shape of the earth is given by the plane to a first, the sphere to a second, the ellipsoid of rotation to a third, degree of approximation : we reserve the right of further approximations, each of which in succession approaches a higher degree of correctness, but none attains the absolute truth.

This reflection on a particular case may be generalized, and remains when we extend it to our attempts at grasping the states, changes, and occurrences of Nature. Whenever we talk of physical laws, we must bear in mind that we are dealing with human processes of thought, that are subjected to a succession of judgments, courts of appeal, as it were, excluding, however, a final court beyond which no appeal is possible. Each new experience in the course of natural phenomena may render necessary a new trial before a higher court, whose duty is then to give a more definite or different form to the law formulated by us, so as to attain a still higher degree of approximation to the truth.

If we call to mind some of the most valuable statements made by modern investigators about the nature of natural laws, we recognize that they are all connected by a single thread of thought, namely, that even in the most certain law there is left a remainder that has not been accounted for, and that obliges us to consider a greater approximation to the truth as possible, even if a final stage is not attainable.

Mechanics furnishes us with the expression of its laws in equations, whose importance Robert Kirchhoff explained in 1874 by a definition that has been considered conclusive by scientists. According to him, it is the object of mechanics to describe completely (and not to explain) in the simplest manner the motions that occur in Nature.

The postulate of simplicity is derived from the fundamental view of science as an economy of thought. It expresses the will of man's mind to arrive at a maximum of result by using a minimum of effort, and to express the greatest sum of experience by using the smallest number of symbols. Let us consider two simple examples quoted by Mach. No human brain is capable of grasping all the possible circumstances of bodies falling freely, and it may well be doubted whether even a supernatural mind like that imagined by Laplace could succeed in doing so. But if we take note of Galilei's Law for Falling Bodies and the value of the acceleration due to gravity, which is quite an easy matter, we are equipped for all cases, and have a compendious formula, accessible to any ordinary mind, that allows us to picture to ourselves all possible motions of falling bodies. In the same way no memory in the world could retain all the different cases of the refraction of light. Instead of trying to do the impossible task of grasping this infinite abundance, we simply take note of the sine law, and the indices of refraction of the two media in question ; this enables us to picture any possible case of refraction, or to complete it, since we are free to relieve our memories entirely by having the constants in a book. Thus we have here natural laws that give us a comprehensive yet abbreviated statement of facts, and satisfy the postulate of simplicity to a high degree.

But these facts are built up on experiences, and it is not impossible that some new unexpected experience will reveal a new fact, which is not sufficiently taken into account in the law. This would compel us to correct the expression for the law, and to seek a closer approximation for the enlarged number of facts.

The Law of Inertia, according to our human standard, seems unsurpassable in simplicity and completeness ; it seems to us fundamental. But this law, which prescribes uniform rectilinear motion to a body subject to no external forces, selects only one possibility out of an infinite number as being valid for us. It does not seem evident to a child, and it is easy to imagine a good scholar in some branch of knowledge other than physics, to whom it would likewise not seem evident.

For it is by no means necessary *a priori* that a body will move at all when all forces are absent.   If the law were self-evident, it would not need to have been discovered by Galilei in 1638. Nevertheless, it appears to us, now, to be absolutely self-evident, and we can scarcely imagine that it can ever be otherwise. This is simply because we are bound to the current set of ideas that cannot extend beyond the sum of sense-data and experiences that have been inculcated into us by heredity and environment.   At a very distant date in the future the average mind may surpass that of Galilei to the same extent as Galilei's surpasses that of a child, or of a Papuan native.   And of all the infinite possibilities one may occur to a Galilei of the distant future, which, when formulated as a law, may serve to describe motions of a body subject to no forces better than the law of inertia, proposed in 1638.

These reflections are not mere hallucinations, but have to do with scientific occurrences that we have observed in the twentieth century.   Newton's equation that gives the Law of Attraction is beyond doubt a model of simplicity, and it would have occurred to no thinking person of even the last generation to doubt its accuracy.   The easily grasped expression $k\dfrac{m.m^1}{r^2}$ apparently expresses truth in a law which is valid for all eternity.   In this expression, he denotes a gravitational constant, that is, a quantity which is invariable in the whole universe ; m and m^1 are two masses that act attractively on one another ; and r is the distance between them.   But Newton has been followed by Einstein, who has proved that this expression represents only an approximate value, that leaves a small remainder as an error that may be detected if the greatest refinement be made in our methods of observation.   The equations that have been set up by Einstein represent the approximation that is to be considered final for the present, and that may remain valid for thousands of years.   They are certainly very complicated, being included in a system of differential equations of awe-inspiring length, and we may feel tempted to object with the question : how do they agree with Kirchhoff's postulate that the simplest description of the motions must be sought ?   But this objection falls to the ground if we look carefully into the question.   For simplicity consists not merely in being brief or in excluding difficulty from a formula, but rather in asserting the simplest relation to the universe as a whole, which is independent of all systems of reference. When this independence is proved—and in Einstein's case it is so—the complicated aspect of the formula disappears entirely in the light of the higher simplicity and unity of the world-system that presents itself—a world-system that is directed in conformity with the one fundamental law of general relativity as well in the motion of the electrons as in motion of the most distant stars. With regard to the other postulate, that of completeness, *i.e.* absolute accuracy, we have been furnished with proofs that have rightly excited the wonder of the present generation. But are we then to recognize the Principle of Approximation in every direction ? Is there then nothing that can be proved rigorously, nothing that is unconditionally valid in the form of knowledge that corresponds exactly to truth ?

We are led to think of mathematical theorems, which, when they have once been proved, are evident to the same degree as the axioms from which they have been derived, by virtue of logic which cannot be disputed since a contradiction leads to absurdity. It has been said that mathematics *est scientia eorum, qui per se clara sunt*, that is, is the science of what is self-evident.

But here again doubts arise. If we should get to know only a single case, in which the self-evident came to grief, the road to further doubts becomes open. Such a case will now be quoted.

As we know, a tangent is a straight line, which makes contact with a curve at two coincident (or infinitely near) points without actually cutting the curve. The simplest case of this is the perpendicular at the extremity of a radius of a circle. And it agrees fully with what our feeling leads us to expect when it is stated that every curved line that is " continuous," that is, which discloses no break and no sudden bend, has a tangent at every point. Analysis, which treats plane curves as equations in two variables, gives the direction of the tangent in terms of the differential coefficient, and declares accordingly that every continuous function has a differential coefficient, that is, may be differentiated, at every point. The one statement amounts to the same as the other, since there must be an equivalent graphical picture corresponding to every functional expression.

But this apparently rudimentary theorem involves an error, which was not discovered before the year 1875. The theory of curves has been in existence for centuries, but it occurred to no one to doubt the general validity of this theorem of tangents. It was regarded as self-evident, as a mathematical intuition. And certainly neither Newton, nor Leibniz, nor Bernoulli, not to mention the mathematicians of olden times, even dreamed that a continuous curve without a tangent, or a continuous function without a differential coefficient, was possible.

Moreover, a proof of the theorem had been accepted. It appeared in text-books, and was often to be heard in lecture rooms ; nor was a shadow of a doubt suggested. For it was not merely a *demonstratio ad oculos*, but it appeared directly to our sense of intuition. And we may safely say that up to the present day no one has ever been able to *imagine* a continuously curved line which has no tangent ; no one has been able to picture even one point of such a curve at which no tangent could be drawn.

Nevertheless, scientists appeared who began to entertain doubts. In the case of Riemann and Schwarz these doubts assumed a concrete form, in that they proved that certain functions are refractory at certain points. But Weierstrass was the first to make a real breach in the old belief that was so firmly rooted. He set up a function that is continuous at every point, but differentiable at *no* point. The graphical picture would thus have to be a continuous curve having no tangent at all.

What is the appearance of such a configuration ? We do not know, nor shall we presumably ever get to know. During a conversation in which this problem of Weierstrass arose, Einstein said that such a curve lay beyond the power of imagination. It must be remarked that, although the mathematical expression of the Weierstrass function is not exactly simple, it is not inordinately complex. Moreover, seeing that one such function (or curve) exists, others will soon be added to it (Poincaré mentions that Darboux actually gave other examples even in the same year that the first was discovered) ; there will, indeed, be found an infinite number of them. We may go still further, and say that, corresponding to each curve that has tangents, there are an infinite number that have no tangents, so that the former form the exception and not the rule. This is an overwhelming confession that shakes the foundations of our mathematical convictions, yet there is no escape.

How may we apply the principle of " approximation " to these considerations ? May we say that the theorem that was believed earlier is an approximation to a mathematical truth ?

This is possible only conditionally, in a certain extremely limited sense, namely, if we picture to ourselves that point in the development of science at which the conception and properties of tangents first began to be investigated. Compared with this stage of science, the above theorem denotes a first approximation to the truth, in spite of its incorrectness ; for it makes us acquainted with a great abundance of curves that are very important for us and that exhibit tangents at every point. This knowledge brings us a step nearer to the more approximate truth given by Weierstrass's example. In the distant future, the earnest student will learn this theorem only as a curious anecdote, just as we hear of certain astrological and alchemistic fallacies. He will learn, in addition, other theorems that are looked on as proved by us of the present day, although actually they were proved only approximately. For what does it mean when Gauss, for example, repudiated certain proofs of earlier algebraists as being " not sufficiently rigorous," and replaced them by more rigorous proofs ? It signifies no more than that, in mathematics, too, what appears to one investigator as flawless, strict, and evident, is found by another to have gaps and weaknesses. Absolute correctness belongs only to identities, tautologies, that are absolutely true in themselves, but cannot bear fruit. Thus at the foundation of every theorem and of every proof there is an incommensurable element of dogma, and in all of them taken together there is the dogma of infallibility that can never be proved nor disproved.

It must appear extremely interesting that, at first sight, this example of the tangent has its equivalent in Nature herself, namely, in molecular motions the investigation of which is again largely due to Einstein.

Jean Perrin, the author of the famous book, *Atoms,* describes, in the introduction, the connexion between this mysterious mathematical fact and results that are visible and may be shown by experiment, to which we have been led by the study of certain milky-looking (colloidal) liquids.

If, for example, we look at one of those white flakes, which we get by mixing soap solution with common salt, we at first see its surface sharply outlined, but the nearer we approach to it, the more indistinct the outline becomes. The eye gradually finds it impossible to draw a tangent to a point of the surface ; a straight line which, viewed superficially, seems to run tangentially, is found on closer examination to be oblique or even perpendicular to the surface. No microscope succeeds in dispelling this uncertainty. On the contrary, whenever the magnification is increased, new unevennesses seem to appear, and we never succeed in arriving at a continuous picture. Such a flake furnishes us with a model for the general conception of a function which has no differential coefficient. When, with the help of the microscope, we observe the so-called Brownian movement, which is molecular by nature, we have a parallel to the curve which has no tangent, and the observer is left only with the idea of a function devoid of a differential coefficient. . . . We find ourselves obliged, ultimately, to give up the hope of discovering homogeneity at all in studying matter. The farther we penetrate into its secrets, the more we see that it, matter, is spongy by nature and infinitely complex ; all indications tend to show that closer examination will reveal only more discontinuities.

I have not yet had an opportunity of seeing these Brownian movements under the microscope, but I must mention that Einstein has repeatedly spoken to me of them with great enthusiasm, of an objective kind, as it were, for he betrayed neither by word nor by look that he himself has done research leading to definite laws that have a recognized place in the history of molecular theory.

As soon as we approach the question of molecular ir-regularities we recognize that, when we earlier spoke of the figure of the earth in discussing the principle of " approximation," we were still very far from the limit that may be imagined. We had set up the three stages : plane—sphere—ellipsoid of revolution, as relative geometrical steps, beyond which there must be still further geometrical approximations. If we imagine all differences of level due to mountains and valleys to be eliminated, for example, and if we suppose the earth's surface to consist entirely of liquid, undisturbed by the slightest breath of wind, even then, the ellipsoid is by no means the final description. For now the discontinuities from mole-cule to molecule begin, the infinite number of configurations without tangents, the macroscopic parallels of what the white flake soap solution showed as microscopically, and no conceiv-able geometry would ever be adequate to grasp these pheno-mena. We arrive at a never-to-be-completed list of functions which can never be described either in words or in symbolic expressions of analysis.

But even if the ultimate geometrical truth is hidden behind the veils of Maya,* we are yet left with the consolation that the method of approximation, even when applied to a relatively modest degree, produces remarkable results in the realm of numbers. Let us consider for a moment in the simple figure of a circle the ratio between the circumference and the radius.

As we know, this ratio is constant, and is called in honour of the man who first gave a trustworthy value for it, Ludolf's number, namely, π (pi). Thus it makes no difference whether we consider a circle as small as a wedding-ring, or as large as a circus arena, or even one the radius of which is as great as the distance of Sirius. And it makes just as little difference what happens to the circle whilst it is being measured ; the above ratio must remain constant.

But here, too, a contradiction makes itself heard, issuing from one section of modern science. It calls to mind the saying of Dove that when professors are not quite sure about a thing they always preface their remarks with the phrase : "it is well known that " . . . We should be well advised in avoiding this method of expression altogether, for even when we feel quite sure, the ghost of the unknown lurks behind what we fain would call well known.

The theorem that all circles without exception are subject

* Maya=appearance.

to the same measure-relation belongs *a priori* to the synthetic judgments. But fields of thought have been discovered in which the *a priori* has lost its power. Mathematics—once a quintessence of synthetic statements *a priori*—is now regarded as being dependent on physical conditions. Physical conditions, however, are empirical and subject to change. Therefore, since the *a priori* is not subject to change, we encounter a discrepancy. It leads to the question : Is the Euclidean geometry with which we are familiar the only possible geometry ? Or, in particular : Is π the only possible measure-relation ?

Einstein replies in the negative. He not only shows how another geometry is possible, but he also discloses what once seemed inconceivable, namely, that if we wish to describe the course of the phenomena of Nature exactly by means of the simplest laws, it is not only impossible to do so with the help of Euclidean geometry alone, but that we have to use a different geometry at every point of the world, dependent on the physical condition at that point.

From the comparatively simple example of two systems rotating relatively to one another, Einstein shows that the peripheral measurement of a rotating circle, as viewed from the other system, exhibits a peculiarity which does not accompany the radial measurement. For, according to the theory of relativity, the length of a measuring rod is to be regarded as being dependent on its orientation. In the case quoted, the rod undergoes a relative contraction only when applied along the circumference, so that we count more steps than when we measure the circumference of the same circle at rest, that is, in non-rotation. Since the radius remains constant in each case, we get a relatively greater value for π, which shows that we are no longer using Euclidean geometry.

Yet, formerly, before such considerations could even be conceived in dreams, this π was regarded as absolutely established and immutable ; and observers used every possible means of determining its value as accurately as possible.

In Byzantium there lived during the eleventh and twelfth centuries a learned scholar, Michael Psellus, whose fame as the " Foremost of Philosophers " stretched far and wide, and whose mathematical researches were regarded as worthy of great admiration. This grand master had discovered by analytical and synthetical means that a circle is to be regarded as the geometric mean between the circumscribed and the inscribed square, which gives to the above quantity, as may easily be calculated, the value $\sqrt{8}$, that is, $2\cdot8284271$. . . . In other words, the length of the circumference is not even three times that of the radius.

We have the choice of regarding the result of Psellus as an approximation, or as mere nonsense. Every schoolboy who, in a spirit of fun, measures a circular object, say a top, with a piece of string, arrives at a better result, but the contemporaries of Psellus accepted this entirely wrong figure with credulous reverence, and continued to burn incense at the feet of the famous master. It is all very well for us of the present to call him a donkey. We have just as much right in saying that mathematicians differ, not in their natures, but only in the order of their brain functions. If a man like Psellus missed the mark by so much, it is possible that men like Fermat or Lagrange may also have erred occasionally or even consistently.

No heavenly power will give us a definite assurance to the contrary, and all of us may be just as false in our judgment of accepted celebrities as were the Byzantines eight hundred years ago in their estimate of Psellus.

Whereas the latter had obtained a value " less than 3," there are learned documents of about the same date that have been preserved, according to which the value of π comes out as exactly 4. Compared with this grandiose bungling, even the observations mentioned in the Old Testament are models of refinement. For, as early as three thousand years ago, it is stated of the mighty basin in the temple of Solomon (First Book of Kings, chapter vii.) : " And he made a molten sea, ten cubits from the one brim to the other : it was round all about, and his height was five cubits ; and a line of thirty cubits did compass it round about." Thus π here appears as 3, an approximation which no longer satisfied later generations. The wise men of the Talmud went a step further, in saying 3 plus a little more ; and this agrees roughly with the actual value.

The view became more and more deeply rooted that this

π was a main pillar of mathematical thought and calculation. The more the problem of the quadrature of the circle seized on men's minds, the greater were the efforts made to find the exact value of this "little more" of the Talmud. Since 1770 we know that this is not possible, for π is not rational, that is, it can be represented only as an infinite and irregular (that is, non-repeating) decimal expression. It occupies, further, a special rank as a transcendental quantity; this fact was proved by Lindemann as late as 1882 for the first time. Yet, even nowadays, there are incorrigible devotees of quadrature, who are still hunting a solution because they cannot rid themselves of the hallucination that such a simple figure as the circle must submit ultimately to a constructive process.

The correct way was to carry out an even more accurate determination of the decimal figures. The above-mentioned Ludolf van Ceulen got as far as the 35th place of decimals ; at the turn of the eighteenth century the 100th decimal place was reached. Since 1844, thanks to the lightning calculator Dase, we have its value to the 200th decimal place, and this should satisfy even the most extravagant demands. This number, associated with the circle, is a classical example of how an approximation that is expressible in figures of very small value gives an order of accuracy that can be described only by using fantastic illustrations.

If we take a circle of the size of the equator, and also multiply the value of the diameter of the earth by π, we know that the latter result will not be exactly equal to the former, and that there will always be a small remainder. If this discrepancy were less than a metre, the order of exactness would be extraordinarily high, for a metre is practically insignificant compared with a mighty circle of the dimensions of the earth's circumference.

Let us stipulate still greater accuracy. We demand that the error is to be less than the thickness of the thinnest human hair. We find, then, that we must take for π at most 15 places of decimals. Thus, if we use $\pi = 3\cdot14159265358973$, we are applying a means of calculation that reduces the possible error in all measurements of circles on the earth to a degree beyond the limits of human perception.

If we pass beyond the world out into celestial space, and consider circles of the dimensions of a planetary orbit, nay, further, if we pass on to the Milky Way or even to the limit of visible stars, to find space for our circle, and if in this case we still reduce the discrepancy so as to be less than any length that is observable under a microscope, then the last given value of π still suffices. Yet we must not forget the proviso : *semper aliquid haeret*, something unsolved still clings to the problem.

Such numerical approximations, however instructive they may be, nevertheless retain a comparatively playful character, and furnish only a superficial analogy to the most important approximations that are contained in our natural laws themselves. It is these, above all, that manifest themselves so clearly in Einstein's life-work, and they bear the same relation to the former as truth bears to correctness. Truth comprises the greatest conceivable circle of ideas and passes far beyond the sphere of correctness, which deals only with measure-relations, and not with the things in themselves. If Einstein, as we learn, emphatically declares truth to be the only object of science, he means the strictly objective truth that is to be derived from Nature, the true relationship of phenomena and occurrences, independently of whether restless philosophy assigns a question mark to this ultimate objectivity. A great discoverer in the realm of Nature cannot and dare not proceed otherwise. For him there is behind the veil of Maya not a phantom that finally vanishes, but something knowable, that becomes ever clearer and more real as he detaches each successive veil in his process of approximation.

During this conversation, when we were talking of the " Future of the Sciences," Einstein gave his ideas free rein, shooting far ahead of the views and prognostications of the above-mentioned scientists :

" Hitherto we have regarded physical laws only from the point of view of *Causality*, inasmuch as we always start from a condition known at a definite cross-section of time, that is, by taking a time-section of phenomena in the universe, as, for example, a section corresponding to the present moment. But, I believe," he added, with earnest emphasis, " that the laws of Nature, the processes of Nature, exhibit a much higher degree of uniformity of connexion than is contained in our time-causality! This possibility suggests itself to me particularly as the result of certain reflections concerning Planck's Quantum Theory. The following may be conceived: What belongs to a definite cross-section of time may in itself be entirely devoid of structure, that is, it might contain everything that is physically conceivable, even such things (so I understood him to say) as, in our ordinary physical thought, we consider impossible of realization, for example, electrons of arbitrary size, and having an arbitrary charge, iron of any specific gravity, etc. By our causality we have adjusted our thought to a lower order of structural limitations than seems realized in Nature. Real Nature is much more limited than our laws imply. To use an allegory, if we regard Nature as a poem, we are like children who discover the rhyme but not the prosody and the rhythm." I interpret this as meaning that children do not suspect the restrictions to which the form of the poem is subject, and just as little do we, with our causality, divine the restrictions which Nature imposes on occurrences and conditions even when we regard them as governed by the natural laws we have found.

Thus a leading problem of science in the future will be to discover the restrictions of Nature as compared with the apparent causality implied in physical laws.

We have in this an example of the transcendental perspectives that are opened up when we accompany Einstein on one of his excursions of thought. In this case it is actually a question of ultimate things, of a region of discovery of which we cannot yet form a conception, and it appears doubtful whether the problems latent in it are to be treated by making investigations into physical nature, or whether they are to be allotted to speculative philosophy.

In the first place, Einstein's remark seems to aim at nothing less than a revision of the conception of causality. However much has been done to purify this conception and to make it clear, we have here, perhaps, a new possibility of refining it by making a synthesis of scientific and abstract philosophical views. We shall just touch very lightly and superficially on the possibility of a synthesis giving us an avenue to truth. Whoever has heard these words of Einstein, feels the need of getting on to firm ground to rescue himself out of the turmoil of ideas into which he has been plunged.

What is Causality ? A physiological answer may be given by saying that it is the irrepressible animal instinct, rooted in our brain-cells, that compels us to connect together things that we have experienced and imagined. Poets have defined Hunger and Love as the fundamental elements of our social lives ; we need only add the thirst for causality to this to complete the list of primary instincts. For this mental thirst is not less intense than our bodily hunger, and is even greater in that it never forsakes us for a moment. It is easier for the body to check breathing than for the soul to still the question of the why and wherefore, of the cause and effect, of the ante-cedent and consequent.

This ceaseless search for a connexion between occurrences has become organized into a fixed and immovable form of thought, which remains mysterious even when we imagine that we have eliminated all the mystery from it. The rela-tions that we seek and that we regard as being of an elementary character are totally foreign to Nature herself. David Hume, the first real, and at the same time the most penetrating, explorer into this form of thought, said that, in the whole of Nature not a single case of connexion is disclosed which we are able to grasp. All happenings appear, in reality, dis-connected and separate. One " follows on " another, but we can never detect a connexion between them. They appear " co-joined," but never " connected." And since we can form no idea of what has never presented itself to our outer or inner perception, the necessary conclusion seems to be that we have absolutely no idea of causal connexions or causative forces, and that these expressions are quite devoid of meaning, how-ever much they may be used in philosophical discussions or in ordinary life. This " Inquiry concerning Human Under-standing," with its atmosphere of resignation, has been ela-borated in manifold ways, particularly by Kant and the Kantians ; for it is impossible to take up a philosophic thread without entering on an examination of the fundamental question concerning the existence of a causality which lies outside our instinct for causality. It is also inevitable that, whenever we start out in this direction, we encounter the

further question: What is Time? For causality directs
itself to the problem of succession, both of sensations and
phenomena, consequently the two questions are not only
intimately connected, but are really only different expressions
of one and the same question. Time, which according to
Descartes and Spinoza is a *modus cogitandi*, not an *affectio
rerum*, and, according to Kant, is an *a priori* form of thought,
dominates our intelligence with the same sovereign power, as
the imagined course of things: what we perceive in the corresponding act of thought is regarded as temporal and causal,
and impossible of further analysis.

Now, the conception of time has been entirely revolu-
tionized by Einstein himself; and it may be expected that
the conception of causality, too—which, in accordance with
custom, we still endow with a separate existence—will also be
affected by this revolution.

We thus approach a relativization of causality, and we
may advance a step further in this direction, if we call to mind
the differences of time-perception that Nature herself leaves
open to us. It must be clearly understood that we are not
dealing at present with the theoretical time of physics, in
the sense of Einstein's theory, but with something physiological that ultimately, however, resolves itself into a relativization of time, and hence also of the causal connexions in
time.

To do this, we have to follow the lines of reasoning developed by the celebrated St. Petersburg academician, K. E.
von Baer, and we need extend it only very little to get at
the heart of causality, if we start from his address of 1860:
" Which View of Living Nature is correct ? " For the human
brain is a part of living nature, and hence the processes of
thought may also be conceived as expressions of life.

The starting-point is a figment, the fictitious character
of which vanishes as soon as we approach its results. The
bridge of thought may be destroyed later ; it suffices to carry
us temporarily, as long as it lands us in safety on the other
side.

The rapidity of perception, of the arbitrary motions, of
intellectual life seems in the case of various animals to be
proportional approximately to the rapidity of their pulse-

bèats. Since, for example, the pulse of a rabbit beats four times as quickly as that of a bull, it will, in the same interval of time, also perceive four times as quickly, and will be able to execute four times as many acts of will, and will experience four times as much as the bull. In the same astronomical length of time the inner life and perceptual world, in the case of various animals, including Man, will take place at different specific rates, and it is on these rates that each of these living creatures bases its subjective measure of time. Only when compared with our own measure of time does an organic individual, say, a plant, appear as something permanent in size and shape, at least within a short interval. For we may look at it a hundred times and more in a minute, and yet notice no external change in it. Now, if we suppose the pulse-beat, the rate of perception, the external course of life, and the mental process of Man, very considerably accelerated or retarded, the state of affairs becomes greatly changed, and phenomena then occur, which we, fettered by our physiological structure, should have to reject as being fantastic and supernatural, although, on the supposition of a new structure they would be quite logical and necessary. If we suppose human life from childhood to old age to be compressed into a thousandth part of its present duration, say, into a month, so that the pulse beats a thousand times more quickly than occurs in our own experience, we should be able to follow the course of a discharged bullet very exactly from point to point with our eyes, more easily than we can at present observe the flight of a butterfly. For now the motion of the bullet in a second will be distributed among at least 1000 pulse-beats, and will induce at least 1000 perceptions, and accordingly, in comparison with our everyday perception, it will appear 1000 times slower. If the duration of our life were *again* to be reduced to a thousandth of its first reduced value, that is, shortened to about forty minutes, then our flowers and herbs would seem just as motionless and immutable as rocks and mountains, in which we only infer the changes without having directly observed them. We would in the course of our lives see little more of the growth and decay of a bud and a flower in full bloom than we at present see of the geological changes in the earth's crust. The acts of animals would be much too slow to be seen ; at most, we could infer them as we do the motions of the stars at present. If life were shortened still further in the same way, light would cease to be an optical occurrence to us. Instead of seeing the things on which light falls, we should become aware of them as being audible, and what we at present call tones and noises would long have ceased to have an effect on the ear.

If, however, we let our fancy roam in the opposite direction, that is, if, instead of compressing the duration of human life, we expand it enormously, what a different picture of the world would present itself ! If, for example, the pulse-beat, and hence the rate of perception, were to be made a thousand times slower, so that the average human life would be spread out over, say, 80,000 years, and that we should experience in one whole year only as much as we now experience in a third of a day, then, in every four hours winter or any other season would pass by, vegetation would spring up and as rapidly die. Many a growth would not be perceptible, on account of its relative rapidity compared with the rate of the pulse-beat. For example, a mushroom would suddenly come into existence, like a newly formed spring. Day and night would alternate as a light and a dark minute ; and the sun would appear to fly over the heavens like a fiery projectile. If we were again to make the duration of human life a thousand times longer still, and hence the rate of life a thousand times slower still, we should, during the whole of an ordinary year, be able to have only 190 distinct perceptions, so that the difference between day and night would vanish entirely, and the sun's path would be a glowing circular band in the heavens, and all changes of form that seem to us to happen quietly and regularly, and to preserve a certain permanency, would melt together in the wild stream of happening, engulfed in its onward rush.

Are we justified in opposing to this relative perception of time " our own " time, which is something specific and dependent on our constitution as human beings ? Should we not rather adopt the view that this specific time, adapted to our particular pulse-beat, gives only a very limited picture of the world, which is conditioned and determined by the limitations of our own definite intelligence ? Is it, perhaps, only a distorted picture, a caricature, of actual occurrences ?

An intelligence infinitely superior to our own would no longer be dependent on the separate sensations such as are presented to us with the rhythm of the pulse. For such a mind there would be no metronomic foundation in the sequence of occurrences, beyond what represents itself as time to our understanding. He would be situated outside of time in what Thomas Aquinas called the *nunc stans*, in the stationary present, without a retrospect of the past and without expectation of a future. Without the Before and the After, the occurrences of the world would acquire the clearest and simplest meaning, like that given by an equation of identity. What presents itself to us as a " succession " of events would merge together into one whole, just as a succession of numerical calculations become summarized in a rule of calculation, or as a series of logical operations resolves into a logical self-evident truth. If the mind conceived by Laplace actually existed, it would stand above the necessity of introducing time as a quantity into its world-equations, for time is a purely anthropomorphic quantity, produced by our perception, and regulated by our own characteristic pulses. Accordingly, the conception of causality, too, which is indissolubly connected with time, must be regarded as anthropomorphic, as something that we read into, and not out of, Nature. We should at least have to recognize that if there is a causality outside ourselves, then we can learn only a minimum about it, and even this only in a world displaced or distorted by the accidental rate of our pulse-beat.

Let us now repeat Einstein's assertion "that the laws of Nature, the processes of Nature, exhibit a much higher degree of uniformity of connexion than is contained in our time-causality ! It is possible that what belongs to a definite cross-section of time may in itself be entirely devoid of structure, that is, it might contain everything that is physically conceivable, even such things as, in our ordinary physical thought, we consider impossible of realization, for example, iron of any arbitrary specific gravity." It seems to me that the non-physicist will, perhaps, gain a clearer insight into these highly significant words of Einstein, now that he has received the assistance of these physiological considerations. It must be granted that the philosophic grounds of Einstein are quite different and lie much deeper than those of von Baer, who starts from organic functions and ends by arriving at a mysterious relativity that is yet consistent in itself. Nevertheless, there is one point of contact, inasmuch as in each case possibilities that lie apparently *extra naturam* are suggested.

Einstein says : " Hitherto we have regarded physical laws only from the point of view of *causality*, inasmuch as we always start from a condition known at a definite cross-section of time, as, for example, a section corresponding to the present moment." At our own risk an easy paraphrase of his words will be attempted :

The time-section of the present contains for us the sum of all previous experiences, out of which the necessary course of our thought sifts out the category of causality.

What is not present in experience cannot appear in our causality. Let us consider for a moment Hume's example of the Indian who has never known ice. Without being told, and if he is dependent only on his own sensations, he would never learn that water freezes in cold climates. The influence of cold on water is not gradual, corresponding to an increase of cold, and not one that may be anticipated in all its consequences, but at the freezing-point water, which a moment before was a very mobile liquid, passes into a very rigid solid. The causality of the Indian cannot account for this. If we tell him of this phenomenon, he has two courses open to him. Either he refuses to believe it—and this would be quite natural, since rigid water is to him as meaningless as is a square circle to us. Or else he believes the story, and then his list of categories incurs a break, passing through the middle of causality. He has then to reconcile himself to the assumption that something that is meaningless to him and that stands outside the connexion of cause and effect is possible of realization. Up to that moment, in his time-section of the present, there was no room for it in his causality. To Torricelli the conception of liquid air, which we have been able to prepare only since 1883, would have appeared impossible and incompatible with his causality.

So there is no room in our causality for the idea of iron

with the specific gravity of air, or with one several times that of gold. For, reasoning along the lines of our causality, we should conclude that a substance that is so light or so heavy may, indeed, exhibit chemical relationship with iron, but it would not itself be sufficiently defined by the term *iron*.

Now Einstein also said: "Real Nature is much more limited (or bound) than our laws imply." A sceptic might be disposed to take these statements separately in order to construe a contradiction out of them. For, if there are limiting conditions in Nature, which are foreign to the views expressed in our laws, how would it then be possible for phenomena, which cannot be imagined, to become realized? If Nature can do this, surely she must have more liberty than we seek to impose on her. This apparent contradiction vanishes if we treat the conception of structural design or uniformity as something distinct from the measure of all experience up to the present. This would give us the following interpretation :

Out of the manifold of occurrences that are possible in mechanical Nature, real Nature selects a very closely defined manifold. Thus the true laws imply a much greater degree of limitation than those known to us. For example, the laws known to us at present would not be affected if we should discover electrons of arbitrary size or iron of arbitrary specific weight. But Nature realizes only electrons of a quite definite size and iron of a definite specific weight.

. . . .

Let us bear in mind that in aiming at ultimate truths we have no final courts of appeal. Nor are the latter to be assumed even when, in pursuing a theory, we encounter a difficulty, which at first exhibits all the signs of a direct conceptual contradiction. It should rather be realized that a fiction containing an initial but only provisional contradiction serves as a starting-point for just those investigations that are most subtle and that have far-reaching consequences. We should have no Infinitesimal Calculus, no Algebra, no Atomic Theory, no Theory of Gravitation if, to avoid all initial contradictions, we surrender the fiction of differentials, of imaginary quantities, of the atom, of action at a distance. In short, it may, indeed, be said that not only knowledge, but also life, the holding together of people by convention, law, and duty, would become impossible if we did not accept the fiction of free will, which directly contradicts the determinate character of all happening, including actions and motives, which, physically, alone seems recognizable.

Fiction (not to be confused with hypothesis) and anthropomorphism, in spite of their inner inconsistency, are the two poles about which our thoughts and our lives revolve. And no doctrine will ever soar to such heights that it will be able to deny completely its origin from these roots of all thought. The Archimedean thought-centre of the universe, which would enable us to lift the world out of its hinges, is unattainable, because it does not exist at all.

Is this also to apply to the new physics, whose results are to be regarded as the last word in scientific knowledge ? Many a hypercritical thinker might be led away by the current of the preceding statement, and feel disposed to answer in the affirmative, were it not that, here too, a contradiction intrudes itself. This is expressed in the fact that not one of the present-day philosophers is in a position to pursue the threads of this theoretical fabric to their hidden ends.

Thus we arrive at a parting of the ways. Whoever aims at becoming thoroughly familiar with Einstein's new world-system finds that the study of the theory claims so much attention that there is scarcely a possibility left of proceeding to an ultimate philosophical analysis. And whoever is absorbed only by the desire of making philosophic investigations soon enough arrives at border-lines of thought, at which his conscience warns him to beware of insufficient scientific knowledge. He will be attacked by doubts as to whether he has properly understood the theory. And he will be confronted with the question whether he is justified in drawing ultimate philosophical conclusions before he has mastered all the mathematical details.

As far as can be judged at present, only one thinker has, so far, had sufficiently wide knowledge to enable him to correlate the physical theory methodically with the theory of knowledge. I mean Professor Moritz Schlick of Rostock, who has set out his ideas systematically in his book *Erkenntnislehre*, which is extraordinary in itself and in its great scope ; it takes us beyond Kant. In Schlick's opinion Einstein's theory furnishes us with the key to new and unexpected chambers of thought ; it is a wonderful instrument for opening up new avenues, and would appear more wonderful still if we could use this instrument without having recourse to anthropomorphism. This limitation may lead to a Utopia, or may entail a *circulus vitiosus*. But we have one philosophy nowadays which applies to what cannot be fulfilled " AS IF " it really is capable of fulfilment. Among the disciples of Vaihinger, the founder of the As-If-doctrine of thought, we, however, notice the tendency to follow anthropomorphic and fictitious paths also in his field of thought.

From numerous utterances of Einstein, I have gathered that he himself does not give his unqualified approval to all attempts at unravelling the ultimate problems by means of philosophy, that is, by using metaphysics alone. He does not deprecate these endeavours, but even expresses admiration for some of the newer works, as for that of Schlick, yet he sees certain obstacles in the purely philosophical methods, that at least restrain him from taking a systematic interest in them. This reluctant acceptance of, and doubt in, the processes of philosophy, that has never forsaken the exact investigator, this suspicious attitude which scents traces of sophistic and scholastic machinations in all metaphysical arguments, also asserts itself in him in a noticeable form. He feels the absence of rigour and of consistency of direction, which is a guarantee of progress in passing from one result to another, in the method of thought of those who are pure philosophers : and he deplores the spongy and murky appearance of certain expressions of thought, which, it must be admitted, form a poor contrast to the completeness and the crystal clearness of mathematico-physical reasoning. There was an inscription on the portals of the Athenian Academy which stated that entrance was forbidden to all who had had no mathematical training ; we may imagine next to it an academy of pure transcendental philosophy, bearing the inscription : No exact research allowed ! I believe that this clear-cut distinction would tally with Einstein's view.

In the case of the great Ernst Mach, for whom Einstein has intense admiration, we observe a similar attitude, or we may say that, in the language of allegory, he sang openly the same refrain in another key. He never ceased reiterating that he was properly " no philosopher at all, but only an investigator of Nature." At the beginning of the introduction to one of his works we read his confession : " Without in the slightest degree being a philosopher, or even wishing to be one . . ." ; and some lines further on he calls himself sarcastically " a mere amateur sportsman " in philosophical regions. Yet, Mach's initial remark is followed by a remarkable result, for the book in question, *Knowledge and Error* (Erkenntnis und Irrtum), is to be reckoned among the most important works in philosophical literature ; and he himself, the amateur sportsman, who did not even desire to be called a philosopher, accepted in 1895 the post of Professor of Philosophy at Vienna University. It was merely his timidity in the face of the philosophical fraternity that had made him emphasize repeatedly the distinction between his own work and that of the philosophers, whereas in his heart he had nourished a passion for Philosophy, the first mother of Science. And in my opinion such a moment may arrive for even the most rigorous investigator when he succumbs to the siren strains from the shores of philosophy.

As far as Einstein himself is concerned, I cannot venture on a prognostication. Even though he belongs to the category and rank of Descartes, Pascal, d'Alembert, and Leibniz, in whom Mathematics and speculative Philosophy are intermingled, he is yet characterized by such a pronounced individuality, that it is quite inadmissible to draw conclusions about him from others. He has no need to experience a day of Damascus, for he carries the gospel of salvation in himself, and it radiates from him. One thing seems possible, in my opinion, namely, that Einstein will occasionally roam into the neighbouring realm merely from æsthetic motives. Although the means of philosophy are nebulous and more indefinite than those of exact science, which are almost glaringly distinct, philosophy itself for this reason is the more closely related to Art. And a theory that applies to the whole universe must assuredly contain many germs that may come to life if subjected to the methods of Art. The connecting link between Kant and Schiller shows in what sense this is to be understood. Even at present there are indications in Art which tend to show that it is ready to establish points of contact with Knowledge. In France symphonic poems were written on the measure relations of the circle, and on logarithms : these are at present only curiosities, but may in future become models. At a much later date, perhaps, the four-dimensional universe may become ripe for treatment by such methods of Art. On the way to this goal there is the treatment with the symbolic, non-rigorous, and semi-poetic means of expression used by Philosophy. Many will use their efforts to achieve this, and perhaps they will come within closer range of success, if Einstein himself lends a helping hand. It will not be possible to arrive at new physical truths by following this path, but those that are actually known will be traced more readily to the great mainstream of philosophy. To fathom the secrets of the world is the work of a recluse, but to make it comprehensible to a wide circle, a preacher is necessary, who uses the beautiful methods of philosophical rhetoric. Cosmos denotes the World and its Ornamentation ; its creator, Demiurge, is a master who fashions his forms along the lines of Art.

Thus we have learned what Einstein regards as the sole purpose of Science, namely, the search after Truth. For him, the latter is something absolute in itself, and the possibility of getting nearer to it is as great as the impossibility of deriving results of scientific use from, say, ethical discoveries. For ethics is a field which is haunted by the conceptual ghosts, and the manner of treatment, *ordine geometrico*, that Spinoza wished to apply to it, is reserved for physics. Einstein leaves the inverse philosophical query : " Is not Truth in itself only something that we have constructed in imagination ? " to those who find pleasure in sauntering along paths of thought that are totally unconnected, whereas he himself advances in a straight line with the consciousness that even if the goal is unattainable, he will at least not lose the right direction !

CHAPTER VIII

HIGHWAYS AND BY-WAYS

I

AGAIN we chanced to refer to the great subject : Can or should theoretical science also pursue practical aims ?

It is impossible to overrate the importance of this question. It haunts us daily and often enough looms up threateningly on the horizon of mankind. Observe what form the discussions of educated people take when the finest and most sublime achievements of mind are being debated : one talks of the wonders of research in the remotest corners of astronomy where the structures of world-wide star-systems are being investigated ; we hear observations about the theories that aim at tracing the cosmogonic development of universes from the original chaos of countless ages ago. We hear mention of exalted sciences, the Theory of Functions and Numbers, whose founders and representatives are just as remarkable in propounding problems as in solving them, and inevitably the following question obtrudes itself : Of what use is it, ultimately ? What can one do with it ? Can it be admitted that theoretical science has an object of its own, or have we at least the right to maintain the hope that, sooner or later, it will bring us a real " Utility " expressible in practical terms ?

And just as the devotees of pure art have framed the expression, " L'art pour l'art," so Einstein proclaims that science is its own object, " Science for its own sake ! " It carries its aims absolutely in itself and must not, through aiming at other purposes, stray from its own highways. " It is my inner conviction," said he, " that the development of science itself seeks in the main to satisfy the longing for pure knowledge, which, psychologically, asserts itself as religious feeling."

" To yourself, Professor, the practical aspect seems comparatively insignificant ? "

" I did not say that, and it was not implied in the question. We must not lose sight of our premises. As long as I am interested in working along lines of research—this was the assumption—the practical aspect, that is, every practical result that is found simultaneously or arises out of it later, is a matter of complete indifference to me."

Far be it from me, even in thought, to wish to question this confession of faith, particularly as the fact that it comes from a searcher of the truth gives it the more weight. Yet a certain uneasiness has crept over me because voices have recently made themselves heard that demand for science a totally different tendency. They arise not only from the public at large, but also from academic circles. Just a short time ago I read an exposition by a well-known scientist, W. Wien, in which he indulged in a violent polemic against the view that purely scientific objects are alone valid. Professor Wien addressed himself particularly to German physicists, reproaching them with underestimating technical science, and with regarding it as a " lowering of status " when a physicist enters into practical life.

To this Einstein remarked : " I do not know at whom this reproach is aimed, but I venture to think that my own attitude can never have given rise to an attack of this kind. For I make no divisions of rank, and recognize no higher and no lower status. I affirm only what is the nature of science herself, and the objects according to which she, objectively, has to direct her gaze. Whatever further orientation individual investigators may seek for themselves depends on the determining conditions of life of each, although these conditions do not serve as a means for deducing the main lines of research. The accusation that I am unwarranted in putting forward this view will, I hope, not be levelled at me, for my connexions with practice are manifold enough, and up to the present moment I have often collaborated with practical physicists. . . ."

" As I have regretfully observed when you were obliged to interrupt a conversation with me to give an audience to impatient persons seeking advice in technical matters ! "

" My own associations with the world of practice are not, indeed, of recent date. My own parents originally wanted me to become a technical scientist, and I was expected to choose this profession to earn my livelihood. I was not, however, sympathetically inclined to it, for even at an early age these practical aims were to me, on the whole, indifferent and depressing. My idea of human culture did not coincide with the current view, that cultural development is to be measured in terms of technical progress. Doubts, indeed, arose in me as to whether technical improvements and advances would actually contribute to the well-being of mankind. I must add that, later, when I came into actual touch with technical science, my opinion became somewhat modified, for the reason that, here too, pleasures of theory often visited me."

The true position is probably that the technical worker who does not merely think out improvements for machines, but occupies himself with inventions on a higher plane, never ceases to feel himself a theorist, since his achievements are dependent for their inspiration on the fruits of theory. The practical results of to-day are rooted in the theoretical results of decades ago, and what is nowadays regarded as an idea of pure research may in later decades acquire practical value. Whether it actually becomes of value, or not, is of little account in judging the idea. At any rate experience has shown that the beginning of theoretical investigations hardly ever gives us the chance of making prognostications. We spoke of the discoveries of Volta, Ampère, and Faraday. When these were first known, the world might have asked : Why have they been disclosed ? To what can they be applied ? Of what use are they ? Nowadays we know the answers that still lay hidden at that time, and we proudly point to modern dynamos. But does a dynamo really represent the significance of these discoveries ? Would the importance and rank of Volta, Ampère, and Faraday be less if the dynamo had not come into existence ? Only an out-and-out materialist would affirm this, and, strictly speaking, the question should not even be raised. For it is in a sense equivalent to wishing to judge of the importance and significance of the Polar Star from its usefulness to the navigator on the earth's surface in finding his bearings. We may put the question (although only in the spirit of psychological curiosity, and without expecting much elucidation) : Would these discoverers have been particularly happy if they had divined the far-reaching consequences of their work ? Did they, indeed, in the course of their abstract researches, have a pre-vision of the future dominated by the dynamo ? Einstein refused to answer this in the decisive negative. He left room, if ever so little, for doubts— that is, he considered that, in all probability, these three discoverers had no presentiment of these consequences, and even if they had in a dream caught a glimpse of our present electrical age, their zest for discovery, their " pleasure in theory," could scarcely have been increased ; for they were discoverers by nature, who, swept along by their own spirits, did not need to wait to satisfy the desires of practical application.

In Einstein's opinion, the presentiment that a discovery may have practical applications in the future may react on pure research. He quoted bacteriology as a proof of this. In the series of eminent bacteriologists, ranging from Spallanzani to Schwann and Pasteur, there were certainly some whose desire for knowledge was directed primarily towards discovering purely scientific relationships. Pasteur himself started from the theoretical question of the creation of life, that is, from the problem of the origin of organic creatures from inorganic matter without the medium of parent organisms. As a pan-spermist he took up a negative attitude, that is, he tried to prove that it is impossible to discover a bridge between organic and inorganic matter. Yet he doubtless knew that his theoretical efforts stretched out into practical regions, and he may easily have foreseen that they would exert a very important influence on Medicine and Hygiene, although he could not measure its full extent. In this case, then, we cannot fail to recognize that a certain connexion between the desire for pure knowledge and the impulse to apply it practically is possible, serviceable, and justified in itself.

An influence in the opposite direction is also possible, and when, during the course of our conversation, we went in search of examples, we came across one of great interest. It shows us that a question may arise out of ordinary practice that may open up an immense field of pure knowledge, nay, it may lead to a science of very wide scope. As this example is not well known, I shall mention it here ; I do so with additional pleasure as the scientist involved is one of those whom Einstein quotes most frequently and for whom he has the greatest admiration, namely, Johannes Kepler. First we have the surprising fact that Kepler, who, even when at the height of his fame, was not free from care, was once the possessor of some money. In the year 1615, his blessed year of fortune, the great astronomer owned a comfortable home in Linz, and even dared to conceive the idea of placing some well-filled casks in his cellar; nay, more, he was in a position to publish a new scientific work at his own expense, and thus appear as his own publisher.

This production of Kepler and his casks of wine are directly connected, as we see clearly from the title : *Doliometrie*, literally, " The Measurement of Casks." But the title of the work gives not the slightest hint of its importance. For these investigations relating to wine-casks actually became the foundation of a science of sovereign power, the *Infinitesimal Calculus*.

What was Kepler's aim ? It was something entirely practical, and directed to a definite purpose, quite independent of " pleasures of theory," to repeat Einstein's expression. His problem was a question of economy, of using material sparingly and appropriately, in accordance with the requirements of the careful head of a house. How must such a cask be constructed from a minimum of wood to give the greatest cubical content ?

His deliberations began by regarding wine as the precious content enclosed by a figure in space, and then conceiving the cask as representing a particular class of " bodies of revolution," that is, of figures in space that may be regarded as produced by the revolution of a curved line about an axis. At this point he at first endeavoured to gain a complete survey of the question. He varied the boards along the sides, the staves, and formed successively ninety-two such bodies of revolution, some of which he named after the fruits which they resembled in shape, as, for example, apple-shaped, lemon-shaped, olive-shaped bodies. He started out by measuring casks, and the final result was that his work, *Doliometrie*, became the source of all future cubatures or measurements of volume.

Now we come to the deciding point. What conditions has the limiting surface of such a cask-like body of revolution to fulfil, if the body is to have a maximum volume ? An epochal discovery here came to light. The practical head of the house soars up into the sublime realms of the theory of magnitudes. Kepler discovered the conception of changes in functions, and their peculiarities at the maximum point. (He did not, of course, use these modern terms.) By this means, long before Newton and Leibniz, he laid the foundations of Infinitesimal Calculus, which later became the heart and soul of mathematics, of astronomy, of theoretical physics, and of technical science, in so far as it is founded in mechanical relations.

On the other hand, Einstein who now, three hundred years later, has set up his differential equations, and, with them, a new world-system, stands before us as a pure discoverer, devoid of practical aims. But in these equations there are elements of analysis that once came to light in a happy idyll. This event did not come out of the grey obscurity of abstraction, but out of a region of earthly happiness, when a ray of light found its way into Kepler's gloomy existence. No poet has yet expressed this curious complex of events in a ballad, telling how Truth, the only object of Science, was pressed out of the grape, and how Practice, inspired by the inquiry of a cooper, found its way to a Theory that stretches to the confines of the Universe.

II

The conversation touched on famous expressions, words carved in stone, in particular a saying of Kant which seeks to fix the foundation and the limits of knowledge. " Every science of Nature," the great philosopher of Königsberg had said, " contains just as much Truth as it contains mathematics." And since, ultimately, Nature includes everything

—for a demarcation between physical and mental science no longer seems possible—then, if we follow Kant, we should have to regard mathematics as the sole measure of science.

It is certainly not yet possible to enter into a discussion on this point with historians, medical or legal practitioners. They would be justified in refusing it, since, in their subjects, " truth " is not the sole factor, and because we cannot see at present how the conception of a comprehensive mathematical truth is to find a place in them. But when we question a physicist on this point, who unceasingly uses mathematics as his chief instrument, we should surely expect him to answer with an unconditional affirmative. At least, I should not have been surprised if Einstein had answered in this way, and if he had indeed claimed its validity for every branch of science.

But Einstein considered this quotation to be true only conditionally, in that he accepted it as a principle, but did not regard it as universal. That is, he does not recognize mathematics as the only test of truth.

" The sovereignty of mathematics," said Einstein, " is based on very simple assumptions ; it is rooted in the conception of magnitude itself. Its dominant position is due to the fact that it gives us much more delicate means of distinguishing between infinitely varied possibilities than any other method of thought that expresses itself in language and is restricted to the use of words. The greater the field taken into consideration, the clearer does this become ; but even in such a narrow range as 1 to 100, an estimate such as 27 is incomparably more exact than can be expressed in words in any other way. If we think of a series of sensations, ranging from pleasure to pain, or from sweet to bitter, we find that words leave us in an uncertain, confused state, and we do not succeed in fixing on a point of the series with the same precision as we above fixed on the 27 out of the 100. But when the theory of magnitude plays a part in the question, as, for example, in a series of tones, whose vibrations exhibit a mathematical sequence, we immediately attain a much higher order of precision by using numbers. . . ."

That is why there is a sort of scientific pleasure in the sequence of tones, so my thoughts ran on. Leibniz remarks that " Music is the pleasure of the human soul, which arises from counting without knowing that it is counting." Here Pythagoras' " Number is the essence of all things " is verified. As soon as we arrive at the stage at which we feel the psychological essence of number, we fall into a sort of ecstasy, because, in our subconscious minds, we experience not only the pleasure of sense but also the underlying truth.

Einstein resumed : " Kant's remark is correct in the sense that it sets up two things in clear contradiction to one another. On the one hand, he has in view the fruits of knowledge of ordinary life, in which our ordinary perceptions and experiences are intermingled and cannot be disentangled by inductive methods and deductive considerations. Opposed to these, and to be regarded of higher rank, are the properly scientific constructions—that is, such in which we find a neat differentiation of connected thoughts that are based on regular foundations and that form the links of a chain of deduction. Whenever our science succeeds in detaching this logically ordered knowledge from its sense-sources, it has a mathematical character, and the amount of truth contained in it will accordingly be determined by Kant's criterion. But Kant demands too much when he asks us to apply this scale to all attainable knowledge of science. It would seem advisable to draw limitations if his remark is to serve as a regulative measure. A great part of biological science will in future still be obliged to make its way independently of purely mathematical considerations."

" Your reflections, Professor, would then also apply to the saying of Galilei : The book of Nature lies open before us, but is written in letters other than those of our alphabet ; its characters are composed of triangles, quadrilaterals, circles, and spheres."

" With all due honour to the beauty of this observation, I cannot refrain from doubting its universal validity. If we were to accept it unconditionally we should have to regard the paths of all research as purely mathematical, and this would exclude certain very important possibilities, above all, certain forms of intuition that have shown themselves to be extremely fruitful. Thus, according to Galilei's interpretation, the book of Nature would have been illegible for Goethe, for his spirit was entirely non-mathematical, indeed anti-mathematical. But he possessed a particular form of intuition that expressed itself as a feeling which put him into direct contact with Nature, with the result that he obtained a clearer vision than many an exact investigator."

" Do you then consider intuitive gifts to be separable at all in form and in kind ? "

" It would be pedantic to seek to establish a fundamental difference, even if we may regard the non-mathematical intuition of Goethe as a very striking case. Moreover, as I have often emphasized, all great achievements of science start from intuitive knowledge, namely, in axioms, from which deductions are then made. It is possible to arrive at such axioms only if we gain a true survey of thought-complexes that are not yet logically ordered ; so that, in general, intuition is the necessary condition for the discovery of such axioms. And it cannot be denied that, in the great majority of minds with a mathematical tendency, this intuition exhibits itself as a characteristic of their creative power."

" From these remarks it would appear that you value deduction considerably higher than induction. Perhaps in using these catchwords I am expressing myself a little vaguely ; it seems to me that great things have been achieved, too, by using inductive processes."

" Let us first define what each of these terms means. Deduction is the derivation of the particular from the general, whereas induction is the process of deriving the general from the particular case. Now, quote any example of a brilliant achievement, which you feel illustrates the power of the inductive method. Of whatever kind your example may be, you will soon become aware of the difference in the significance of the two processes."

" For me the most perfect example of induction is given by certain reasoning of Euclid. The question was whether there is a finite or an infinite number of primes (that is, numbers that cannot be divided without leaving a remainder except by unity). Euclid found an elegant proof that the total number is infinite by the following strictly inductive reasoning. If the total number were finite there would have to be a *greatest* prime. Let us call it n, and then form the product of all primes up to n and including it, finally adding one, thus : $2 \times 3 \times 5 \times 7 \times 11 \times 13 \ldots n$, plus 1. This new number, say Y, is certainly greater than n, and now there are two possibilities, either n is prime or it is not prime.

" If it is not prime, it must be divisible by some existing prime. But the primes up to and including n cannot divide exactly into Y, as there is always a remainder, namely, 1. Hence Y must be divisible by an existing prime X greater than n. This contradicts the assumption that n is the greatest prime, for X is shown to be greater than n.

" Secondly, if Y *is* a prime, it immediately follows that n cannot be the greatest prime, for Y is greater than n. Hence, however great may be any prime that we may assume, there will always be one that is greater, and even if we do not succeed in expressing it in figures, we see that it must certainly exist. Thus by studying carefully a particular case—the prime n, which was assumed to be the greatest possible one— we have arrived at a general theorem which states that there is no limit to the number of primes. Is not that, too, a triumph of intuition ? "

" Certainly," said Einstein. " But you must not overlook the fact that a theorem of this kind cannot be ranked with a theorem of a fundamentally axiomatic character. The one you have discussed has been derived by a clever process of reasoning, but it does not exhibit the characteristic of a momentous discovery. This theorem of Euclid can be im- agined absent from science without the content of truth in science being essentially effected. Compare with it a theorem of axiomatic significance, such as Galilei's Law of Inertia, or Newton's Law of Gravitation. Theorems such as the latter are characterized by being starting-points of knowledge that are inexhaustible in the consequences that may be deduced from them. Your question, earlier, as to whether I consider the deductive method superior to the inductive, was not formulated in correct terms. To this I answered above that the inductive method as a means of discovering general truths usually appears over-estimated. The proper form of the question is : Which truths are of the higher order, those that are found inductively, or those that lead to further deduction ? There can scarcely be doubt about the answer."

" No, that is certainly true. If I understand your meaning rightly, the answer may be expressed by an allegory. Intuition of the highest order creates treasure-mines, those of lesser degree individual articles of value that are significant in themselves, although they cannot be compared with the inestimable value of the mines. The fact that the highest intuition is found in minds with a mathematical trend makes it appear possible that Kant's remark may gain more and more credence in the future. It already applies in a measure to subjects to which it seemed inapplicable during Kant's lifetime, for example, in Psychology, in which the relations between stimulus and response have been established mathematically only since the Weber-Fechner Law was set up ; and also, since the time of Quetelet, in Moral Science and Sociology, we learn from mathematical methods of statistics and probability that even Man as an active being is subjected to mechanical causality. At any rate it seems manifest that Kant's remark, that in every science there is just as much truth as there is mathematics, has received additional support in recent times."

" That may be admitted," concluded Einstein, " without recognizing his remark as an axiom. It is still far removed from making possible unassailable deductions, and will never quite succeed in doing so ; yet it may claim equal significance as a beautifully expressed idea with that of Pythagoras, which asserts number to be the nature of all things."

III

" The lines of demarcation between ' conceptual knowledge ' (*Erkennen*) and ' perceptual knowledge ' (*Kennen*) are being drawn more and more closely nowadays. The former is regarded as being the exclusive possession of the highly developed human mind, and the latter as being characteristic of the lower intelligence of other living creatures. Is this not a pronounced case of anthropomorphism, and does it not mislead us to form opinions that we should at once disown if we succeed in stepping out of our human frames even for a moment ? "

" We have to rest satisfied with anthropomorphism once and for all," answered Einstein, " and there is no sense in wishing to escape from it, for the arguments *about* anthropomorphism are necessarily also diffused with it, itself. We are thus moving in a circle if we imagine we can deduce something outside of human knowledge. As soon as we have argued around the circle, we find ourselves again at the starting-point, and so we are compelled to mark clear lines of division between instinctive knowledge, derived directly by perception, from conceptual knowledge, derived by processes of abstraction and reflection ; in this way we award the palm of supremacy to the human mind."

" But what if the following contradiction were to assert itself ? Suppose that the logical ' circle ' is not a circle at all, but a spiral, so that the final point of the argument lies just a trifle above the initial point. I feel instinctively that such apparently fruitless circuitous arguments might finally lead to a definite piece of knowledge. For example, a certain insect, the ichneumon-fly, although devoid of a knowledge of science in our sense, infallibly plants its sting in a definite point in the rings of a caterpillar, at just the point that serves its purpose of paralysing the caterpillar without killing it. It acts instinctively, and it is open to me to interpret this occurrence in other words. The fly discloses that it ' knows ' the anatomy of the foreign creature, although it has no conceptual knowledge of it in our sense. But it immediately follows from this analogy that, from the point of view of the fly, its *perceptual* intelligence stands higher than our *conceptual* intelligence—that is, by changing the perspective, I am led to declare the anatomical knowledge of the fly to be of higher rank than the analogous knowledge of the most learned anatomist. In the same way I might persuade myself that the mathematics of a bird of passage stands above the cartographic knowledge of any human explorer. The migratory bird that flies from the interior of Africa in a straight line to its nest in Mecklenburg must have something in the nature of a co-ordinate system in its organism. The real reason that we assign a higher position to our conceptual knowledge is that we are equally proud of our intelligence as of our science ; this is perhaps a deception depending on some compromise, a sort of illicit deal in which the mind draws bills of exchange on science, and, as a return, science meets its obligations by paying in cheques drawn on the mind ! "

I must confess that these hazardous suggestions received no welcome from Einstein, and were not even met with the friendly smile with which he usually accompanies his refutations. Nor do I disguise from myself that the question of conceptual or perceptual knowledge can in no way serve as a basis of proof ; we may at most base certain conjectures on the difference of these types of knowledge, conjectures that suggest in words what eludes our clear comprehension. Einstein's refusal to allow this possibility certainly rests on much firmer ground than the somewhat Bergsonian views that I tried to present. Perhaps they are of a hair-splitting nature, and deal with things lying on different planes ; and are deduced by unjustifiably altering the perspective with a sort of sophistic somersault ; perhaps I may be reproached with seeking, like Münchhausen, to reach a higher standpoint without having a support from which to start. Yet how is it that I find it impossible to free myself from this chain of thought ? No reason is forthcoming, for it is a purely metaphysical question, and there has never yet been a clear system of metaphysics free from ambiguities and sophism.

Let us rather confine ourselves to the conceptual intelligence characteristic of human beings, with which, according to Einstein, so many pleasures of theory are available. I asked him whether he would recognize differences of degree in these pleasures, dependent on their intensities. Although I rightly felt that he would answer in the affirmative, his answer took a totally different turn from what I had expected. It was, indeed, a great surprise, for in the matter of happiness of spirit he expressed a view, according to which he—a great discoverer !—does not regard Science as the deepest source of happiness !

" Personally," said Einstein, " I experience the greatest degree of pleasure in getting contact with works of *Art*. They furnish me with happy feelings of an intensity such as I cannot derive from other realms."

" This is indeed a remarkable revelation, Professor ! " I exclaimed. " Not that I have ever doubted your receptivity for products of art, for I have often enough observed how you are affected by good music, and with what interest you yourself practise music. But even at such moments when you gave yourself up to the pleasures of the Muses, and were soaring in regions far removed from the earth, I used to say to myself : This is a delightful arabesque in Einstein's existence ; but I should never have surmised that you regard this decorative side-issue as the greatest source of happiness. But your confession seems to go further, perhaps even beyond music ? "

" At the moment I was thinking particularly of literature."

" Do you mean literature in general ? Or had you a definite writer in mind, when you were speaking of the felicitous effect of works of art ? "

" I meant it generally, but if you ask in whom I am most interested at present, I must answer : Dostojewski ! " He repeated the name several times with increasing emphasis. And, as if to deal a mortal blow at every conceivable objection, he added : " Dostojewski gives me more than any scientist, more than Gauss ! "

" If, Professor," said I, after a pause that may easily be accounted for—" if you mention in the same breath the names of two such powerful but essentially different intellects, you open the way to a discussion that cannot be settled by a mere positive assertion. It is possible to admire intensely Dostojewski as one who moulds personalities and who analyses the inner struggles of the soul, and yet to deny him perpetual fame. This depends on individual judgment, and, as for my own, I believe that Dostojewski, in spite of his direct artistic appeal, will not have his name perpetuated through the centuries like that of many another member of Parnassus. It seems to me to be a more important matter whether a common measure can be found for Art and Discovery at all. Perhaps the test of how far a work can be replaced may be regarded as valid for each. When you say that Dostojewski gives you more than Gauss, this probably corresponds with the feeling that without Dostojewski you would have no ' Karamasoffs ' and hence would lack a certain life-value that cannot be replaced. But if Gauss had failed to produce one of his fundamental theorems of Algebra, probably some other Gauss would have appeared, who would have achieved this result.

According to this, then, our instinct increases the value of a work of art, as we feel that we are dependent on one being alone for its creation."

" But this is only to be admitted conditionally," said Einstein, " for the best that Gauss has given us was likewise an exclusive production. If he had not created his geometry of surfaces, which served Riemann as a basis, it is scarcely conceivable that anyone else would have discovered it. I do not hesitate to confess that to a certain extent a similar pleasure may be found by absorbing ourselves in questions of pure geometry."

" Perhaps we may use a different characteristic as a means of comparison," I suggested, " namely, the permanency of the impression produced on the subject receiving it. For example, a fine piece of music never loses its influence. We can listen to the first movement of Beethoven's Ninth Symphony a hundred times, and, although we know at every beat what will follow, the state of pleasure continues unweakened ; indeed, it might rather be said that the expectation of pleasure increases from one hearing to the next."

" This characteristic, too," answered Einstein, " cannot be claimed as the exclusive property of works of art. Its existence cannot be doubted, inasmuch as it belongs to every eminent example of art. Yet we encounter it outside the realm of art, too, in great advances of science, with which we never cease occupying ourselves, and yet the impression continues unweakened."

" Do you include among them the impressions that a discoverer experiences when he reviews in his mind the progress due to his own efforts ? "

" Naturally, and these, indeed, quite particularly ; and if this question were put to me directly, I should answer unhesitatingly that I find pleasure in reflecting on my own discoveries, and never experience feelings of weariness in passing over them again. So that, to return to our original thesis, we must adopt a new basis of value if we wish to account for the fact that the greatest degree of happiness is to be expected of a work of art. It is the moral impression, the feeling of elevation, that takes hold of me when the work of art is presented. And I was thinking of these ethical factors when I gave preference to Dostojewski's works. There is no need for me to carry out a literary analysis, nor to enter on a search for psychological subtleties, for all investigations of this kind fail to penetrate to the heart of a work such as " The Karamasoffs." This can be grasped only by means of the feelings, that find satisfaction in passing through trying and difficult circumstances, and that become intensified to exultation when the author offers the reader ethical satisfaction. Yes, that is the right expression, ' ethical satisfaction ' ! I can find no other words for it."

His whole face lit up, and I was deeply touched by his expression. At that moment it seemed to me that he had drawn the last veil from his soul to allow me to share in his ecstasy. Was that the same physicist who interprets the events of the world in terms of mathematics, and whose equations encompass phenomena from electrons to universes ? If so, it was a different soul ; one which gave utterance, like that of Faust, to the words :

> " And when in the feeling wholly blest thou art,
> Call it then what thou wilt.
> Call it Bliss ! Heart ! Love ! God !
> I have no name for it !
> Feeling is all in all !
> Name is but sound and reek,
> A mist round the glow of heaven ! "

And, certainly, the book need not have been one of Dostojewski's to excite this feeling in him. He chose the latter to give expression to a mood that may change according to what he reads, but undergoes no fluctuations in its ethical foundation. From other occasions we know how little ethics, that is conducted along systematic lines, signifies to him, and that he does not even include it in the sciences. But at the same time we see now that his inner life is dominated entirely by the ethical principle. His deep love of Art is characterized by it, and receives full satisfaction from the source of ethical joy of which Art is the centre.

IV

During the autumn of 1918 Einstein was feeling indisposed, and, on the advice of his doctor, did not leave his bed. When

I entered his room, I saw at once that there was no reason for alarm, for pieces of paper covered with mysterious symbols were lying about, and he was absorbed in making additions to some of them. Nevertheless, I considered it my duty to treat him as a patient under medical care, and did not conceal my intention of leaving him after having inquired about his condition. But he would not accept my visit as a mere call to ascertain his progress towards recovery, and insisted that I should remain with him a while, to converse about amusing little problems as usual.

I pointed out to him that there were two objections to this, the first being that he was unwell, and the second that I was intruding on his work.

" How illogical ! " he answered. " If I interrupt my work to chat with you, I am putting aside exactly what the doctor would deny me if I were to allow him. So, let us make a start. You have probably some conundrum weighing on your mind."

" That may not be far wrong. I have been troubled by something in connexion with Kepler's second law. It almost robbed me of my night's sleep. My thoughts kept returning to a certain question, and I should like to know whether there is any sense in the question itself at all."

" Let us hear it ! "

" The law in question states that every planet in describing its elliptic path, sweeps out with its radius vector equal sectorial areas in equal intervals of time. But this seems only half a law, for the radius vectors are only considered drawn from the one focus of the ellipse, namely, the gravitational centre. Now, another focus exists, that may be situated in space somewhere, perhaps far away in totally empty regions, if we assume the orbit to be very eccentric. My question is : What form does this law take if the radius vectors are drawn from this second focus and if the corresponding sectorial areas are considered, instead of these quantities being referred to the first focus exclusively ? "

" This question is not devoid of sense, but it serves no useful purpose. It may be solved analytically, but would probably lead to very complicated expressions, that would be of no interest for celestial mechanics. For the second focus is only a constructive addition, that has nothing real in space corresponding to it. What else is troubling you ? "

" My next difficulty is a little problem that sounds quite simple and yet is sufficiently awkward to make one rack one's brains. It was suggested to me by an engineer who certainly has a keen mind for such things, and yet, as far as I could judge, he did not get a solution for it. It concerns the position of the hands of a clock."

" You surely are not referring to the children's puzzle of how often and when both hands coincide in position ? "

" By no means. As I said just now, it is really quite perplexing. Let us assume the position of the hands at twelve o'clock, when both hands coincide. If they are now interchanged, we still have a possible position of the hands, giving an actual time. But, in another case, say, exactly six o'clock, we get a false position of the hands, if we interchange them, for on a normal clock it is impossible for the large hand to be on the six whilst the small hand is on the twelve. The question is now : When and how often are the two hands situated so that when they are interchanged, the new position gives a possible time on the clock ? "

" There, you see," said Einstein, " that is just the right kind of distraction for an invalid. It is quite interesting, and not too easy. But I am afraid the pleasure will not be of great duration, for I already see a way to solve it."

Supporting himself on his elbow, he sketched a diagram on a sheet of paper that gave a clear picture of the conditions of the problem. I can no longer recollect how he arrived at the terms of his equation. At any rate, the result soon came to hand in a time not much longer than I had taken to enunciate the problem to him. It was a so-called indeterminate (Diophantic) equation between two unknowns, that was to be satisfied by simple integers only. He showed that the desired position of the hands was possible 143 times in 12 hours, an equal interval separating each successive position; that is, starting from twelve o'clock, the two hands may be interchanged every 5 minutes $\frac{2}{143}$ seconds, and yet give a possible time.

. . . .

I mention this little episode, which is insignificant in itself, merely to give an example of how a great discoverer, too, finds amusement in such distractions. In Einstein's case this tendency to practise his ingenuity on unimportant trifles is so much the more pronounced from the fact that he requires an outlet for his virtuosity in calculation, and gratefully welcomes every suggestion that helps him to relieve his mental tension. Similar characteristics are reported of the great Euler, as well as of Fermat, whereas many another eminent mathematician feels decidedly unhappy if he drifts within reach of the realm of actual numerical calculation. In my mind's eye I still see Ernst Kummer, the splendid savant (who, in his time, conferred distinction on Berlin University by his very presence), suffering agonies whenever ordinary arithmetical tables threatened to appear in the working-out of his formulæ. As a matter of fact, these two things, a mastery over mathematics and a talent for ingenious calculation, are to be considered as quite independent, even if we now and then find them present in the same person.

In the case of Einstein this tendency is a symptom of an incredible universality of spirit. It moreover presents itself in the pleasantest forms, and a character-sketch of Einstein would be incomplete if this trait were not mentioned. Every problem which is in any way amusing excites in him a willing interest and enthusiasm. I once directed our conversation to the so-called *Scherenschnitte*. These are made from long strips of paper or canvas, the ends of which are caused to overlap a little and then pasted together, but instead of being fixed so that a flat wheel results, which rolls on one side of the strip, the strip is twisted one or more times before the ends are fastened together. If now the strip is cut lengthwise right along its centre, various unexpected results occur, depending on the number of twists that have been made before pasting.

Some very complex geometrical difficulties are involved in these problems. This is shown by the fact that learned mathematicians have written extensive disquisitions on these curious constructions (for example, Dr. Dingeldey's book, published by Teubner, Leipzig). Einstein had never taken notice of these wonders of the scissors, but when I began to form these strips, to paste them, and to cut them, he immediately became interested in the underlying problem, and predicted in a flash what puzzling chain constructions would result in each case, with a certainty that would lead one to imagine that he had spent days at it. On another occasion a space-problem dealing with dress came up for discussion : Can a properly dressed man divest himself of his waistcoat without first taking off his coat ? One would not have dared to confront Copernicus or Laplace with such a problem. Einstein at once attacked it with enthusiasm, as if it were an exercise in mechanics, the body being the object ; he solved it in a trice, practically, with a little energetic manipulation, much to the amazement and joy of the beholder, who asked himself : Is this the same Einstein who developed the work of Copernicus and Newton ? A little later, perhaps, the conversation centres around some serious point drawn from politics, political economy, sociology, or jurisprudence. Whatever it may be, he knows how to spin out the suggested thread, to establish contact with his partner in conversation, to open up his own perspectives without ever insisting on his point of view, always stimulating and showing a ready sympathy for the subject of discussion and for all the ideas which it crystallizes, the prototype of the scientist, in the mouth of whom Terence put the words : " I am a human being ; nothing that is human is alien to me ! "

CHAPTER IX

AN EXPERIMENTAL ANALOGY

" I WISH to ask you, Professor, to help me over a difficulty and to treat me as the spokesman of a great number who are similarly troubled. In most accounts of your theory of relativity, there is a dearth of definite, concrete, illustrative examples on which we can fix our minds whenever the theorem is to be applied generally without limitation. Let me express this more precisely : Your simplified picture of the structure of the universe is achieved in the theory of relativity by emancipating all observations from fixed co-ordinate systems, and by proclaiming the equivalence of all systems of reference. One of your earliest theorems states that physical laws describing how the states of physical systems alter, remain the same, no matter to which of two co-ordinate systems these states are referred, provided that the co-ordinate systems are moving rectilinearly and uniformly relatively to one another. This theorem entails the following statement. If we—erroneously—adopt a non-relativistic view, we shall come to the conclusion that physical laws depend on the particular system of reference chosen, and will thus assume a different form for each different system. At this point we experience a desire to hear definite examples. What varying forms may a certain given physical law, known under a definite form, assume, and how can we use this law to show that it must adapt itself to the postulate of relativity ? "

Einstein explained that such examples cannot be given in special cases, but only in very general terms. If we were to suggest the elliptic orbits of the planets (at which I had hinted in my remarks), we should fall into error, for the law of elliptic orbits is no such law. For, from another point of view, the elliptic paths of the planets might be drawn out into wavy lines, or into spirals, and they would remain ellipses only as long as the lines of motion are referred to the central attracting body. But the constancy of the velocity of light is such a law, as also is the law of inertia, according to which a body that is left to itself moves uniformly in a straight line.

I confessed to him that this limitation to a few very general laws would be a painful matter for many an enthusiast of average attainments, who has great difficulty in distinguishing the laws that are *generally* valid from those that hold only within circumscribed limits. But if this were not so, we should have to alter our conception of what is conveyed by a popular exposition. For it is called *popular*, not because it now and then uses the patronizing words " dear reader," but because it anticipates the questions and doubts of the man of average sense, and examines them, proving some to be unjustified and others to be reasonable or unreasonable, as the case may be. " Then there is a further matter that troubles me," I continued. " Let us suppose an ordinary reader of such a popular account to get a first insight into the new conception of Time. He is glad to feel the ideas dawning in him, and, to get a more lasting view of the idea, he repeats the arguments through which he has just threaded his way, and, in doing so, again encounters the phrase ' uniform motion.' At the first reading he imagined that he understood the expression quite well, but the second time he pauses and considers. For now that he knows how much depends on it, he is anxious to find out the exact meaning of a ' uniform motion.' He looks for a definition, and if he cannot find one in the book he is perusing, he endeavours to reason it out for himself. With good luck he arrives at the usual statement : a body moves with ' uniform motion ' if it traverses equal distances in equal intervals of time. But equal intervals of time are clearly those during which a body in uniform motion traverses equal distances. In other words, he explains A by means of B, and B by means of A, so that he has involved himself in a vicious circle from which he cannot escape. This is his hour of need, due to the difficulty of ' time.'

"He hopes that further study will remove this obstacle. He meets with the conception of 'simultaneity,' which is defined for him anew, and is disclosed as being 'relative.' He manœuvres further towards the fundamental theorem that every body of reference has its own particular time.

"His popular booklet makes this clear to him by quoting the example of a flying-machine, or, better still, a railway train that is rushing along an embankment at a very great speed, and that carries a passenger. Two strokes of lightning I and II are to take place at two widely distant points on the embankment. The question is then : When are these two flashes of lightning to be considered 'simultaneous'? What conditions must be fulfilled to ensure this ? It is found—incontrovertibly—that the light-rays starting out from the two strokes of lightning must meet at the mid-point of the embankment.

"It now follows from a short chain of argument that the observer in the train will see flash II earlier than flash I, if they reach the observer, who is at rest, at the same moment. That is, two events that are simultaneous with respect to the embankment are not simultaneous for a moving system (such as a train or a flying-machine) ; the converse is, of course, also true.

"Here, again, the eager layman encounters difficulty, for he asks himself : Why should the two events be characterized or defined by lightning-flashes in particular ? If acoustic signals were used instead, nothing would be altered in the fundamental determination, for the sound rays (sound-waves) would likewise meet at the mid-point of the line joining the sources of disturbance. What is the reason that the relativity of time arises only when phenomena are regarded optically, and that rays of light play the deciding part in all later developments ?

"And this particular query is followed by one which is more general : Why does the popular pamphlet not read this question in my mind ? I know that the author of it is more skilled in these matters than I, but just this superiority should help him to divine what is passing in my mind when I make efforts to follow his reasoning."

Einstein had listened to me patiently, and then he explained to me at considerable length why in this case optical signals cannot be replaced by sound signals : light is the only mode of motion that shows itself to be entirely independent of the carrier of the motion, of the transmitting medium. Thus the constancy of velocity is assumed in the above argument, and as this constancy is an exclusive property of light, every other method must be discarded as unallowable for investigating the conception " simultaneity." Furthermore, he showed me how, on the basis of relativity, starting from the embankment-experiment, we may arrive at a perfectly consistent representation of the conception of Time. He certainly did this by applying subtle physical arguments that exceed the scope of the present book.* He added, in substance, that it was futile and impossible to discuss in detail all the conceivable objections that might arise in the mind of one reading a popular work of this kind : it was a futile undertaking, because the true purpose was defeated, inasmuch as a clear development of the fundamental thought would be almost impossible under the cross-fire of so many random questions.

Thus, in this matter, Einstein takes the same stand as Schopenhauer in the preface of his chief work, in which he says : " To understand this work no better way can be advised than to read it *twice* (at least), inasmuch as the beginning assumes the end, almost as much as the end assumes the beginning ; the smallest part cannot be understood if the *whole* has not already been understood." Whoever accepts and follows this advice will find that the intermediate objections will gradually balance and cancel one another, and that it is not necessary that they should interrupt the steady and consistent line of development.

The position would be different if a disciple of the new theory should resolve to dispense with strictly scientific reasoning altogether, and should wish to meet the wishes of his readers or hearers by discarding accuracy entirely. Such a programme seems quite feasible.

---

* In these arguments, arrangements of synchronous clocks occur, which are fixed into the co-ordinate systems, the positions of their hands being compared with one another. The " time " of an event is then defined as the position of the hands of a clock immediately adjacent to the scene of the event.

" This would be merely following the sketchy method of a magazine," Einstein remarked, " but you do not seriously think that it would lead to anything ? "

" It would not be a true explanation, which is reserved for technical productions. But I can imagine that it would not be unprofitable to help one who is entirely ignorant on these questions by using makeshifts, in the form of allegories or analogies, which will serve as supports if he should take fright during the course of his earlier studies. These shocks are bound to occur, as, for instance, when he learns that a moving rigid rod undergoes contraction in the direction of motion."

" But this is *proved* to him ! "

" Nevertheless, he does not easily accept it. For the general reader will say to himself : ' A superhuman effort is imposed on my mind. A rigid rod is the most constant of all things, and never before has one been compelled to regard something that is constant as variable.' "

" If he does not grasp it, no analogy will teach him."

" But perhaps it is possible. The analogy is to show him that the effort is not *superhuman*, and that thinking Man has already had occasion to become familiar with such transformations from constant to variable factors."

" I am afraid your analogy will prove a failure."

" From the scientific point of view this is probably true, inasmuch as all comparisons are imperfect, but the analogy may yet be of service as a last resort. For example, I should say to my general reader : ' Picture to yourself a savant of the Middle Ages who reflects on the constitution of animals and plants. One fact seems to him to be irrevocably true, namely, that the species are unchangeable ! A palm tree is a palm tree, a horse is a horse, a worm a worm, and what is once a reptile remains a reptile. A species in itself denotes something absolutely *invariant*."

" The expression is wrong when taken in this connexion ; you mean *invariable*."

" A little inaccuracy more or less does not affect the analogy. For the sake of my picture I should like to retain the conception-couple, *variable* and *invariant*. Well, then, the species give our savant the impression of invariance, as in the view that was held by Linné and Cuvier. This view necessarily has its counterpart in his thought. He argues that every species has its own original root, and that, in this sense, there is very extensive *variation*. The fundamental roots are extremely manifold ; Nature has produced innumerable variations in her individual acts of creation. But now the *Theory of Descent* of Lamarck, Goethe, Oken, Geoffroy St. Hilaire, enters the field and produces a complete inversion of these two elements ; the two parts of the earlier point of view change places. Our savant has to revise his whole world of thought. Now all organisms are to be traced back to a single original root : the latter, which was variable before, becomes an invariable unicellular primitive organism, but the apparently unchangeable species now becomes variable, in the widest possible sense. And even if this savant should exclaim : ' How am I to reconcile myself to this view ? ' his descendants later find no difficulty in accepting the idea that the organic roots are uniform, and that it is the species that are subject to all manner of variation as a compensating feature.''

Einstein expressed himself very little pleased with this attempt at an analogy, and found that it was so far fetched that it could not be considered admissible.

'' Then I must ask your permission to continue my attempt ; perhaps something useful may yet result from it. I now picture to myself a human being who lived in classical times and who, following Ovid and the great majority of his contemporaries, regards the earth as a disc. On this disc, each inhabitant of the earth has his own particular position, for the disc has a centre with reference to which the position of a person can be specified if his distance and his angular displacement from a given initial radius is specified. Thus, there is a variation of position if various persons are considered. On the other hand, the *Above* and the *Below* is absolutely invariable for all persons, for the lines running between *Above* and *Below* are all parallel for them, since they all have uniformly the same disc under their feet and the same heaven above their heads. Ovid would therefore have refused to entertain for a moment the suggestion that *Above-Below* is a variable. But his distant descendants accepted the view that the earth is spherical and that there are antipodes as self-evident, and they found not the slightest difficulty in considering the line *Above-Below* to vary with their own position, making all possible angles with an initial line extending to direct oppositeness. Referred to the centre of the sphere, all people have now an 'invariant' position, whereas, in compensation, the *Above-Below* is subject to every conceivable variation. And now I again address myself to the average reader, and say that the meaning of these analogies is that every doctrine that leads to a great *uniformity* converts what was formerly invariant into a variable quantity, and vice versa. The theory of relativity makes all considerations about the physical world independent of all co-ordinate systems ; it establishes completely invariable uniformity, removed from all changes due to varying points of view. Hence what was previously invariable—such as a rigid measuring-rod—will now become variable. It is not surprising that this requires a new method of thought, a revision of our mode of reasoning, for the above analogies show that these radical adjustments are characteristically necessary in the case of comprehensive theories, and that such theories are able to overcome apparently firmly established ideas. The parallels that I drew above will at least inspire the average reader with a certain confidence, for they show him how results of reasoning that were once considered incredible were regarded as self-evident by later generations."

I have already emphasized sufficiently that Einstein regards as inadequate these auxiliary pictures that have presented themselves to me. Yet in the course of the conversation I gained the impression that his judgment grew somewhat milder, and that, with certain reservations, he was disposed to let them pass as tolerably useful helps—and they are not intended to be more than this. I think, therefore, that I am not acting counter to his wishes in citing these allegorical examples here, particularly as they arose in the course of our talks.

Since then, I have had many opportunities of testing these examples on certain persons, and may mention that they proved quite useful. Analogies of this kind may offer a friendly help in moments when the uninitiated feel themselves in peril, and encounter a difficulty which they imagine to be insurmountable. They do not remove the difficulty, but they impart a certain power of expansion to the intellect and encourage a continuation of effort, which would probably otherwise be relaxed at the first sign of something which is imagined to be inconceivable. There is thus no room in textbooks for such helps, but they may justifiably find a place in a book that departs from the methodical route, and hopes to discover in by-ways things that are suggestive and instructive.

CHAPTER X

DISCONNECTED SUGGESTIONS

Conditionality and Unconditionality of Physical Laws.—Conception of Temperature.—Grain of Sand and Universe.—Are Laws unalterable ?—Paradoxes of Science.—Rejuvenation by Motion.—Gain of a Second.—Deformed Worlds.—Atomic Model.—Researches of Rutherford and Niels Bohr.—Microcosmos and Macrocosmos.—Brief Statement of the Principle of Relativity.—Science with reduced Sense-Organs.—Eternal Repetition.—Higher Types of Culture.

IN all branches of reasoning, no word and no conception has played a more important part than that of *law*. Physical laws denote the barrier that separates strictly chance and arbitrariness from necessity, and it seems to us that the region of the latter must ever extend so that finally nothing will be left of the former, which will have become amalgamated with necessity. We shall be constrained to believe more and more in a supreme law that will be a complete expression of all the partial laws which science presents to us as more or less permanent results of individual researches.

Our conversation was centred about these individual laws, such as those that are taught in the theory of gases, optics, etc., and that are associated with the names, Boyle, Gay-Lussac, Dalton, Mariotte, Huyghens, Fresnel, Kirchhoff, Boltzmann, and others. In connexion with these I asked Einstein whether he regarded the laws as things unconditioned in themselves, and capable of proof under every set of circumstances ; and whether absolutely valid laws existed or could exist.

Einstein's answer was essentially in the negative. " A law cannot be final, if only for the reason that the conceptions, which we use to formulate it, show themselves to be imperfect or insufficient as science progresses. Let us consider, for example, an elementary law such as Newton's Law of Force. From our more recent point of view we find the conception of direct action at a distance to be inexact in Nature. For it has been shown that action at a distance is not an ultimate factor, but must be resolved into a multiplicity of actions between immediately neighbouring points (The Theory of Action by Contact or Contiguous Action). Another example is provided by the conception *Temperature*. This conception becomes meaningless if we endeavour to apply it to molecules : it leads to no result if we try to impose it on the smallest parts of matter as such. The reason is that the state, the velocity, and the inner energy of the individual molecules fluctuates between very wide limits. The conception ' temperature ' is applicable only to a configuration composed of many molecules, and even then it is not applicable quite generally. For let us picture to ourselves an extremely rarefied gas contained in a closed receiver. Two opposite walls are to be at different temperatures, the one being cold and the other being hot In a gas at such very low pressure the molecules come into collision so seldom that, practically, we have to take into account only the collisions of the molecules with the confining walls. The molecules that rebound from the hot wall have greater velocities than those coming from the colder wall, and hence the conception of temperature becomes untenable for this gas."

" Would the temperature-scale on the thermometer then denote nothing ? " I asked. " The greater or lesser degree of warmth of a body, in this case of the mass of gas, depends on the more rapid or less rapid motion of its smallest parts. The motions are in any case present, so what would a thermometer indicate ? "

" It would betray only that it had nothing to indicate. If a thermometer that is blackened on one side were inserted into the vessel containing the gas, then *different* temperatures would be recorded if the thermometer were gradually turned about its own axis ; and this signifies that the conception of temperature has become meaningless for this configuration of molecules. And passing beyond the quoted examples, I should maintain that all our conceptions, however subtly they may have been thought out, are shown in the course of progressive knowledge to be too rough hewn, that is, too little differentiated."

.   .   .   .

We spoke of the " Properties of Things," and of the degree to which these properties could be investigated. As an extreme thought, the following question was proposed :

Supposing it were possible to discover *all* the properties of a *grain of sand*, would we then have gained a complete knowledge of the *whole universe* ? Would there then remain no unsolved component of our comprehension of the universe ?

Einstein declared that this question was to be answered with an unconditional affirmative. " For if we had completely and in a scientific sense learned the processes in the grain of sand, this would have been possible only on the basis of an exact knowledge of the laws of mechanical events in time and space. These laws, differential equations, would be the most general laws of the universe, from which the quintessence of all other events would have to be deducible."

[This thought may be spun out in yet another direction. Every piece of research, however specialized it may appear and of whatever minor importance it may be, retains a relationship with researches into the universe, and may prove to be valuable for this latter task. If we accept the view that science is capable of realizing perfection, then every contribution to knowledge, even the most insignificant, is essentially indispensable for attaining this goal.]

.   .   .   .

Can a physical law alter with time ? In more precise language, can time, as such, enter explicitly into laws, so that, for example, an experiment that is carried out at different times leads to different results ? This question has been treated several times, among others, by Poincaré, who answered it with an emphatic " No ! " but also by others to whom the invariability of physical laws did not seem to hold for all eternity. If my memory does not play me false, Helmholtz once expressed faint doubts about the constancy of laws.

Einstein answered this question with a decided negative. " For a law of physical nature is, by definition, a rule to which events conform wherever and whenever they take place. Thus, if we were to be compelled as a result of experience to make a law dependent on time, it would be a necessary step to seek a law independent of time, which would include in itself the law dependent on the time as a special case. The latter would be excluded from the category of physical laws, and would henceforward play the part only of a result deduced from the law which is independent of the time."

.   .   .   .

What attitude should we adopt if, in studying a scientific doctrine, we encounter paradoxical results even though the inferences have been drawn correctly—that is, if we meet with a deduction to which our reasoning powers object, although no fallacy is discoverable in the argument ?

Before we deal with cases which seem to me, personally, to be interesting, let us hear what is Einstein's attitude in general. " As soon as a paradox presents itself, we may, as a rule, infer that inaccurate reasoning is the cause, and should thus examine in each particular case whether an error of logic is discoverable, or whether the paradoxical result denotes only a violent contrast with our present views."

Let us first take examples from an entirely modern science, from the *Theory of Aggregates* founded by Georg Cantor of Halle. We shall follow the argument by the only possible method for this book, namely, by rough indications that will serve our purpose and do not claim to be accurate in expression or in sense.

If we take an aggregate of three objects, for example, an apple, a pear, and a plum, we may, by definition, form six partial aggregates, namely :

> the apple
> the pear
> the plum
> the apple and the pear
> the apple and the plum
> the pear and the plum.

The aggregate of the partial aggregates, which contains six elements, is thus greater than (actually twice as great as) the original aggregate, in which only three elements occur.

If the original aggregate contains an additional element,

for example, a nut, the following partial aggregates may be formed :

```
the apple
the pear
the plum
the nut
the apple and the pear
the apple and the plum
the apple and the nut
the pear and the plum
the pear and the nut
the plum and the nut
the apple, the pear, and the plum
the apple, the pear, and the nut
the apple, the plum, and the nut
the pear, the plum, and the nut.
```

Thus, in this case, the aggregate of the partial aggregates is already considerably greater than the original aggregate. This numerical excess increases rapidly with each successive increase in the original aggregate, so that if we apply the same reasoning to an infinite aggregate, the aggregate of partial aggregates becomes an infinity of a *higher order*. This is expressed by saying that the infinite aggregate of partial aggregates has a greater *potentiality* than the infinity of the elements of the original aggregate.

So we see that the one infinity is, in popular language, much more comprehensive, more powerful than the other. Our minds do not find it impossible to grasp this. But in a definite imaginary experiment it is found that this theorem of progression not only fails in its application, but leads to flagrant contradiction.

For if we start from the primary aggregate of " all conceivable things," its infinity can certainly not be transcended by any other infinity. But according to the above theorem the " aggregate of all partial aggregates " would have a greater potentiality, although it itself cannot extend further than to the conception of the maximum of all conceivable things. We thus arrive at an insoluble paradox, a typical example of how, in the system of conceptions involved, something is insufficient or not in conformity with logical thought. And this sceptical view receives support from various remarks of Descartes, Locke, Leibniz, and particularly Gauss, who, long before the advent of the Theory of Aggregates, raised a protest against inexact definitions of infinity.

In another case, however, the same theory seems to arise by perfectly logical processes, although it again leads to a statement that does not seem correct to "common sense." For it shows by a very subtle and ingenious method that all the surface-points of a surface infinitely extended in all directions may be brought to correspond in a reversible single manner to the linear points of a line, however small; so that to every point of the unlimited plane there corresponds a definite point of the line, and vice versa. The same theorem may be extended to three-dimensional space, with the result that we have to reconcile ourselves with the incredible fact that, expressed in popular language, a straight line of however small length exhibits the same potentiality with regard to the number of its points, as all the points in the universe.

For my own part, I must confess that no means suggests itself to me to make this paradox intelligible. But the *sacrificium intellectus* comes within dangerous proximity. Einstein, who values and marvels at the theory of aggregates as a science, or perhaps more as a work of art built up from the materials of science, gives whole-hearted support to the proof. He refuses to accept the notion of a paradox—that is, he recognizes a contradiction not in our process of reasoning, but only in a habit of thought that is open to correction. I should give much to discover the means of correction !

.　　.　　.　　.　　.　　.　　.　　.

A third example arises out of the special theory of relativity. It has a mysterious paradoxical character that vanishes when a clear view of the relationships involved has been obtained.

According to this theory the rate at which events happen alters according to the state of motion of the system under consideration. Let us now consider two twins A and B, that, although born at one place on the earth, are immediately separated, B remaining at rest, whilst A rushes out into space at an enormous rate, describing what, viewed from the earth, is an inconceivably great circle. In this way the rate of happening of all events is reduced very considerably for A in a manner that may be calculated. If A then returns to

B, it may happen that the twin who stayed at home is now sixty years old, whereas the wanderer is only fifteen years of age, or is perhaps only an infant still.

The first introduction to this flight of imagination naturally causes profound perplexity. Nevertheless, we are dealing not with a realm of miracles, but with something that is within the range of comprehension.

" In the case of these two twins," Einstein declared, " we have merely a paradox of *feeling*. It would be a paradox of *thought* only if no sufficient ground could be suggested for the behaviour of these two creatures. This ground, which accounts for the comparative youth of A, is given, from the point of view of the special theory of relativity, by the fact that the creature in question, and only this creature, has been subject to accelerations. A proper grasp of the reason is furnished only when we adopt the *general* theory of relativity, which tell us that, from the point of view of A, a centrifugal field exists, whereas it is absent from the point of view of B. This field exerts an influence on the relative rate of happening of the events of life."

It certainly requires a prodigious mechanism to allow the moving twin to gain even only one second of time. If he were to spend a year in a merry-go-round whose circumference were about 19 milliard miles in length, he would have to travel in it at the rate of over 600 miles per second if he is to gain a second on his brother.

This inevitable result that is immediately apparent to a trained scientific mind throws light on the nature of " common sense," the validity of which, as an ultimate criterion, Kant too has refused to recognize, in so far as this " common sense " is incapable of passing beyond the examples offered in its own experience. It circulates, as Einstein says, in the " realms of feeling and analogy." It finds no analogy for a phenomenon like that described above, and since it can apply rules only concretely, many things appear to it paradoxical that, in the light of intensified abstraction, appear logical and necessary.

. . . .

Let us speculate on the following question. If all things in the universe should increase or decrease enormously in dimensions, and if, at the same time, in a manner totally concealed from us, certain physical conditions should become changed, we should lack all means of discovering the difference between things before and after the change. For since all measuring-rods, including those furnished by our senses, would have become changed in the same proportion, the two conditions could not be differentiated from one another. It may easily be shown that this would necessarily occur, if an extra-mundane power were non-uniformly to displace, deform, compress, or bend all things in the universe, provided that our instruments and senses participated in this transformation. Accordingly it is permissible also to regard the universe known to us as one that is deformed, and one that is derived from another, the original form of which will ever remain a secret to us.

Is there any connexion between this grotesque speculation and the theory of relativity ?

We can establish only one that is negative and that arises *e contrario*. " These deformations," said Einstein, " are in themselves abstractions that are physically meaningless. Only *relations between bodies* have a physical meaning, for example, the relation between measuring-rods and the objects they measure. Therefore, it is reasonable to talk of deformations only when we are dealing with the deformations of two or more bodies with respect to one another, whereas the conception of deformation has no sense, unless a real object is specified, to which it is referred. The philosophical merit of the general theory of relativity, as compared with previous views of physics, consists in the fact that the former avoids entirely these meaningless abstractions with respect to space and time."

[According to this, it is not purposeless to enter on these grotesque trains of thought, even if they are untenable physically. For since the new physics teaches us to avoid these false tracks, it seems of value to know what it is that is to be avoided. Just as we must study scholastic thought if we wish to grasp thoroughly the philosophy which sprang up after the scholastic fetters were burst. Moreover, these reflections on concealed universes are not without a certain attraction, reminiscent of the sorcerer's wand, if they pursued any other goal than that of making universes distorted. It is true that they hold out latent temptations that may in some cases lead us on to dangerous ground, in encouraging us to venture on analogies beyond the scope of geometry and physics. Would it be possible to enter suddenly into a world that is distorted and deformed with respect to its ethics, its culture, and its reasoning intellects, without our observing the difference ? Are we ourselves perhaps living under such deranged conditions, of which we cannot become aware, because our perceptual organs have likewise become deformed ? I must frankly confess that I do not regard it as quite inconceivable that this argument of deformation may be spun out in this direction, but I must add that Einstein rejects absolutely all such extensions, since, as he emphasizes, they lead to regions that are merely fields for the exhibition of " verbal gymnastics."]

. . . .

The question whether Nature makes leaps or not is very old. In the theory of descent it forms the foundation of the difference between revolutionists and the evolutionists, who uphold the axiom *natura non facit saltus*, with all its consequences. Recently attempts have been made, particularly by psychologists, to propound and justify a natural principle of discontinuity. They assert that our own perceptions and sensations are discontinuous in themselves, and that the mechanism of every perception is akin to that of a cinematograph with its extremely rapid interruptions. If this should actually be the case, we should scarcely have a means of solving definitely the question whether continuity reigns, or not, in Nature.

Einstein does not recognize the possibility of this alternative for a moment. If a doubt had ever arisen, the researches of Maxwell would in themselves have been sufficient to dispel it. Our universe that is to be described in terms of differential equations is absolutely continuous.

" But," I interjected, " does not modern physics offer a certain support to the assumption of a discontinuity ? Does not the Quantum Theory point to an atomistic structure of energy, and hence also of events that are to be imagined as happening in jerks and as involving relations expressible in whole numbers ? "

Einstein gave an answer of epigrammatic brevity and

flavour. " The fact that these phenomena are expressible in whole numbers must not be construed into an argument against continuous happening. Just imagine to yourself for a moment that beer is sold only in whole litres ; would you then infer that beer, as such, is *discontinuous* ? "

.   .   .   .

What achievements are to be expected of astronomy in the present era ?

This question would have a special meaning if it were assumed that the astronomer who works in observatories is surrounded by solved problems, and can no longer hope to solve problems having the universal significance of those of Copernicus or Kepler. This assumption, however, would not be in agreement with the actual state of affairs.

Einstein indicated to me a number of fundamental problems that present themselves to modern astronomy, and the solution of which he expected of future times.

Above all, the geometrical and physical constitution of the stellar systems will, in the main, become revealed.

At present we do not yet know whether Newton's Law of Attraction holds, at least approximately, for configurations of the type of the Milky Way and of the spherical clusters of stars—that is, in extents of space in which the influence of space-curvature would become appreciable. The rapid progress of recent astronomy justifies our great hopes that the solution of this universal problem will be found within the coming decades.

In distant connexion with this we also touched on the question of the habitability of other worlds. This theme of Fontenelle, " la pluralité des mondes habités," which has again become a centre of public interest, owing to investigations of Mars, has evoked a storm of discussion. We hear the noisy war-cries of geocentric scientists who wish to regain for the earth her shattered supremacy in astronomy, and who claim the existence of organic forms as the sole prerogative of our planet. It is scarcely necessary to mention that Einstein rejects the motives of these human and all-too-human individuals as small-minded and short-sighted. Creatures in distant worlds are derived from, and are subject to, conditions of organic nature, of which we can form no idea by deductions from the world which we inhabit. But to deny their existence on numberless constellations, or to demand an ocular proof of their presence, is no better than to assume the point of view of an infusoria to whom there is no life other than that in a dirty drop of ditch-water.

.   .   .   .   .   .

The idea of the atom as the ultimate structural element involves a philological as well as a conceptual contradiction. For *atomos* signifies the indivisible, the no-further-divisible, whereas the idea of a body, however small, an element of structure differing from zero, demands, at least geometrically, further divisibility. Even the original founders of the theory of atoms, Leukippus, Epicurus, and Democritus, assigned definite forms to the ultimate components, and we may read in the splendid work of Lucretius how he infers from the nature of substance that the ultimate particles are smooth, round, or rough, or have the shapes of hooks and eyes. The further analysis pressed forward, the more the simplicity of the original idea vanished. Microcosms came to be regarded as copies of macrocosms, and the atoms of present-day science actually exact from us that we should regard them as worlds in themselves.

Einstein acceded to my request that he might give a sketch of the latest achievements of science sufficient to provide an approximate idea of the *atomic model*. According to the researches of Rutherford and Niels Bohr, we are to picture it as a planetary system.

The central body of this system is represented by a positively charged nucleus, which constitutes almost the whole mass of the atom, surrounded by a certain number of electrons, negative charges, that move in uniform circular or elliptic orbits about the nucleus. There is thus a certain analogy that allows us to regard the nucleus as the sun, and the electrons as the planets of this system.

The number of these electrons varies between the limits 1 and 92, according to the chemical constitution of the element. The smallest number occurs in the case of helium (in which there are two), and of the hydrogen atom, in which only one electron-planet describes its circular path about the nucleus. In other atoms there are probably more complicated orbits, although they are more or less approximately circular. According to this still very new theory, which is supported by very convincing facts, the electrons are to be imagined as arranged in concentric shells (like the layers of an onion), among which the innermost shell plays a distinctive part inasmuch as the number of the electrons arranged in it decides the chemical character of the atom in question. It sometimes occurs that electrons spring, under external influence, from one orbit to another ; when the electron jumps back to the original orbit, light is emitted. An essential fact is to be noted : Whereas any arbitrary orbits of any arbitrary radius may occur in a planetary system of the celestial regions, the manifold of these orbits in the case of the electrons is restricted, in that only certain orbits are possible, namely, those that are determined mathematically by the quantum condition.

" Perhaps," I interrupted, " the whole analogy may be inverted. If the atom is considered analogous to a planetary system in the model, it should be admissible to regard our true planetary system as a cosmic atom. And then, long after we have become accustomed to regard our earth as playing the part of a grain of sand, the sovereignty of the sun, too, would be past. The whole majesty of the solar system as far as the orbit of Neptune would then shrink to a configuration compared with which the world of a grain of sand would be infinitely complex."

" This fantastic inversion is permissible up to a certain extent," said Einstein, " but we must not lose sight of the fact that there is a cardinal difference. If we disregard the enormous disparity in dimensions, the analogy is far from exact owing to the circumstance that the atom is only an element of structure, whereas the true planetary system is an extraordinarily complex structure in itself. Thus the difference between a simple thing and one that is very highly complex still remains."

" But, Professor, may not a similar complexity yet be discovered in the atom ? It may be merely a difference of philosophical view from the primary idea to that of regarding the electrons as circulating like planets. May we not conjecture that in each successive step we are merely carrying out a true *regressus in infinitum* ? "

"That seems highly improbable," he replied, "although, of course, structural investigations can never cease. At first they are directed at the more remote object of finding out why certain atoms are radioactive, that is, exhibit a tendency to disintegrate. It has already been established that this tendency is a property of the positive nucleus, of which little is as yet known. This means that the nucleus is not simple, yet it does not open up the possibility of an unending regression. Our aim must be to get a clear insight into the constitution of the nucleus, as regards the positive and negative charges, and it is my opinion," he concluded, "that beyond this there will be no further subdivision of matter."

When Goethe writes of the immovable pole in the flux of phenomena, we recognize that his beautiful remark pronounces an elegy to the possibility of attaining ultimate simplicity. Einstein's utterance, if I understand him aright, converts this elegy into a song of hope. If the subdivision of matter actually has an end somewhere, then we are now on the threshold of ultimate things, we are near the immovable pole, which we are capable of reaching.

.   .   .   .

"Every new truth of science must be such that, in ordinary writing, it may be communicated completely within the space of a quarto leaf." Kirchhoff made this remark, and gave a sufficient, if not literal, demonstration of its truth. When Bunsen and he published the first notice about spectral analysis, they compressed their publication into the small space of three printed pages.

But what is to happen if the new truth should be built up of very comprehensive materials, when it requires many links, of which none can be omitted if the truth is to be made intelligible? Would Kirchhoff's quarto page still be sufficient?

"Certainly," said Einstein, "provided, of course, that it is addressed to a reader who has already mastered what went before—that is, to one who is so far acquainted with the older facts that he has to learn only the really new part of the new truth."

"That sounds very hopeful," I remarked, "for then it

should also be possible to describe very briefly the theory of relativity."

" Let us rather say its essentials—the heart of the matter. Well, then, get your Kirchhoff page ready. We shall see whether we can set out on it the special theory of relativity."

The totality of our experience compels us to assume that light travels with a constant velocity in empty space. Likewise, our whole experience in optics compels us to recognize that all inertial systems are equivalent ; these are systems that are produced from an allowable one by means of a uniform translation. An allowable system is one in which Galilei's and Newton's Law of Inertia holds. (This law states that a moving body that is left to itself retains its direction and velocity permanently.)

Now, the law of the constancy of light propagation seems to conflict with the classical principle of relativity, according to which the velocity of a ray of light assumes different values in the moving system according to the direction of the ray.

This apparent incompatibility arises from the following unproved assumptions :

(*a*) If two events are simultaneous with regard to one inertial system, they are also simultaneous with regard to any other inertial system.

(*b*) The length of a measuring-rod, the shape and size of a rigid body, and the rate of a clock are independent of their motion with respect to the system of reference used, provided this motion is rectilinear and non-rotational.

These assumptions must be discarded if this disagreement is to be eliminated. If we substitute for them the assumption that all inertial systems are equivalent and that the velocity of light *in vacuo* is constant, we get :

(1) That the dimensions of bodies and the rate of clocks have a functional relation to the motion.

(2) That the equations of motion of Newton require to be modified ; this modification leads to results that, for rapid motions, differ appreciably from those of Newton.

This is, in a very compressed form, the meaning of the special theory of relativity.

As there is still some space left on our quarto page, we

may add a remark that, it is hoped, will make a little clearer the above-mentioned discrepancy.

Let us choose as our system of reference an express train 18 miles long. There are two passengers—Mr. Front, right at the front of the train, and Mr. Back, at the extreme end of the train, so that a rigid distance of 18 miles separates the two passengers. The carriages are transparent, so that the two passengers can signal to one another. They are, moreover, furnished with ideal clocks that run at exactly the same rate.

First, suppose that the train is at rest. Back is just opposite milestone 100, whilst Front is opposite milestone 118. By means of a flash, Back signals to Front his time, exactly 12 o'clock. It takes light very nearly $\frac{1}{10,000}$ second to traverse the length of the train—18 miles ; hence the flash will reach Front at 12 o'clock $\frac{1}{10,000}$ second. Exactly the same result would have come about if Front had signalled his time to Back. Light makes no difference in travelling forwards and backwards. If the train moves at a great speed, the two travellers can conduct the same experiment as when the train was at rest. They will then set the time that light takes to travel from Back to Front equal to the time that it takes to traverse the same way in the reverse direction. But this phenomenon will assume a different aspect if viewed from the railway embankment. An observer on the latter would affirm that light does not take the same time in travelling the length of the train in one direction as it does when travelling in the opposite direction.

For the ray of light moving in the forward direction has to traverse not only the distance between Back and Front, but also the very short distance that Front has moved forward during the interval that the light has been moving ; whereas, inversely, the flash sent out by Front to Back will traverse a distance that is correspondingly less than that between the passengers, since Back is moving towards the signal.

Thus the duration of the two phenomena of light propagation is the same or different, respectively, according as it is judged from the train or from the embankment. In other words, *the judgment of the length of time depends on the state of motion of the observer.*

All further pronouncements of the special theory of relativity are based on the preceding arguments of the relativity of time.

. . . .

Would Man be able to construct a Science if he possessed one sense less than at present—for example, if he were deprived of sight ? Let us apply this to a definite case. In the new physics the velocity of light plays a decisive part as a world-constant. At first sight it would appear impossible for us to determine it and recognize its importance, if we had not at our disposal some organ which enabled us to become aware of optical phenomena.

But, as Einstein explained to me, even under such difficult circumstances, it would be possible to build up a science, for the reason that phenomena, as far as they are perceptible, may be transformed so that they become manifest to other senses if one sense should be absent. For example, the electrical conductivity of selenium is strongly influenced by the amount of illumination that falls on it. Thus light acts on a selenium cell, causing changes of current intensity, which in their turn may be perceived by feeling, or by chemical action on the mucous fluid of the tongue. Ultimately we are concerned only with a differentiation that enables us to refer identical experiences to identical events. We should certainly encounter enormous difficulties in endeavouring to form a physical picture of our surrounding world if the number of our senses should become less than the organs with which we actually operate. Yet, in principle, we should be able to overcome all difficulties by means of much lengthened and complicated lines of research, even if we should have only *a single sense* left, or if we had only one at the very outset. The construction of a Science would then be possible, and would give the same results, although it might be propounded only after a delay of perhaps millions of years.

[It is naturally assumed that the intellect is retained, as this is the necessary condition for all scientific research. Since the degree of understanding depends on the senses—*nihil est in intellectu, quod non prius fuerit in sensu*—we may conjecture that a human being with only one sense organ would work with a minimum degree of understanding, which would be insufficient for the acquirement of any knowledge whatsoever.

This transcendental question, which lies almost beyond the bounds of discussion, was not touched on in our conversation, as the subject was restricted so that it should not drift into metaphysical regions.

Nevertheless, I should like to mention that a speculation of this kind is recorded in the history of science. Condillac, in a study teeming with ideas, investigates the behaviour of a " Statue," that he represents as a human being, with the assumption that there is at first no idea in the soul of this statue-person. This living creature is enclosed in a marble envelope, the sole exterior organ of which is at first the organ of smell. He then shows that by means of this single sense all manner of sensations and expressions of will may develop in his " statue." Condillac does not, however, undertake to give a convincing proof that this creature, restricted to the organ of smell, would be able to discover physically the relationships that hold in physical nature, and thus to build up a scientific system. Thus Einstein, in his discussion, goes considerably further than the author of this statue.]

. . . .

Has the " eternal repetition," as outlined by Nietzsche, any meaning ?

The sage of Sils-Maria tells us that this revelation came to him midway between tears and ecstasy, as a fantasy with a real meaning. The crux of his idea is a finite world built up of a finite number of atoms. From the fact that the present state emerges out of the immediately preceding one, the latter from the one just before, and so on, he concludes that the present state exhibits repetition both forwards and backwards. All becoming recurs and moves in a multiple cycle of absolutely identical states.

Let us discard for the moment all philosophical objections, above all this, that the recurrence of the same disposition of atoms may not necessarily entail the recurrence of the same psychical states. Furthermore, let us suppress the cynical thought that in the return to the same state the world would have reason to enjoy extreme happiness only for moments, but to lament for æons. Then we are left with the comparatively simple question : Is this repetition, from the point of view of physics, conceivable and possible ?

It would be the death-knell of Nietzsche's idea if the answer of a great physical research scientist were entirely in the negative. But Einstein still allows it a small measure of life. " Eternal repetition," so he expressed himself, " cannot be denied by science with absolute certainty." The disciples of Nietzsche will have to rest satisfied with this very small concession. For what, in Nietzsche's eyes, is a logical necessity becomes transformed by Einstein's supplementary remark into a vague assumption, the product of fantasy. From the point of view of physics the recurrence of the same condition is to be regarded as "enormously improbable." This statement is founded chiefly on the famous second Law of Thermodynamics, according to which the processes of Nature are in the main irreversible, so that a one-sided tendency is expressed in natural phenomena. The fact that the course of phenomena is in only one sense or direction speaks in favour of the view that the events of the world are to be regarded as occurring only once.

So that when Nietzsche, in contradistinction to this, vigorously supported the doctrine of repetition, he contradicted at least one important recognized theorem of physics. The fact that he did not become conscious of this contradiction, but that, on the contrary, he regarded his idea as the most important event in the development of his intellect, may be regarded as an example of a *docta ignorantia*. But it is allowable, too, that philosophic fantasies that complete the poetical picture of the universe should be given expression. And Nietzsche would presumably have been deprived of a degree of pleasure if he had been aware of this second law.

" Truth is the most expedient error " ; this statement may be traced back to a sequence of thought developed by Nietzsche. But the Eternal Repetition is shattered by just this remark, for judged by its consequences it would be a very inexpedient error.

.   .   .   .

Supposing we should succeed in exchanging thoughts with the inhabitants of distant worlds and should, through them, acquire the elements of a civilization *superior to our own*, would this knowledge prove a blessing to us or the reverse ?

The word " superior " must, of course, be treated circumspectly. It is to denote only that, relatively, this distant civilization bears somewhat the same relation to our civilization of to-day as our own bears to that of an Australasian negro or an anthropoid ape. There are fanatics of progress whose wishes plunge headlong and without restraint into the future, and to whom nothing could be more desirable than the sudden appearance of a civilization that, as they opine, would at one stroke carry us " forward " many thousands of years.

But the view of these magicians with their seven-league boots is untenable. Let me cite a mere outline of the many opposing arguments in a few words of Einstein. " Every sudden change in the conditions of existence, even if it occurred in the form of a higher development, would come upon us like a doom, and would probably annihilate us, just as the Indians succumb to the civilization that has outstripped them. The tragedy of our own highly civilized times is that we cannot create the social organizations that have become necessary as a consequence of the technical advances of the last century. This has given rise to the crises, impasses, and senseless competition between nations, and to the impoverishment of defenceless individuals. These deplorable conditions would become inconceivably accentuated if we were to be invaded by extra-mundane technical sciences of a higher order."

.   .   .   .

Nevertheless, there is still a possibility that the " superior civilization " might contain indications of the organizations which we lack. Instead of entering on the question of this Utopia, we confined ourselves to comparing past conditions in our world with present ones. Did we not have the most promising preliminaries for an organization that was devoid of friction and tended to reduce the competition between nations in the numerous international institutions that drew together a great section of the intellectual world to work in co-operation ? Are there hopes that this international coalition will be resumed ?

Einstein expressed himself optimistically, not to do homage to an organization artificially formed, but to extol the world-wide mastery of intellect. " Even if international congresses were to be swept away," he said, " international co-operation would not be abolished, as it effects itself automatically." I should venture to assert that if all these congresses were to cease, we should not even have cause to fear that there would be an appreciable diminution in the combined effort of research. If certain developments are hindered by political conditions, it is only due to the resulting economic hardships affecting individuals in their work and robbing them of their intellectual freedom. The real friends of Truth have always clung together, and do so actually now ; indeed, many feel the tie to be closer than that connecting them to their own country. In spite of all obstacles and boundaries they will never cease to find contact with one another !

CHAPTER XI

EINSTEIN'S LIFE AND PERSONALITY

W E know from the biographies of great thinkers that they seldom personify the character of a dramatic ideal. They are not heroes of fiction who pass through complex experiences and struggle with mysterious problems of existence that may unduly excite the imagination of observers. Whoever follows their development remarks in the majority of cases the predominance of the inner life, the course of which is discoverable only by study of their works, no clue being given in the confusion of ordinary exterior manifestations. An eminent man of thought, whose energies are concentrated on mental effort, rarely finds time to present in addition an interesting figure in the epic sense. The poet who moulds his forms from life finds little scope in him as a model, and only in exceptional cases has he succeeded in idealizing the savant in a work of art.

It would be a fruitless undertaking to treat Einstein's life as one of these exceptional cases. It is possible to trace the various phases of his development, yet neither the writer nor the reader must disguise from himself the fact that such outlines give only the external picture of the man and chronological events of importance. Nevertheless, a book of which he forms the theme cannot pass over the task of giving his *curriculum vitæ*. And if it should partly appear aphoristic and disjointed, it must be borne in mind that this account originated from conversations and scraps of conversation that touched on various episodes of his life, according as they had a bearing on the subject under discussion.

The story of Einstein's life begins at Ulm, the town which possesses the highest building in Germany. Gladly would I stand on the belfry of the Ulm Cathedral in order to obtain a general survey of Einstein's youth. But the view discloses nothing beyond the bare fact that he was born there in March 1879. The detail which has already been mentioned above, namely, that it was something physical that first arrested the child's attention, remains to be noted. His father once showed the infant, as he lay in his cot, a compass, simply with the idea of amusing him—and in the five-year-old boy the swinging metal needle awakened for the first time the greatest wonderment about unknown cohesive forces, a wonderment that was an index of the research spirit that was still lying dormant in his consciousness. The remembrance of this psychical event has a significant meaning for the Einstein of to-day. In him all the impressions of early childhood seem to be still vivid, the more so as all other physical occurrences, such as the falling of an unsupported body, left no impression on him. His attention was fixed on the compass, and the compass alone. This instrument addressed him in oracular language, indicating to him an electromagnetic field that was in later years to serve him as a domain for fruitful research.

His father, who had a sunny, optimistic temperament, and was inclined towards a somewhat aimless existence, at this time moved the seat of the family from Ulm to Munich. They here lived in a modest house in an idyllic situation and surrounded by a garden. The pure joy of Nature entered into the heart of the boy, a feeling that is usually foreign to the youthful inhabitants of cities of dead stone. Nature whispered song to him, and at the coming of the spring-tide infused his being with joy, to which he resigned himself in happy contemplation. A religious undercurrent of feeling made itself manifest in him, and it was strengthened by the elementary stimulus of the scented air, of buds and bushes, to which was added the educational influence of home and school. This was not because ritualistic habits reigned in the family. But it had so happened that he learned simultaneously the teachings of the Jewish as well as the Catholic Church ; and he had extracted from them that which was common and conducive to a strengthening of faith, and not what conflicted.

Youthful impetuosity, which in boys of a similar age usually expresses itself in rash enterprises and loose tricks, did not appear in him. His spirit was adjusted to contemplation, and an inborn fatalism, diffused with a super-sensuous element appertaining to dreams, restrained him from responding to external impulses. He reacted slowly and hesitatingly, and he interpreted what his senses offered him and all the little experiences of early days in terms of a reverence reflected from within. Words did not easily rise from his lips, and measured by the ordinary scale of rapidity of learning and readiness in answering questions, he would scarcely have been judged to possess unusual gifts. As an infant he had started to talk so late that his parents had been in some alarm about the possibility of an abnormality in their child. At the age of eight or nine years he presented the picture of a shy, hesitating, unsociable boy, who passed on his way alone, dreaming to himself, and going to and from school without feeling the need of a comrade. He was nicknamed " Biedermaier," because he was looked on as having a pathological love for truth and justice. What at that time seemed to be pathological, to-day appears as a deeply rooted and irrepressible natural instinct. Whoever has got to know Einstein as a man and as a scientist knows that this failing of his boyhood was but the forerunner of a very healthy outlook.

Signs of his love for music showed themselves very early. He thought out little songs in praise of God, and used to sing them to himself in the pious seclusion that he preserved even with respect to his parents. Music, Nature, and God became intermingled in him in a complex of feeling, a moral unity, the traces of which never vanished, although later the religious factor became extended to a general ethical outlook on the world. At first he clung to a faith free from all doubt, as had been infused into him by the private Jewish instruction at home and the Catholic instruction at school. He read his Bible without feeling the need of examining it critically ; he accepted it as a simple moral teaching and found himself little inclined to confirm it by rational arguments inasmuch as his reading extended very little beyond its circle.

Painful inner conflicts were not wanting. Jewish children formed a small minority in the school, and it was here that the boy Albert felt the first ripples of the anti-semitic wave that, sweeping on from without, was threatening to overwhelm master and pupil alike. For the first time he felt himself oppressed by something that was not in harmony with his simple temperament. His modesty made him a prey to injustice, and in defending himself his originally gentle and restrained nature gained a certain independence and individuality.

If one may speak of achievements at all in a preparatory school, those of Albert were of the average modest level. He was careful as a pupil, generally satisfied requirements, but in no way betrayed special talents : indeed, so much the less, as he showed himself to be possessed of a very uncertain memory for words. The methodic plan of the elementary school that he attended to his tenth year was, however, not other than the usual scheme mapped out by drill-masters ; it made up for what was lacking in an understanding of the pupils by applying drastic strictness. The beautiful sentence of Jean Paul : " Memory is the only paradise from which we cannot be banished," finds no echo in Einstein's school memories, of which he has often spoken to me without a shadow of regret for a lost paradise. He told me with bitter sarcasm that his teachers had the character of sergeants—those later in the *gymnasium* (secondary school) were of the nature of lieutenants. Both terms are used in the pre-armistice sense, and his words were directed against the self-opinionated tone and customs of these garrison-schools of earlier days.

The next stage of his development was a course of study at the Luitpold-Gymnasium in Munich, which placed him in the second class. In Einstein's retrospect of these days more friendly recollections present themselves, connected, however, only with particular persons, and not breathing praise in general ; on the contrary, from his account, it is clear that although he conceived affection for individual teachers, he felt the tone of the institute as a whole to be rough. As we know, many things have been changed in these schools since then, following on a revulsion from the convict atmosphere that used to characterize them, and which meant suffering enough for the pupils. The result was that the schoolboy Einstein developed a contempt for human institutions and assigned little value to the subjects of study which he was obliged to absorb in schematic form without the application of his own mental energy. This gloomy picture is relieved at points by the presence of several teachers, above all, one called Ruëss, who took pains in exposing the beauty of classical antiquity to the fourteen-year-old boy. We learn elsewhere that Einstein at present admits the humanistic ideal for the school of the future only under very restricted limitations. But when he thinks of this teacher and his influence, a warm appreciation of classical study vibrates in his words, occasionally rising, indeed, to an unbounded enthusiasm for the treasures of Greek history and literature. His instruction was not restricted to the acquisition of a perspective of the antique. Under the direction of the same teacher, he was introduced into the poetic world of his native country, and learned the magic of Goethe in his " Hermann and Dorothea " ; this poem, as he confesses, was explained to him in a really model manner. Thus there were some oases in the desert of schematic teaching : they served as refreshing halts for the spirit of the eager young searcher after knowledge.

We must go back one or two years to note a weighty experience, which occurred when he made his first acquaintance with elementary mathematics ; this subject presented itself to him with the intensity of a revelation. It did not happen in the ordinary course of school-work, but was due to a sort of wizard-like inquiring inner spirit that plied him with questions and that gave him inward thrills of joy when he found a sharp-witted solution. From the very beginning Albert proved himself to be a good solver of problems, even before he achieved an arithmetical virtuosity, and before he knew the technique of equations. He helped himself by means of little tricks, experimented roundabout inventions, and was happily excited when they led to the goal. One day he asked his uncle, Jacob Einstein, an engineer who lived in Munich, a certain question. He had heard the word " algebra " and surmised that his uncle would be able to explain the term to him. Uncle Jacob answered : " Algebra is the calculus of indolence. If you do not know a certain quantity, you call it x and treat it as if you do know it, then you put down the relationship given, and determine this x later." That was quite sufficient. The boy received a book containing algebraic problems that he solved all alone in accordance with this not exhaustive but expedient direction. On another occasion Uncle Jacob told him the enunciation of

Pythagoras' theorem without giving him a proof. His nephew understood the relationship involved, and felt that it had to be founded on some reasoning. Again he set about all alone to furnish what was wanting. This was, however, not a case for the " calculus of indolence " with an x that was to be determined. Here it was a question of developing a facility for geometric argument, such as very few possess at such an early stage of development. The boy plunged himself for three weeks into the task of solving the theorem, using all his power of thought. He came to consider similarity of triangles (by dropping a perpendicular from one vertex of the right-angled triangle on to the hypotenuse), and was thus led to a proof for which he had so ardently longed ! And although it concerned only a very old well-known theorem, he experienced the first joy of the discoverer. The proof that he had found proved that the ingenuity of the worrying young mind was awakening.

A new world was opened for him when he made the acquaintance of A. Bernstein's comprehensive popular books on scientific subjects. This work is looked on nowadays as being somewhat antiquated and, in the eyes of many a professional scientist, has sunk to the level of a pseudo-scientific " shocker " ; even when Einstein as a boy made explorations in it, there were signs of rust and decay in the work, for it originated in the fifties of the previous century and, in point of subject-matter, had long been transcended. Yet it could be read then—and even now—as a story containing thousands of interspersed physical, astronomical, and chemical wonders, and for the boy Einstein it came to be a true book of Nature, which presented to his mind, greedy for knowledge, as much as it did to his imagination.

Other vistas were opened up to him by Büchner's *Kraft und Stoff (Force and Substance)*, a book the cheapness of which he could not yet discern, but which called up wonder in him without rousing his criticism. In addition, his attention was chiefly occupied by a handbook of elementary planimetry, containing an abundance of geometrical exercises, which he fearlessly attacked and within a very short time solved almost· in their entirety. His delight grew when he ventured into the difficulties of analytical geometry and infinitesimal calculus quite apart from the curriculum of his school-work. Lübsen's textbook had fallen into his hands, and these directions sufficed for his audacious spirit. Whereas many of his school companions were still standing undecidedly before the pools of theorems of congruence and repeating decimals, he was already disporting himself freely in the ocean of infinitesimals. His work did not remain concealed, and gained appreciation. His mathematical teacher declared that the fifteen-year-old boy was ripe for university study.

Yet he was not to find a way into the open by matriculating very early, but through an event that unexpectedly threw him into new surroundings of life. In 1894 his parents transferred their abode to Italy. The chronicler has nothing to report of pangs of separation in Albert when he left Bavarian soil. He was glad to get away from the drill academy, Luitpold, and, as an inhabitant of Milan, he enjoyed the change in his existence, and was not encumbered by attacks of home-sickness. All in all, he had felt himself in an unhappy position under school compulsion in Munich, in spite of the mathematical delights he had provided for himself, and in spite of the rapturous moments that musical revelations had created for him since his twelfth year. Defiance and distrust against outside influences had remained active in him as forces that did not allow the happy disposition proper to his age to assert itself. But now the fetters had fallen and the pent-up joy of life burst forth as if through opened sluices. The sun and landscape of the South, Italian manners of life, art freely displayed in the market-place and on the street, realized for him dream-pictures that had appeared to him earlier during the hours of oppression. Whatever he saw, felt, and experienced lay outside the ordinary course of his life, awakened his sense for natural and human things, and set his spirit free from all bonds. There was no question of his going to school in the first six months. He enjoyed complete freedom, occupied himself with literature, and undertook extended excursions. Starting from Pavia, he wandered all alone over the Apennine to Genoa. Whilst he was being intoxicated with the sublime Alpine landscape, he came into contact with the lower stratum of the people, who aroused his deepest sympathy. The tour took him over a short stretch of the Italian Riviera, the beauties of which, as depicted by Böcklin, do not seem to have revealed themselves to him. At that time he was probably subject to a feeling of upward striving such as possessed Zarathustra.

With all their joys and inspirations the experiences in Italy remained but a short episode. Einstein resolved on a new tour, which was not without a professional purpose. He made a pilgrimage to Switzerland with the intention of studying mathematics and physics at the Zürich Polytechnical Institute. But he was not to be successful in his first effort to gain entrance. The conditions of entry required a standard in descriptive sciences and modern languages that he had not yet reached. So he turned to Aarau, where he was allowed to extend his knowledge with the help of excellent methods at the Canton school. Even at the present day Einstein talks with extreme enthusiasm of the organization of this model school that corresponds in rank approximately to a German Realgymnasium (or an English Grammar School). There was nothing to remind him of the continual manipulation of the sceptre of authority at the Luitpold school barracks ; he easily obtained his leaving certificate, and now the portals of the Zürich Polytechnicum were open for him.

He himself was probably not aware that he carried a marshal's baton in his own mathematical equipment. But, in looking back, we come across astounding things. For it is a fact that even in the pupil at Aarau problems had taken root that already lay in the vanguard of research at that time. He was not yet a finder, but what he sought as a sixteen-year-old boy was already stretching into the realms of his later discoveries. We have here simply to register facts, and to abstain from making an analysis of his development, for how are we to trace out the intermediate steps, and to discover the sudden phases of thought that lead a very young Canton pupil to feel his way into a still undiscovered branch of physics ? The problem that occupied him was the optics of moving bodies, or, more exactly, the emission of light from bodies that move relatively to the ether. This contains the first flash of the grandiose complex of ideas that was later to lead to a revision of our picture of the world. And if a biographer should state that the first beginnings of the doctrine of relativity occurred at that time, he would not be making an objectively false statement.

The ambitions of the youth by no means reached these flights of imagination, for whereas the latter signified the coming power of his wings, he himself set a modest goal. He wished to become a schoolmaster, and imagined that in choosing this career he was allowing his hopes to run high. This was in conformity with the esteem in which he held the status of teachers. In the Zürich Technical School there is a section equipped as a department for preparing teachers, and in this Einstein studied from the age of seventeen to the age of twenty-one, perfectly satisfied with the thought of sitting, not on the pupil's bench, but at the master's desk, and of exercising a beneficial if limited influence as a preceptor of the young.

He was still under the sway of the feeling that he was not sufficiently experienced in life and that he dare not venture out into the fight for existence in the great turmoil of the world. He saw in this struggle, which pitted man against man, led to exhibitions of violence, and aroused ambition for glittering unrealities, cause only for disgust and alienation. The prospect of personal success did not lure him to try force against force. Thus, for the time being, it was his ideal to lead a very modest existence. From various quarters he had been given hopes of a position as assistant to some professor of physics or mathematics. But for unknown reasons he was everywhere refused. These apparently obscure grounds, it must be said with regret, become clearer when we bear in mind his confession of faith. Nor did his hopes of teaching at a gymnasium seem near fulfilment, as certain conditions of birth raised obstacles. In the first place, he was not a Swiss ; in fact, since his stay in Milan he was without a nationality at all in the bureaucratic sense, and then he had no personal connexions, without which, at least at that time, there was no chance of progress even for a talented person. Yet the young student who was entirely without protection of any sort had to overcome the cares and satisfy the needs of daily life. He could not rely on material help from his parents, who themselves lived in restricted circumstances, and thus we find him a little later in Schaffhausen and Bern, where he earned a small pittance as a private tutor.

He found consolation in the fact that he preserved a certain independence, which meant the more to him as his instinct for freedom led him to discover the essential things in himself. Thus, earlier, too, during his studies at Zürich he had carried on his work in theoretical physics at home, almost entirely apart from the lectures at the Polytechnic, plunging himself into the writings of Kirchhoff, Helmholtz, Hertz, Boltzmann, and Drude. Disregarding chronological order, we must here mention that he found a partner in these studies who was working in a similar direction, a Southern Slavonic student, whom he married in the year 1903. This union was dissolved after a number of years. Later he found the ideal of domestic happiness at the side of a woman whose grace is matched by her intelligence, Else Einstein, his cousin, whom he married in Berlin.

In 1901, after living in Switzerland for five years, he acquired the citizenship of Zürich, and this at last gave him the opportunity of rising above material cares. His University friend, Marcel Grossmann, lent him a helping hand by recommending him to the Swiss Patent Office, the director of which was his personal friend. Einstein occupied himself here from 1902 to 1905 as a technical expert, that is, as an examiner of applications for patents, and this position gave him the chance of moving about in absolute freedom in the realms of technical science. Whoever has a strong predilection for discovery will perhaps feel estranged to find Einstein so long in the sphere of " invention," but, as Einstein himself emphasizes very strongly, both regions make great demands on clearly defined and accurate thought. He recognizes a definite relationship between the knowledge that he gained at the Patent Office and the theoretical results that appeared at the same time as products of intensive thought.

In 1905, in the midst of his work, the storm broke loose in him with the suddenness of a hurricane. In quick succession his mind disburdened itself of the abundance of ideas that had stored themselves up in the work of the preceding years, and these ideas signify more to us than a definite stage in the development of an individual. What physicists have come to regard as an elaboration of the heritage of Galilei and Newton had matured in him. We merely record the title of dissertations, which appeared in 1905 in the *Annalen der Physik* : " Concerning a Heuristic Standpoint towards the Production and Transformation of Light "—" Concerning the Inertia of Energy "—" The Law of Brownian Movement." —Then the most important contribution : " The Electrodynamics of Moving Bodies," that contained the revolutionary ideas underlying the special theory of relativity. To these is to be added a dissertation for his doctorate in the same year : " A New Determination of Molecular Dimensions."

In all, these represent a life-work that belongs to the history of science. It was certainly some considerable time before his work began its triumphal march in the sight of the world, and it may be added that treasures were hidden in these disquisitions that were not understood till long years afterwards. Yet the youthful discoverer was not passed over without signs of friendly appreciation. He received a letter, couched in very warm terms, from the celebrated physicist, Max Planck, who was a complete stranger to him at that time ; it spoke in glowing words of his essay, " The Electrodynamics of Moving Bodies." This letter was the first diploma, the forerunner of all the honours that later swept over him like a tidal wave.

It was his intention to obtain a tutorial position at the University. An appointment to Bern was at first again hindered by certain obstacles which he would probably have overcome if he had applied himself energetically to attaining his goal. He finally received his appointment, but exercised his duties for only a very short time, as Zürich now opened her arms to him. In 1909 he accepted the position of Professor extraordinarius there for theoretical physics, and soon assembled a grateful audience about himself. Nevertheless, during the earlier stages of his professorship he found it difficult to suppress a longing for the quiet, unexcited life of his patent-office work, in which he seemed to have had a still greater degree of independence. In 1911 he accepted a new appointment as Professor ordinarius to Prague, which offered him more favourable emoluments as an inducement. In the autumn of 1912 he returned to Zürich as a Professor at the Polytechnic, and in the early part of 1914 he was drawn into the strong magnetic field of the northern capital ; he arrived at the Spree, and has, since then, lived among us. He is now a Swiss by nationality, a world citizen by conviction, and, professionally, a member of the Berlin Academy and attached in a lecturing capacity to the University. Here he perfected his works on relativity, ending in the superlative elaboration of the theory of gravitation, the beginnings of which stretch back to the year 1907. He had spent eight years in a concentrated effort of severe thought to bring it to completion, and perhaps centuries will be necessary before the world will gain a complete perspective of all the consequences of his theory.

For the theory asks us to brush aside habits of thought that have claimed an hereditary position in pre-eminent minds. One of the foremost physicists, Henri Poincaré, had confessed as late as 1910 that it caused him the greatest effort to find his way into Einstein's new mechanics. Another whole year passed before he gave up his last doubts. Then he passed with flying colours into Einstein's camp, and recommended Einstein's appointment to the Professorship at Zürich, in conjunction with the discoverer of radium, Madame Curie, in an exuberant letter which may add its note of appreciation here :

" Herr Einstein," so wrote the great Poincaré, " is one of the most original minds that I have ever met. In spite of his youth he already occupies a very honourable position among the foremost savants of his time. What we marvel at in him, above all, is the ease with which he adjusts himself to new conceptions and draws all possible deductions from them. He does not cling tightly to classical principles, but sees all conceivable possibilities when he is confronted with a physical problem. In his mind this becomes transformed into an anticipation of new phenomena that may some day be verified in actual experience. . . . The future will give more and more proofs of the merits of Herr Einstein, and the University that succeeds in attaching him to itself may be certain that it will derive honour from its connexion with the young master."

We may be tempted to look back and ask whether the criteria that Wilhelm Ostwald once set up as a test of great men are verified in Einstein's case. He has certainly not broken the first and most general rule, the principle of " early maturity." This showed itself clearly when his impulse towards mathematical knowledge and discovery asserted itself, and when he penetrated far into the future with his optical problems. The history of science and of art may offer more striking examples in this connexion, but at any rate in Einstein's case the indications are sufficient to serve as a confirmation of the rule. On the other hand, the second test of Ostwald seems to be valid only conditionally when applied to Einstein. For Ostwald takes up arms against a " gradual intensification " of ability, and proclaims it as an almost universal rule that the exceptional achievement is the privilege of quite young persons : " what he achieves later is seldom as impressive as his first brilliant achievement." Thus, in Einstein's case, the exception is evident. For if we fix on only two chief discoveries, passing over many others, there is no doubt that the second (the theory of gravitation) surpasses the first (special relativity) in both range and significance. Indeed, we cannot escape from the idea of a " gradual intensification," for the second discovery could come about only as a result of the first. Moreover, it is not yet night, and there is nothing to refute the assumption that there will be a further progression.

Furthermore, Ostwald takes into consideration the tempo of the intellectual pulse of inspiration to divide the main types of great men into a classical and a romantic category : this classification cannot, however, be applied to Einstein. He is decidedly classical, in so far as his work seems calculated to serve later generations as a classical foundation for all mechanical investigations of the macrocosm of the heavens and the microcosm of atoms. On the other hand, his versatility, the mobility and resource of his highly imaginative mind, stamp him as a romantic spirit. His delight in teaching would also assign him to this category, for in the case of many classical spirits there is a decided aversion to imparting instruction. So that, although we might well be able to speak of a synthesis of these two forms, it seems better to estimate Einstein, not in the light of a ready scheme, but rather as a type of which he is the unique representative.

. . . .

Just as the external contour of his life is on the whole regular and unbroken, so also his inner life is attuned to simplicity. Nowhere, it might almost be said, do we observe a break, a spasmodic turn, or a sudden intensification. Although he has grasped and suggested so many problems, he himself presents no psychological riddle, and we meet with no singularities in analysing his personality. It has already been remarked several times that Art plays a part in his life. What I learned from him himself about his affection for music coincides exactly with what observation clearly discloses. The expression of his countenance when he is listening to music is a sufficient indication of the resonances induced in him. He is confessedly a classicist, and a sincere devotee of the revelations of Bach, Haydn, and Mozart. What fascinates and enraptures him above all is that which is directed inwards, which is contemplative and erected on a religious basis. The simple masterful flow in musical development and invention is all-important for him. The architectonic structure that we marvel at in Bach, the Gothic tendency towards heavenly heights, perhaps calls up in him sensations that emanate from his hidden wealth of constructive mathematical ideas. It seems to me that this possibility is not unworthy of remark. It suggests a reason for the fact that he gives himself up only unwillingly to the nervous strain of drama directed at emotional upheaval. He does not gladly overstep the boundary that separates the simple from the psychologically subtle, and whenever his desire to understand art requires him to venture beyond it, his appreciation is not accompanied by genuine pleasure. His subjectivity does not fix this boundary in accordance with the ordinary rules of concert æsthetics, which are actually not rules at all, but only changeable valuations and crystallizations of the feelings of certain groups of people. He gives himself up quietly and freely to what is presented, but makes no special effort to assimilate experiences to which his being does not spontaneously react. There would be no meaning in seeking to mark off the limits of his receptivity in accordance with this, and to tell him that it is too limited, and that it should be enlarged, and that he should not regard as an opinionated exaggeration what appears to others to be a deep and mighty revelation, or seems to be possessed of divine sweetness. He would be able to point out that even in the case of masters of the musical art a change of faith was not a rare occurrence, and that they learned anew, or rejected what they once idolized, and very often found no permanent haven in their own faith. Whoever, like Einstein, gives himself up to the simply contemplative, and feels no impulse towards sensationalism, is spared the task of learning afresh, and finds still one world left for him even if many other worlds are inaccessible. To mention only the main features, then, neither Beethoven as a composer of symphonies, nor Richard Wagner, denote the pinnacles of music for him ; he could live without the Ninth Symphony, but not without Beethoven's ensemble music. The number of composers and compositions which are not a necessity of life for him is very considerable. It includes the majority of romanticists, the erotically inclined school of Chopin and Schumann, which revels in sensation, and, as already mentioned, the neo-German dramatic composers. He has much objective admiration for them, yet he does not conceal the fact that he also feels lively opposition in the gamut of his sensations. He regards the properly modern productions as interesting phenomena, and has various degrees of disapproval for them, extending to complete aversion. It costs him an effort to hear an opera of Wagner, and when he has done so, he returns home bearing with him the *leitmotiv* of Meister Eckhard : " The lust of creatures is intermingled with bitterness." In general he seems to take up approximately the point of view of Rossini. Wagner gives him wonderful moments, followed, however, by periods of acute emotional distress. I need hardly add that I myself, who confess to being an ultra-Wagnerite, never strove in my conversations with Einstein to make my opinion prevail against his. For I am deeply convinced that in this matter there is no question of right and wrong, and that every musical valuation represents no more than an accidental judgment dependent on one's own nature, entirely ego-centric and thus objectively of no account.

Einstein also occupies himself in an active sense with music, and has developed into a very fair violinist, without claiming higher degrees of achievement. Among other things I once heard him play the violin part of a Brahms Sonata, and his performance approached concert standard. He draws a beautiful tone, infuses expression into his rendering, and knows how to overcome the technical difficulties. Among the supreme artists of his instrument who have exerted a personal influence on him, Joachim assumes the first place. Einstein still speaks with great enthusiasm of Joachim's performance of Beethoven's Tenth Sonata and of Bach's Chaconne. He himself plays the latter piece, for which the purity and accuracy of his double and multiple stopping fits him. Whoever chooses the right moment—this good fortune has not yet befallen me—may overhear Einstein at his pianistic studies. As he confessed to me, improvisation on the piano is a necessity of his life. Every journey that takes him away from the instrument for some time excites a home-sickness for his piano, and when he returns he longingly caresses the keys to ease himself of the burden of the tone experiences that have mounted up in him, giving them utterance in improvisations.

The regular run of concerts in which displays of bravura play an important part finds little favour with him ; above all, he is not a worshipper of the orchestral conductor, whom he regards only as an interpreter and not as a virtuoso on the orchestral instrument. He expressed this idea in unmistakable words : " The conductor should keep himself in the background." I believe that his dearest wish would be to breathe in the tones without a personal or material medium, merely out of the air or out of space. Furthermore, I believe that there is an unfathomable connexion between his musical instinct and his nature as a research scientist. For the ear, as we know from Mach, is the true organ that enables us to experience space, and thus things may occur within the ear of the investigator of space that may have a different significance from that of music which is representable in tones. I strongly doubt whether traces of compositional form occur in Einstein's tone-monologues, but perhaps they contain examples of an art for which the æsthetics of a distant future may find a name.

With regard to higher literature, and indeed all writings not connected with science, Einstein has little to say. He himself rarely directs conversation on to this topic, and still less rarely does he give vent to an enthusiastic outburst that betrays warm interest. He restricts himself to making short, aphoristic comments, and now and then allows his listener to gather that he can easily imagine an existence without literature. The number of accepted novels, tales, and poetic works which he has not read is legion, and all the pretentiously artistic, historical, and critical writings that are added to them have attracted only a very momentary interest from him.

I have never seen him attracted in any way by the promising aspect of some new book intended for diversion. If such a one happens to get into his hands, he merely places it among the others. At times I was constrained to think of Caliph Omar's words : " If the book contains what is already in the Koran, it is unnecessary ; if it contains something else, it is harmful." It is harmful at least in the sense that it robs us of time that may be better spent in another way. I am purposely exaggerating here to make it quite clear that Einstein finds full satisfaction in a narrow circle of literature, and that he experiences no loss if numerous new works pass by and escape his notice.

Nevertheless, he speaks with reverence of a series of authors, to whom he owes enrichment : among them are the classical writers, who naturally occupy the highest position, with certain exceptions, which he equally naturally wishes to be taken as a personal opinion and not in the sense of a critical valuation. With him the difference reveals itself in the intonation from which we may read a greater or lesser measure of affection. When he says " Shakespeare," the eternal greatness seems to be inherent in the actual sound of the name. When he says " Goethe," we notice a slight undertone of dissonance, which may be interpreted without difficulty. He admires him with the pathos of distance, but no warmth glows through this pathos.

I had ventured to deduce from my knowledge of his nature the men and the works which, in my opinion, should awaken strong echoes in him. A fairly clearly defined line leads to the true path. Outside of any systematic series, I may mention Dostojewski, Cervantes, Homer, Strindberg, Gottfried Keller in the positive sense, Emile Zola and Ibsen in the negative sense. Taken as a whole, this prognostication does not disagree seriously with his own statement, excepting that he lays still greater emphasis on Don Quixote and the Brothers Karamasoff than I had surmised. He expressed himself with reserve about Voltaire. He has no belief in Voltaire's poetic qualities, and sees in him only a subtle-minded and amusing writer. Perhaps if Einstein were to devote himself a little more intensively to Voltaire and Zola, he would assign a higher value to these related spirits. But there is little hope of this occurring, as the wide range of Voltaire's works tends to restrain him. Time, which the physicist Einstein has shown to be relative, has an absolute value for him when measured in hours, and whoever seeks to persuade him to read thick volumes is not likely to gain his goodwill.

Our philosophical literature is not received with acclamation by him. If some one wished to undertake the task of ascertaining Einstein's attitude towards philosophy, he would be well advised to plunge into Einstein's works rather than to ask him personally. In them the questioner would find ample hints, pointing towards a new theory of knowledge, the first indications of which are already perceptible. A great portion of philosophic doctrine will yet have to pass through the Einstein filter to be purified. He himself, it seems to me, leaves this process of filtering mostly to other thinkers, but we must not lose sight of the fact that these others derive their views of space, time, and causality from Einstein's physics. It is thus immediately evident that he does not find revelations about ultimate things in already extant literature, for the simple reason that they are not to be found there. For him famous works represent, in Kant's language, " Prolegomena to every future system of metaphysics which can claim to rank as a science." The accent is to be put on the future that has not yet become the present. He praises many, particularly Locke and Hume, but will grant finality to none, not even to the great Kant, not to mention Hegel, Schelling, and Fichte, whom he barely mentions in this connexion. To Schopenhauer and Nietzsche he assigns a high position as writers, as masters of language and moulders of impressive thoughts. He values them for their literary excellence, but denies them philosophic depth. As far as Nietzsche is concerned, whom, by the way, he regards as too glittering, Einstein certainly experiences ethical objections against this prophet of the aristocratic cult whose views are so diametrically opposed to Einstein's own opinion of the relations between man and man.

Earlier when we were talking of classical poetry he had particularly emphasized Sophocles as one who was dear to him. And this name leads us to the innermost source of Einstein as a man. " I am not here to hate with you but to love with you," is the cry of Sophocles' Antigone, and this cry is the keynote of Einstein's emotional existence. I shall not give way to the temptation to follow those who in the turmoil of the present day refer to Einstein as a political figure. That would lead to a description of policy and party arguments that lie beyond the scope of this book ; so much the less am I inclined to do so as Einstein's convictions may be expressed very clearly without reference to schematic terms of a very elastic nature. An individuality such as his cannot be compressed into a party programme. And if anyone should insist on placing him among the radicals or on assigning him far to the left, I should suggest that it would be better to choose, instead of the classification right and left, that of above and below. I look up towards his idealism, whose altitude may perhaps be reached one day by the raising of our ethical standards. But not by means of paragraphs of laws. I have seldom heard him talk of such schematic recipes, but so much the more have I noted utterances which bore witness to a very intense and ever-present sympathy with every human creature. His programme, which is written not in ink but in heart's-blood, proclaims in the simplest manner the categorical imperative : Fulfil your duty to your fellow-being : offer help to every one : ward off every material oppression. " Well, then, he is a socialist," so the cry runs. If it is your pleasure to call him so, he will not deny you it. But to me this term seems to denote too narrow limits for him. I see no contradiction in applying the term, but there is no perfect congruence. If one word is necessary, I should be rather more inclined to say that he is in the widest sense a democrat of liberal trend.

For him the State is not its own aim, nor does he imagine himself to be the possessor of a panacea. " The attitude of the individual to socialism," he said, " is uncertain owing to the fact that we can never ascertain clearly how much of the iron compulsion and blind working of our economic system may be overcome by appropriate institutions." And I should like to add that such institutions would scarcely have a permanent result, but that more may be expected from the ethical example of those who have the power of renunciation. Whoever realizes the motto of Antigone, " I am here to love with you," brings us nearer the goal. All in all, our longing continually flees from the confusion of political considerations to simple morality. For Einstein this is the primary element, that which is directly evident and not open to misrepresentation. It includes sympathy, and, what is more important, joy in conjunction with others. " The best that life has to offer," he once exclaimed, " is a face glowing with happiness ! "

This look is expressed on his own face when he discusses his ideals, above all the internationality of all intellectual workers and the realization of eternal peace among the nations. To him pacifism is a matter of mind as well as of heart, and he is of the opinion that the course of history so far is but the prelude to its realization. The past, with its bloodstained fingers that reach into the present, does not discourage him He points to the endless city wars of the Middle Ages in Italy, which had finally to cease in answer to the increasing feeling of solidarity. So he believes in the victory of peace, which the unified consciousness of all humanity will one day win over the demonic powers of tyranny and conquest.

The pacifistic goal seems to him to be attainable without the peculiarities of the various States being destroyed. National characteristics arising from tradition and hereditary influences do not signify in his eyes a contradiction to the internationalism that embraces the common intellectual factors of civilized peoples. Thus the desire for the preservation and care of particularities directs him to the secondary goal of Zionism. His blood asserts itself when he supports the foundation of a State in Palestine, which seems to him to be the only means of preserving the national individuality of his race without the freedom of the individual being affected.

We had left Art to talk of the State, and then returned to the former theme to touch lightly on the pictorial arts. Painting was allowed to pass with merely a fleeting remark. It plays no considerable part in Einstein's existence, and he would not suffer great grief if it were to vanish from the plane of culture, a consummation to which definite signs seems to point. I have described these signs in other writings (as in *Kunst in 1000 Jahren*), and maintain the point of view that the latest branches of painting as represented by expressionism and cubistic futurism denote, in essence, the last convulsions of a dying surface art. And even the chief representatives of former flourishing periods are beginning to fade away, and Einstein will not be the only one who will relegate this art, as compared with music, to a lower plane among the inspired arts that bring joy to humanity. He is only more frank than others when he freely confesses that he cannot convince himself that a life without the joys of pictorial art would be hopelessly impoverished. But he bows his head to sculpture, and, for him, architecture is a goddess. It is again his deeply rooted piety that asserts itself when memory recalls to him the Gothic dome with its pinnacles striving towards heaven. Goethe and Schlegel have called architecture " frozen music," and this picture is present in his mind when he sees Gothic architecture as frozen music of Bach. It is open to anyone to analyse this specific impression in another way by seeking the fundamental elements, in which the essence of the art is to provide support for a weighty structure and to overcome gravitation. For a spirit that works with mechanics and that feels within itself the pressures and tensions occurring in external nature, architecture is a kind of statics and dynamics transformed into a thing of beauty, a ravishing picture of his own science.

.   .   .   .

Einstein has told me many a story of his travels, and these reports were characterized by an absence of definite purpose. The conception of something worth seeing in the tourists' sense does not exist for him, and he does not set out in eager pursuit of those things that are marked with two asterisks in Baedeker. The intense romanticism of Swiss scenery, that lay within such easy reach for him, has never enticed him into its magic circle, and he has nothing to do with the abysmal terrors of glaciers and the world of snow-peaks. His enthusiasm for landscape beauty conforms with the behaviour of the barometer : the greater the altitude, the lower the mercury. In simple contact with Nature he prefers the lesser mountains, the seashore, and extensive plains, whereas brilliant panoramic contours like those of the Vierwaldstetter See do not rouse him into ecstasy. It is unnecessary to remark that he does not arrange his living on the standard of the Grand Palace Hotels *en route*. It is nearer the truth to picture him as a vagrant who tramps along without a sense of time and without a goal, in the fairy atmosphere of a joyous wanderer who has unconsciously adopted the old rule of Philander : Walk with a steady step : make your burden small : start early in the morn, and leave home all care !

Am I to record the list of pleasures and hobbies that are foreign to him ? The list would be very long, and I should arrive at my goal more quickly by setting his sporting tendencies equal to zero. I once suspected him of being given to aquatic sport, as I learned that he had taken part in several yachting excursions. But I was mistaken. He sails in the same way as he walks on his tours, without a set purpose, dreaming, and uninterested in what is regarded by members of sailing clubs as a " feat." In the negative list of his games we see even chess, that usually exerts a strong attraction on natures with a mathematical tendency. The particular types of combination offered by this game have never tempted him, and the world of chess has remained *terra incognita* for him. He is just as little interested in every kind of collection, even that of books. I have seldom or never met a savant who attaches so little value to the personal possession of numerous and valuable books. This statement may be extended as far as saying that he experiences no pleasure at all in possession as such : he says so himself, and his whole manner of life proves it. There seems to me to be an element of resignation in his amiable hedonism, a kind of monkish asceticism. He never rids himself of the feeling that he is only paying a visit in this world.

I do not know whether Einstein considers that his lifework can be completed within the span of this visit. At any rate he makes no attempt to extract more out of the day by following a rigid programme of work than the day voluntarily offers. He does not compel himself to cover a definitely circumscribed piece of ground with chronological exactitude. There are brain-workers, especially artists, who actually never shake off the fetters of the twenty-four hours day of work inasmuch as they spin on the threads of daily effort into the nightly fabric of dreams. Einstein can make a pause, interrupt his work, or divert himself into side-channels at leisure and according to the demands of the hour, but dreams offer him no inspiration and do not waylay him with problems.

On the other hand, however, he is waylaid so much the more during the day by things and persons that make an assault on him. This starts as soon as the first post arrives, to see through which requires a special bureau. In addition to the communications of a professional or official nature there appear innumerable letters from everywhere and anywhere asking him to grant a little of his time. Whatever each individual writer has thought about the principle of relativity, all his thoughts and doubts, additions, and, above all, that which he has not been able to understand, all this is to be answered by Einstein. Has he, the child of fame, even a quarter of an hour for himself? There they wait in the hall, the painter, the photographer, the sculptor, and the interviewer; with whatever powers of persuasion and argumentative subtlety his attentive wife may seek to defend his hours of rest, some of these visitors will yet succeed in gaining the upper hand, and will produce something in oil-colours, in plaster of Paris, in black and white, in water-colours, or in print. Fame, too, demands her sacrifices, and if we talk of a hunt after fame, then Einstein is certainly not the hunter, but the hunted.

He sighs under the burden of his correspondence, not only as the recipient, but also with the sender, whose letter has to remain unanswered. Yet he is never roused to anger by the intruder on his time. If this were not so, the aphorism of Cyrus that patience is the panacea of all ills would not hold for him, and how would I myself otherwise have dared to claim so many hours of him? A sense of guilt falls on me!

But even Einstein's patience can come to an end, and this is at the point where "society" begins: I mean the congregation of persons in a salon, society entertainments to which one is invited to be seen, and so that one may claim to have been there. A solemn representation in which he is to be made the cynosure of all eyes is a torture to him. If in a very exceptional case he is compelled to participate in such a gathering, the joy of his hosts will not be entirely unmixed, for it does not require a thought-reader to recognize the longing for solitude imprinted on his countenance : " Could I but escape ! "

So much the happier does he feel himself in the narrow circle of his friends, who offer what means to him much more than admiration, namely, affection, and an appreciation of his human self. He is what one wishes him to be. He is happy when he can forget the doctor profundus, and can yield himself up to the atmosphere of stimulating and un-constrained converse. He is a master in the art of listening, and is not averse to contradiction ; when possible, he even emphasizes the arguments of his opponent. *Audiatur et altera pars !* This is a further manifestation of his altruistic personality, which rejoices when he extracts the true kernel from the husk of the opposing opinion. Here he also displays a characteristic which one does not usually expect to find among abstract thinkers, a sense of humour that runs through the whole gamut from a gentle smile to hearty laughter, and that is the happy source of many a striking sally. It may happen that the subject of conversation excites his anger, especially in political debates when he calls to mind militaristic or feudal misgovernment. He then becomes roused, and, as a cynical philosopher, sarcastically attacks personalities and points out the primary source of perennial hate, immediately afterwards soaring up to happy speculations of the future.

It is a matter for regret that the subjects that he has discoursed on lightly have not been fixed phonographically. Such records would form an interesting supplement to the conversations outlined in this book. It would never occur to him to set down in permanent literary form the inspiration of the moment. What he writes emanates from other regions, and is, to use his own expression, a precipitate of " thick ink." This is obvious, for what he has to proclaim as a scientist cannot be presented in a " thin " form. But many a so-called writer would have reason to congratulate himself, if so much thinly flowing matter occurred to him in writing as to Einstein in speaking.

.   .   .   .

The record of these conversations was begun in the summer of 1919, and completed in the autumn of 1920.

INDEX